Business Guide to Eastern Europe & Russia

Volume 4

Business Guides to the World™

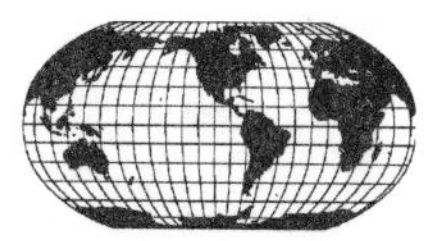

The Internationalist Publishing Company
96 Walter Street, Suite 200
Boston, MA 02131

The Internationalist Business Guide to Eastern Europe & Russia
Volume 4 of 6 volume Business Guides to the World™

Edited by Patrick W. Nee

The Internationalist Publishing Company
96 Walter Street, Suite 200
Boston, MA 02131
(617) 570-0810

ISBN 0-9633905-4-6

A B C D E F G H I J

Table of Contents

Introduction

The *Internationalist® Business Guides* for executives and investors contain the essential, core information about countries around the world. They include information about the economics of a country, its infrastructure, people, government and geography. The data has been compiled from the most authoritative government sources.

The Guides have been designed for ease of use by the busy executive or investor. The Guides are divided into six economic/geographic regions. Information is simply and precisely presented. The compact size permits use when traveling on international business. Important telephone numbers are included.

Fast moving political or economic events may affect certain elements of a country's situation, however, the basic underlying facts about a country remain constant. Those basic facts are what are covered by the guides.

COUNTRIES

AFGHANISTAN

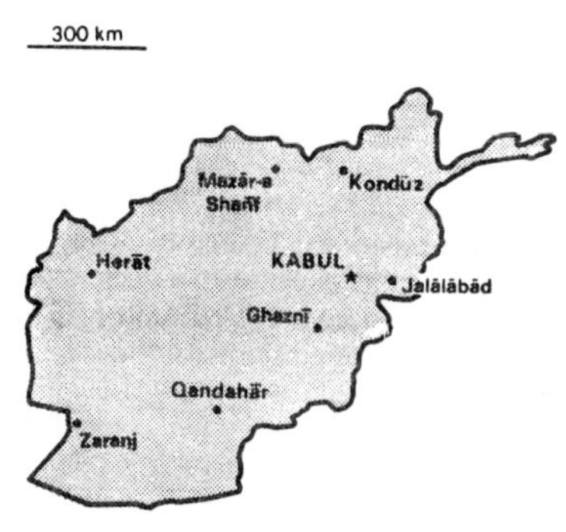

Economy

Overview: Afghanistan is an extremely poor, landlocked country, highly dependent on farming (wheat especially) and livestock raising (sheep and goats). Economic considerations have played second fiddle to political and military upheavals during more than 14 years of war, including the nearly 10-year Soviet military occupation (which ended 15 February 1989). Over the past decade, one-third of the population fled the country, with Pakistan sheltering more than 3 million refugees and Iran about 3 million. About 1.4 million Afghan refugees remain in Pakistan and about 2 million in Iran. Another 1 million probably moved into and around urban areas within Afghanistan. Although reliable data are unavailable, gross domestic product is lower than 12 years ago because of the loss of labor and capital and the disruption of trade and transport.
National product: GDP $NA
National product real growth rate: NA%
National product per capita: $NA
Inflation rate (consumer prices): NA%
Unemployment rate: NA%
Budget:
revenues: $NA
expenditures: $NA, including capital expenditures of $NA
Exports: $243 million (f.o.b., 1991)
commodities: fruits and nuts, handwoven carpets, wool, cotton, hides and pelts, precious and semi-precious gems
partners: FSU countries, Pakistan, Iran, Germany, India, UK, Belgium, Luxembourg, Czechoslovakia
Imports: $737 million (c.i.f., 1991)
commodities: food and petroleum products; most consumer goods
partners: FSU countries, Pakistan, Iran, Japan, Singapore, India, South Korea, Germany
External debt: $2.3 billion (March 1991 est.)
Industrial production: growth rate 2.3% (FY91 est.); accounts for about 25% of GDP
Electricity:
capacity: 480,000 kW
production: 1 billion kWh
consumption per capita: 60 kWh (1992)
Industries: small-scale production of textiles, soap, furniture, shoes, fertilizer, and cement; handwoven carpets; natural gas, oil, coal, copper
Agriculture: largely subsistence farming and nomadic animal husbandry; cash products—wheat, fruits, nuts, karakul pelts, wool, mutton
Illicit drugs: an illicit cultivator of opium poppy and cannabis for the international drug trade; world's second-largest opium producer after Burma (680 metric tons in 1993) and a major source of hashish
Economic aid:
recipient: $450 million US assistance provided 1985-1993; USAID will stop all programs by mid-1994; the UN provides assistance in the form of food aid, immunization, land mine removal, and a wide range of aid to refugees and displacedpersons
Currency: 1 afghani (AF) = 100 puls
Exchange rates: afghanis (Af) per US$1—1,900 (January 1994), 1,019 (March 1993),

850 (1991), 700 (1989-90), 220 (1988-89); note—these rates reflect the free market exchange rates rather than the official exchange rates
Fiscal year: 21 March—20 March

Communications

Railroads: 9.6 km (single track) 1.524-meter gauge from Gushgy (formerly Kushka) (Turkmenistan) to Towraghondi and 15.0 km from Termiz (Uzbekistan) to Kheyrabad transshipment point on south bank of Amu Darya
Highways:
total: 21,000 km
paved: 2,800 km
unpaved: gravel 1,650 km; earth 16,550 km (1984)
Inland waterways: total navigability 1,200 km; chiefly Amu Darya, which handles vessels up to about 500 metric tons
Pipelines: petroleum products—Uzbekistan to Bagram and Turkmenistan to Shindand; natural gas 180 km
Ports: Shir Khan and Kheyrabad (river ports)
Airports:
total: 42
usable: 35
with permanent-surface runways: 9
with runways over 3,659 m: 0
with runways 2,440-3,659 m: 10
with runways 1,220-2,439 m: 17
Telecommunications: limited telephone, telegraph, and radiobroadcast services; television introduced in 1980; 31,200 telephones; numerous cellular telephones; broadcast stations—5 AM, no FM, 1 TV; 1 satellite earth station

Defense Forces

Branches: the military still does not yet exist on a national scale; some elements of the former Army, Air and Air Defense Forces, National Guard, Border Guard Forces, National Police Force (Sarandoi), and tribal militias remain intact but are factionalized among the various mujahedin and former regime leaders
Manpower availability: males age 15-49 4,188,036; fit for military service 2,245,196; reach military age (22) annually 158,335 (1994 est.)
Defense expenditures: the new government has not yet adopted a defense budget

Geography

Location: Southern Asia, between Iran and Pakistan
Map references: Asia, Middle East, Standard Time Zones of the World
Area:
total area: 647,500 sq km
land area: 647,500 sq km
comparative area: slightly smaller than Texas
Land boundaries: total 5,529 km, China 76 km, Iran 936 km, Pakistan 2,430 km, Tajikistan 1,206 km, Turkmenistan 744 km, Uzbekistan 137 km
Coastline: 0 km (landlocked)
Maritime claims: none; landlocked
International disputes: periodic disputes with Iran over Helmand water rights; Iran supports clients in country, private Pakistani and Saudi sources also are active; power struggles among various groups for control of Kabul, regional rivalries among emerging warlords, traditional tribal disputes continue; support to Islamic fighters in Tajikistan's civil war; border dispute with Pakistan (Durand Line); support to Islamic militants worldwide by some factions
Climate: arid to semiarid; cold winters and hot summers
Terrain: mostly rugged mountains; plains in north and southwest
Natural resources: natural gas, petroleum, coal, copper, talc, barites, sulphur, lead, zinc, iron ore, salt, precious and semiprecious stones
Land use:
arable land: 12%
permanent crops: 0%
meadows and pastures: 46%
forest and woodland: 3%
other: 39%
Irrigated land: 26,600 sq km (1989 est.)
Environment:

current issues: soil degradation; overgrazing; deforestation (much of the remaining forests are being cut down for fuel and building materials); desertification
natural hazards: damaging earthquakes occur in Hindu Kush mountains (one measured 6.8 on the Richter scale in 1991); flooding
international agreements: party to—Endangered Species, Environmental Modification, Marine Dumping, Nuclear Test Ban; signed, but not ratified—Biodiversity, Climate Change, Hazardous Wastes, Law of the Sea, Marine Life Conservation
Note: landlocked

People

Population: 16,903,400 (July 1994 est.)
Population growth rate: 2.45% (1994 est.)
Birth rate: 43.46 births/1,000 population (1994 est.)
Death rate: 18.94 deaths/1,000 population (1994 est.)
Net migration rate: 0 migrant(s)/1,000 population (1994 est.)
Infant mortality rate: 155.8 deaths/1,000 live births (1994 est.)
Life expectancy at birth:
total population: 44.89 years
male: 45.53 years
female: 44.21 years (1994 est.)
Total fertility rate: 6.27 children born/woman (1994 est.)
Nationality:
noun: Afghan(s)
adjective: Afghan
Ethnic divisions: Pashtun 38%, Tajik 25%, Uzbek 6%, Hazara 19%, minor ethnic groups (Chahar Aimaks, Turkmen, Baloch, and others)
Religions: Sunni Muslim 84%, Shi'a Muslim 15%, other 1%
Languages: Pashtu 35%, Afghan Persian (Dari) 50%, Turkic languages (primarily Uzbek and Turkmen) 11%, 30 minor languages (primarily Balochi and Pashai) 4%, much bilingualism
Literacy: age 15 and over can read and write (1990 est.)
total population: 29%
male: 44%
female: 14%
Labor force: 4.98 million
by occupation: agriculture and animal husbandry 67.8%, industry 10.2%, construction 6.3%, commerce 5.0%, services and other 10.7% (1980 est.)

Government

Names:
conventional long form: Islamic State of Afghanistan
conventional short form: Afghanistan
former: Republic of Afghanistan
Digraph: AF
Type: transitional government
Capital: Kabul
Administrative divisions: 30 provinces (velayat, singular—velayat); Badakhshan, Badghis, Baghlan, Balkh, Bamian, Farah, Faryab, Ghazni, Ghowr, Helmand, Herat, Jowzjan, Kabol, Kandahar, Kapisa, Konar, Kondoz, Laghman, Lowgar, Nangarhar, Nimruz, Oruzgan, Paktia, Paktika, Parvan, Samangan, Sar-e Pol, Takhar, Vardak, Zabol
note: there may be a new province of Nurestan (Nuristan)
Independence: 19 August 1919 (from UK)
National holiday: Victory of the Muslim Nation, 28 April; Remembrance Day for Martyrs and Disabled, 4 May; Independence Day, 19 August
Constitution: none
Legal system: a new legal system has not been adopted but the transitional government has declared it will follow Islamic law (Shari'a)
Suffrage: undetermined; previously universal, male ages 15-50
Executive branch:
chief of state: President Burhanuddin RABBANI (Interim President July—December 1992; President since 2 January 1993); First Vice President Mohammad NABI Mohammadi (since NA); First Vice President Mohammad SHAH Fazli (since NA); election last held NA December 1992 (next to be held

NA December 1994); results—Burhanuddin RABBANI was elected to a two-year term by a national shura, later amended by multi-party agreement to 18 months.
head of government: Prime Minister Gulbuddin HIKMATYAR (since 17 March 1993); First Deputy Prime Minister Qutbuddin HELAL (since 17 March 1993); Deputy Prime Minister Arsala RAHMANI (since 17 March 1993)
cabinet: Council of Ministers
Legislative branch: a unicameral parliament consisting of 205 members was chosen by the shura in January 1993; non-functioning as of June 1993
Judicial branch: an interim Chief Justice of the Supreme Court has been appointed, but a new court system has not yet been organized
Political parties and leaders: current political organizations include Jamiat-i-Islami (Islamic Society), Burhanuddin RABBANI, Ahmad Shah MASOOD; Hizbi Islami-Gulbuddin (Islamic Party), Gulbuddin HIKMATYAR faction; Hizbi Islami-Khalis (Islamic Party) Yunis KHALIS faction; Ittihad-i-Islami Barai Azadi Afghanistan (Islamic Union for the Liberation of Afghanistan), Abdul Rasul SAYYAF; Harakat-Inqilab-i-Islami (Islamic Revolutionary Movement), Mohammad Nabi MOHAMMADI; Jabha-i-Najat-i-Milli Afghanistan (Afghanistan National Liberation Front), Sibghatullah MOJADDEDI; Mahaz-i-Milli-Islami (National Islamic Front), Sayed Ahamad GAILANI; Hizbi Wahdat (Islamic Unity Party), Abdul Ali MAZARI; Harakat-i-Islami (Islamic Movement), Mohammed Asif MOHSENI; Jumbesh-i-Milli Islami (National Islamic Movement), Rashid DOSTUM
note: the former ruling Watan Party has been disbanded
Other political or pressure groups: the former resistance commanders are the major power brokers in the countryside; shuras (councils) of commanders are now administering most cities outside Kabul; ulema (religious scholars); tribal elders
Member of: AsDB, CP, ECO, ESCAP, FAO, G-77, IAEA, IBRD, ICAO, IDA, IDB, IFAD, IFC, ILO, IMF, INTELSAT, IOC, ITU, LORCS, NAM, OIC, UN, UNCTAD, UNESCO, UNIDO, UPU, WFTU, WHO, WMO, WTO
Diplomatic representation in US:
chief of mission: (vacant); Charge d'Affaires Abdul RAHIM
chancery: 2341 Wyoming Avenue NW, Washington, DC 20008
telephone: (202) 234-3770 or 3771
FAX: (202) 328-3516
US diplomatic representation: none; embassy was closed in January 1989
Flag: three equal horizontal bands of green (top), white, and black, with the national coat of arms superimposed in the middle of the white band and large Islamic lettering superimposed over the green and white bands

---

U.S Government Contacts:

U.S. Trade Desk: (202) 482-2954

ALBANIA

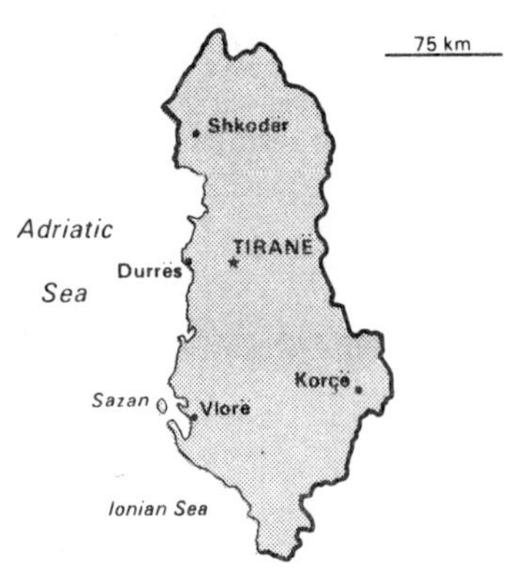

Economy

Overview: An extremely poor country by European standards, Albania is making the difficult transition to a more open-market economy. The economy rebounded in 1993 after a severe depression accompanying the collapse of the previous centrally planned system in 1990 and 1991. Stabilization policies, including public sector layoffs and reduced social services, have improved the government's fiscal situation and reduced inflation. The recovery was spurred by the remittances of some 5% of the population which works abroad, mostly in Greece and Italy. Foreign assistance and humanitarian aid also supported the recovery. Most agricultural land was privatized in 1992, substantially improving peasant incomes. Albania's limited industrial sector, now less than one-sixth of GDP, continued to decline in 1993. A sharp fall in chromium prices reduced hard currency receipts from the mining sector. Large segments of the population, especially those living in urban areas, continue to depend on humanitarian aid to meet basic food requirements. Unemployment remains a severe problem accounting for approximately one-fifth of the work force. Growth is expected to continue in 1994, but could falter if Albania becomes involved in the conflict in the former Yugoslavia, workers' remittances from Greece are reduced, or foreign assistance declines.

National product: GDP—purchasing power equivalent—$3.3 billion (1993 est.)

National product real growth rate: 11% (1993)

National product per capita: $1,100 (1993 est.)

Inflation rate (consumer prices): 31% (1993 est.)

Unemployment rate: 18% (1993 est.)

Budget:
revenues: $1.1 billion
expenditures: $1.4 billion, including capital expenditures of $70 million (1991 est.)

Exports: $70 million (f.o.b., 1992)
commodities: asphalt, metals and metallic ores, electricity, crude oil, vegetables, fruits, tobacco
partners: Italy, The Former Yugoslav Republic of Macedonia, Germany, Greece, Czechoslovakia, Poland, Romania, Bulgaria, Hungary

Imports: $524 million (f.o.b., 1992)
commodities: machinery, consumer goods, grains
partners: Italy, The Former Yugoslav Republic of Macedonia, Germany, Czechoslovakia, Romania, Poland, Hungary, Bulgaria, Greece

External debt: $724 million (1993 est.)

Industrial production: growth rate -10% (1993 est.); accounts for 16% of GDP (1993 est.)

Electricity:
capacity: 1,690,000 kW
production: 5 billion kWh
consumption per capita: 1,520 kWh (1992)

Industries: food processing, textiles and clothing, lumber, oil, cement, chemicals,

mining, basic metals, hydropower
Agriculture: accounts for 55% of GDP; arable land per capita among lowest in Europe; 80% of arable land now in private hands; one-half of work force engaged in farming; produces wide range of temperate-zone crops and livestock
Illicit drugs: transshipment point for Southwest Asian heroin transiting the Balkan route; limited opium production
Economic aid:
recipient: $190 million humanitarian aid; $94 million in loans/guarantees/credits
Currency: 1 lek (L) = 100 qintars
Exchange rates: leke (L) per US$1—99 (January 1994), 97 (January 1993), 50 (January 1992), 25 (September 1991)
Fiscal year: calendar year

Communications

Railroads: 543 km total; 509 km 1.435-meter standard gauge, single track and 34 km narrow gauge, single track (1990); line connecting Titograd (Serbia and Montenegro) and Shkoder (Albania) completed August 1986
Highways:
total: 16,700 km
paved: 6,700 km
unpaved: earth 10,000 km (1990)
Inland waterways: 43 km plus Albanian sections of Lake Scutari, Lake Ohrid, and Lake Prespa (1990)
Pipelines: crude oil 145 km; petroleum products 55 km; natural gas 64 km (1991)
Ports: Durres, Sarande, Vlore
Merchant marine: 11 cargo ships (1,000 GRT or over) totaling 52,967 GRT/76,887 DWT
Airports:
total: 12
usable: 10
with permanent-surface runways: 3
with runways over 3,659 m: 0
with runways 2,440-3,659 m: 6
with runways 1,220-2,439 m: 4
Telecommunications: inadequate service; 15,000 telephones; broadcast stations—13 AM, 1 TV; 514,000 radios, 255,000 TVs (1987 est.)

Defense Forces

Branches: Army, Navy, Air and Air Defense Forces, Interior Ministry Troops
Manpower availability: males age 15-49 906,938; fit for military service 746,945; reach military age (19) annually 33,184 (1994 est.)
Defense expenditures: 215 million leke, NA% of GNP (1993 est.); note—conversion of defense expenditures into US dollars using the current exchange rate could produce misleading results

Geography

Location: Balkan State, Southeastern Europe, on the Balkan Peninsula between Serbia and Montenegro and Greece
Map references: Africa, Ethnic Groups in Eastern Europe, Europe, Standard Time Zones of the World
Area:
total area: 28,750 sq km
land area: 27,400 sq km
comparative area: slightly larger than Maryland
Land boundaries: total 720 km, Greece 282 km, The Former Yugoslav Republic of Macedonia 151 km, Serbia and Montenegro 287 km (114 km with Serbia, 173 km with Montenegro)
Coastline: 362 km
Maritime claims:
continental shelf: not specified
territorial sea: 12 nm
International disputes: Albanian majority in Kosovo seeks independence from Serbia and Montenegro, and the Albanian Government supports the Kosovo position politically
Climate: mild temperate; cool, cloudy, wet winters; hot, clear, dry summers; interior is cooler and wetter
Terrain: mostly mountains and hills; small plains along coast
Natural resources: petroleum, natural gas, coal, chromium, copper, timber, nickel
Land use:
arable land: 21%
permanent crops: 4%

meadows and pastures: 15%
forest and woodland: 38%
other: 22%
Irrigated land: 4,230 sq km (1989)
Environment:
current issues: deforestation
natural hazards: subject to destructive earthquakes; tsunami occur along southwestern coast
international agreements: party to—Biodiversity

Note: strategic location along Strait of Otranto (links Adriatic Sea to Ionian Sea and Mediterranean Sea)

People

Population: 3,374,085 (July 1994 est.)
note: IMF, working with Albanian government figures estimates the population at 3,120,000 in 1993 and that the population has fallen since 1990
Population growth rate: 1.19% (1994 est.)
Birth rate: 22.46 births/1,000 population (1994 est.)
Death rate: 5.32 deaths/1,000 population (1994 est.)
Net migration rate: -5.27 migrant(s)/1,000 population (1994 est.)
Infant mortality rate: 30 deaths/1,000 live births (1994 est.)
Life expectancy at birth:
total population: 73.4 years
male: 70.42 years
female: 76.61 years (1994 est.)
Total fertility rate: 2.78 children born/woman (1994 est.)
Nationality:
noun: Albanian(s)
adjective: Albanian
Ethnic divisions: Albanian 95%, Greeks 3%, other 2% (Vlachs, Gypsies, Serbs, and Bulgarians) (1989 est.)
Religions: Muslim 70%, Greek Orthodox 20%, Roman Catholic 10%
note: all mosques and churches were closed in 1967 and religious observances prohibited; in November 1990, Albania began allowing private religious practice
Languages: Albanian (Tosk is the official dialect), Greek
Literacy: age 9 and over can read and write (1955)
total population: 72%
male: 80%
female: 63%
Labor force: 1.5 million (1987)
by occupation: agriculture 60%, industry and commerce 40% (1986)

Government

Names:
conventional long form: Republic of Albania
conventional short form: Albania
local long form: Republika e Shqiperise
local short form: Shqiperia
former: People's Socialist Republic of Albania
Digraph: AL
Type: nascent democracy
Capital: Tirane
Administrative divisions: 26 districts (rrethe, singular—rreth); Berat, Dibre, Durres, Elbasan, Fier, Gjirokaster, Gramsh, Kolonje, Korce, Kruje, Kukes, Lezhe, Librazhd, Lushnje, Mat, Mirdite, Permet, Pogradec, Puke, Sarande, Shkoder, Skrapar, Tepelene, Tirane, Tropoje, Vlore
Independence: 28 November 1912 (from Ottoman Empire)
National holiday: Liberation Day, 28 November (1944; changed by decree on 12 November 1993)
Constitution: an interim basic law was approved by the People's Assembly on 29 April 1991; a new constitution was to be drafted for adoption in 1992, but is still in process
Legal system: has not accepted compulsory ICJ jurisdiction
Suffrage: 18 years of age, universal and compulsory
Executive branch:
chief of state: President of the Republic Sali BERISHA (since 9 April 1992)
head of government: Prime Minister of the Council of Ministers Aleksander Gabriel

MEKSI (since 10 April 1992)
cabinet: Council of Ministers; appointed by the president
Legislative branch: unicameral
People's Assembly (Kuvendi Popullor): elections last held 22 March 1992; results—DP 62.29%, ASP 25.57%, SDP 4.33%, RP 3.15%, UHP 2.92%, other 1.74%; seats—(140 total) DP 92, ASP 38, SDP 7, RP 1, UHP 2
Judicial branch: Supreme Court
Political parties and leaders: there are at least 18 political parties; most prominent are the Albanian Socialist Party (ASP; formerly the Albania Workers Party), Fatos NANO, first secretary; Democratic Party (DP), Eduard SELAMI, chairman; Albanian Republican Party (RP), Sabri GODO; Omonia (Greek minority party), leader NA (ran in 1992 election as Unity for Human Rights Party (UHP)); Social Democratic Party (SDP), Skender GJINUSHI; Democratic Alliance Party (DAP), Spartak NGJELA, chairman
Member of: BSEC, CCC, CE (guest), CSCE, EBRD, ECE, FAO, IAEA, IBRD, ICAO, IDA, IDB, IFAD, IFC, ILO, IMF, IMO, INTELSAT (nonsignatory user), INTERPOL, IOC, IOM (observer), ISO, ITU, LORCS, NACC, OIC, UN, UNCTAD, UNESCO, UNIDO, UPU, WFTU, WHO, WIPO, WMO
Diplomatic representation in US:
chief of mission: Ambassador Lublin Hasan DILJA
chancery: Suite 1010, 1511 K Street NW, Washington, DC 20005
telephone: (202) 223-4942, 8187
FAX: (202) 628-7342
US diplomatic representation:
chief of mission: Ambassador William E. RYERSON
embassy: Rruga E. Elbansanit 103, Tirane
mailing address: PSC 59, Box 100 (A), APO AE 09624
telephone: 355-42-32875, 33520
FAX: 355-42-32222
Flag: red with a black two-headed eagle in the center

U.S. Government Contacts:

U.S. Trade Desk: (202) 482-4915

ARMENIA

Economy

Overview: Under the old central planning system, Armenia had built up a developed industrial sector, supplying machine building equipment, textiles, and other manufactured goods to sister republics in exchange for raw materials and energy resources. Armenia is a large food importer and its mineral deposits (gold, bauxite) are small. The economic decline in the past three years (1991-93) has been particularly severe due to the ongoing conflict over the Armenian enclave of Nagorno-Karabakh in Azerbaijan. Azerbaijan and Turkey have blockaded pipeline and railroad traffic to Armenia for its support of the Karabakh Armenians. This has left Armenia with only sporadic deliveries of natural gas through unstable Georgia, while other fuel and raw materials are in critical short supply. Inflation, roughly 14% per month in the first nine months of 1993, surged even higher in the fourth quarter. In late 1993, most industrial enterprises were either shut down or operating at drastically reduced levels. Only small quantities of food were available (mostly humanitarian aid), heat was nonexistent, and electricity strictly rationed. An economic recovery cannot be expected until the Nagorno-Karabakh conflict is settled and until transportation through Georgia improves.
National product: GDP—purchasing power equivalent—$7.1 billion (1993 estimate from the UN International Comparison Program, as extended to 1991 and published in the World Bank's World Development Report 1993; and as extrapolated to 1993 using official Armenian statistics, which are very uncertain because of major economic changes since 1990)
National product real growth rate: -9.9% (1993 est.)
National product per capita: $2,040 (1993 est.)
Inflation rate (consumer prices): 14% per month average (first 9 months, 1993)
Unemployment rate: 6.5% of officially registered unemployed but large numbers of underemployed (1993 est.)
Budget:
revenues: $NA
expenditures: $NA, including capital expenditures of $NA
Exports: $31 million to countries outside the FSU (f.o.b., 1993)
commodities: machinery and transport equipment, light industrial products, processed food items, alcoholic products (1991)
partners: NA
Imports: $87 million from countries outside the FSU (c.i.f., 1993)
commodities: grain, other foods, fuel, other energy (1991)
partners: Russia, US, EC
External debt: $NA
Industrial production: growth rate -11% (1993 est.)
Electricity:
capacity: 2,875,000 kW
production: 9 billion kWh
consumption per capita: 2,585 kWh (1992)

Industries: traditionally diverse, including (as a percent of output of former USSR) metalcutting machine tools (5.5%), forging-pressing machines (1.9%), electric motors (9%), tires (1.5%), knitted wear (4.4%), hosiery (3.0%), shoes (2.2%), silk fabric (0.8%), washing machines (2.0%), chemicals, trucks, watches, instruments, and microelectronics (1990); currently, much of industry is shut down
Agriculture: accounts for about 45% of GDP; only 17% of land area is arable; employs 20-30% of labor force as residents increasingly turn to subsistence agriculture; fruits (especially grapes) and vegetable farming, minor livestock sector; vineyards near Yerevan are famous for brandy and other liqueurs
Illicit drugs: illicit cultivator of cannabis mostly for domestic consumption; used as a transshipment point for illicit drugs to Western Europe
Economic aid:
recipient: considerable humanitarian aid, mostly food and energy products, from US and EC; Russia has granted 60 billion rubles in technical credits
Currency: 1 dram = 100 luma; introduced separate currency in November 1993
Exchange rates: NA
Fiscal year: calendar year

Communications

Railroads: 840 km; does not include industrial lines (1990)
Highways:
total: 11,300 km
paved: 10,500 km
unpaved: earth 800 km (1990)
Inland waterways: NA km
Pipelines: natural gas 900 km (1991)
Ports: none; landlocked
Airports:
total: 12
usable: 10
with permanent-surface runways: 6
with runways over 3,659 m: 1
with runways 2,440-3,659 m: 3
with runways 1,060-2,439 m: 2
note: a C-130 can land on a 1,060-m airstrip
Telecommunications: progress on installation of fiber optic cable and construction of facilities for mobile cellular phone service remains in the negotiation phase for joint venture agreement; Armenia has about 650,000 telephones; average telephone density is 17.7 per 100 persons; international connections to other former republics of the USSR are by landline or microwave and to other countries by satellite and by leased connection through the Moscow international gateway switch; broadcast stations—100% of population receives Armenian and Russian TV programs; satellite earth station—INTELSAT

Defense Forces

Branches: Army, Air Force, National Guard, Security Forces (internal and border troops)
Manpower availability: males age 15-49 862,921; fit for military service 690,113; reach military age (18) annually 28,458 (1994 est.)
Defense expenditures: 250 million rubles, NA% of GDP (1992 est.); note—conversion of the military budget into US dollars using the current exchange rate could produce misleading results

Geography

Location: Southwestern Asia, between Turkey and Azerbaijan
Map references: Africa, Asia, Commonwealth of Independent States—European States, Middle East, Standard Time Zones of the World
Area:
total area: 29,800 sq km
land area: 28,400 sq km
comparative area: slightly larger than Maryland
Land boundaries: total 1,254 km, Azerbaijan (east) 566 km, Azerbaijan (south) 221 km, Georgia 164 km, Iran 35 km, Turkey 268 km
Coastline: 0 km (landlocked)
Maritime claims: none; landlocked
International disputes: violent and longstanding dispute with Azerbaijan over

ethnically Armenian exclave of Nagorno-Karabakh; traditional demands on former Armenian lands in Turkey have greatly subsided
Climate: highland continental, hot summers, cold winters
Terrain: high Armenian Plateau with mountains; little forest land; fast flowing rivers; good soil in Aras River valley
Natural resources: small deposits of gold, copper, molybdenum, zinc, alumina
Land use:
arable land: 17%
permanent crops: 3%
meadows and pastures: 20%
forest and woodland: 0%
other: 60%
Irrigated land: 3,050 sq km (1990)
Environment:
current issues: soil pollution from toxic chemicals such as DDT; energy blockade, the result of conflict with Azerbaijan, has led to deforestation as citizens scavenge for firewood; pollution of Hrazdan (Razdan) and Aras Rivers; the draining of Lake Sevan, a result of its use as a source for hydropower, threatens drinking water supplies; air pollution in Yerevan
natural hazards: occasionally severe earthquakes (25,000 people killed in major quake in 1988); subject to drought
international agreements: party to—Biodiversity, Climate Change
Note: landlocked

People

Population: 3,521,517 (July 1994 est.)
Population growth rate: 1.08% (1994 est.)
Birth rate: 24.21 births/1,000 population (1994 est.)
Death rate: 6.72 deaths/1,000 population (1994 est.)
Net migration rate: -6.72 migrant(s)/1,000 population (1994 est.)
Infant mortality rate: 27.1 deaths/1,000 live births (1994 est.)
Life expectancy at birth:
total population: 72.07 years
male: 68.65 years
female: 75.65 years (1994 est.)
Total fertility rate: 3.19 children born/woman (1994 est.)
Nationality:
noun: Armenian(s)
adjective: Armenian
Ethnic divisions: Armenian 93%, Azeri 3%, Russian 2%, other 2%
Religions: Armenian Orthodox 94%
Languages: Armenian 96%, Russian 2%, other 2%
Literacy: age 9-49 can read and write (1970)
total population: 100%
male: 100%
female: 100%
Labor force: 1.578 million
by occupation: industry and construction 34%, agriculture and forestry 31%, other 35% (1992)

Government

Names:
conventional long form: Republic of Armenia
conventional short form: Armenia
local long form: Hayastani Hanrapetut'yun
local short form: Hayastan
former: Armenian Soviet Socialist Republic; Armenian Republic
Digraph: AM
Type: republic
Capital: Yerevan
Administrative divisions: none (all rayons are under direct republic jurisdiction)
Independence: 28 May 1918 (First Armenian Republic); 23 September 1991 (from Soviet Union)
National holiday: Referendum Day, 21 September
Constitution: adopted NA April 1978; post-Soviet constitution not yet adopted
Legal system: based on civil law system
Suffrage: 18 years of age; universal
Executive branch:
chief of state: President Levon Akopovich TER-PETROSYAN (since 16 October 1991), Vice President Gagik ARUTYUNYAN (since 16 October 1991); election last held 16 October 1991 (next to be held NA); results—Levon

Akopovich TER-PETROSYAN 86%; radical nationalists about 7%; note—Levon Akopovich TER-PETROSYAN was elected Chairman of the Armenian Supreme Soviet 4 August 1990 before becoming president
head of government: Prime Minister Hrant BAGRATYAN (since 16 February 1993); First Deputy Prime Minister Vigen CHITECHYAN (since 16 February 1993)
cabinet: Council of Ministers; appointed by the president
Legislative branch: unicameral
Supreme Soviet: elections last held 20 May 1990 (next to be held NA); results—percent of vote by party NA; seats—(260 total) non-aligned 125, ANM 52, DPA 23, Democratic Liberal Party 17, ARF 17, NDU 9, Christian Democratic Party 1, Constitutional Rights Union 1, UNSD 1, Republican Party 1, Nagorno-Karabakh representatives 13
Judicial branch: Supreme Court
Political parties and leaders: Armenian National Movement (ANM), Ter-Husik LAZARYAN, chairman; National Democratic Union (NDU), David VARTANYAN, chairman; Armenian Revolutionary Federation (ARF, Dashnaktsutyun), Arutyun ALISTAKESYAN, chairman; Democratic Party of Armenia (DPA; Communist Party), Aram SARKISYAN, chairman; Christian Democratic Party, Azat ARSHAKYAN, chairman; Greens Party, Hakob SANASARIAN, chairman; Democratic Liberal Party, Rouben MIRZAKHANYAN, chairman; Republican Party, Ashot NAVARSARDYAN, chairman; Union for Self-Determination (UNSD), Paruir AIRIKYAN, chairman
Member of: BSEC, CCC, CIS, CSCE, EBRD, ECE, IAEA, IBRD, ICAO, IDA, IFAD, ILO, IMF, INTELSAT, INTERPOL, IOC, ITU, NACC, NAM (observer), UN, UNCTAD, UNESCO, UNIDO, UPU, WHO, WIPO, WMO
Diplomatic representation in US:
chief of mission: Ambassador Rouben Robert SHUGARIAN
chancery: Suite 210, 1660 L Street NW, Washington, DC 20036
telephone: (202) 628-5766
US diplomatic representation:
chief of mission: Ambassador Harry J. GILMORE
embassy: 18 Gen Bagramian, Yerevan
mailing address: use embassy street address
telephone: 7-8852-151-144 or 8852-524-661
FAX: 7-8852-151-138
Flag: three equal horizontal bands of red (top), blue, and gold

U.S. Government Contacts:

U.S. Trade Desk: (202) 482-0988

AZERBAIJAN

Economy

Overview: Azerbaijan is less developed industrially than either Armenia or Georgia, the other Transcaucasian states. It resembles the Central Asian states in its majority Muslim population, high structural unemployment, and low standard of living. The economy's most prominent products are oil, cotton, and gas. Production from the Caspian oil and gas field has been in decline for several years. With foreign assistance, the oil industry might generate the funds needed to spur industrial development. However, civil unrest, marked by armed conflict in the Nagorno-Karabakh region between Muslim Azeris and Christian Armenians, makes foreign investors wary. Azerbaijan accounted for 1.5% to 2% of the capital stock and output of the former Soviet Union. Azerbaijan shares all the formidable problems of the ex-Soviet republics in making the transition from a command to a market economy, but its considerable energy resources brighten its prospects somewhat. Old economic ties and structures have yet to be replaced. A particularly galling constraint on economic revival is the Nagorno-Karabakh conflict, said to consume 25% of Azerbaijan's economic resources.

National product: GDP—purchasing power equivalent—$15.5 billion (1993 estimate from the UN International Comparison Program, as extended to 1991 and published in the World Bank's World Development Report 1993; and as extrapolated to 1993 using official Azerbaijani statistics, which are very uncertain because of major economic changes since 1990)

with runways over 3,659 m: 0
with runways 2,440-3,659 m: 8
with runways 1,220-2,439 m: 23

Telecommunications: domestic telephone service is of poor quality and inadequate; 710,000 domestic telephone lines (density—9 lines per 100 persons (1991)), 202,000 persons waiting for telephone installations (January 1991); connections to other former USSR republics by cable and microwave and to other countries via the Moscow international gateway switch; INTELSAT earth station installed in late 1992 in Baku with Turkish financial assistance with access to 200 countries through Turkey; since August 1993 an earth station near Baku has provided direct communications with New York through Russia's Stationar-11 satellite; a joint venture to establish a cellular telephone system (Bakcel) in the Baku area is supposed to become operational in 1994; domestic and Russian TV programs are received locally and Turkish and Iranian TV is received from an INTELSAT satellite through a receive-only earth station

Defense Forces

Branches: Army, Air Force, Navy, Maritime Border Guard, National Guard, Security Forces (internal and border troops)

Manpower availability: males age 15-49 1,884,458; fit for military service 1,525,123; reach military age (18) annually 68,192 (1994

est.)
Defense expenditures: 2,848 million rubles, NA% of GDP (1992 est.); note—conversion of the military budget into US dollars using the current exchange rate could produce misleading results
National product real growth rate: -13.3% (1993 est.)
National product per capita: $2,040 (1993 est.)
Inflation rate (consumer prices): 20% per month (average 1993); above 50% per month (February 1994)
Unemployment rate: 0.7% includes officially registered unemployed; also large numbers of underemployed workers (December 1993)
Budget:
revenues: $NA
expenditures: $NA, including capital expenditures of $NA
Exports: $355 million to outside the FSU countries (f.o.b., 1993)
commodities: oil and gas, chemicals, oilfield equipment, textiles, cotton (1991)
partners: mostly CIS and European countries
Imports: $240 million from outside the FSU countries (c.i.f., 1993)
commodities: machinery and parts, consumer durables, foodstuffs, textiles (1991)
partners: European countries
External debt: $NA
Industrial production: growth rate -7% (1993)
Electricity:
capacity: 6,025,000 kW
production: 22,300 kWh
consumption per capita: 2,990 kWh (1992)
Industries: petroleum and natural gas, petroleum products, oilfield equipment; steel, iron ore, cement; chemicals and petrochemicals; textiles
Agriculture: cotton, grain, rice, grapes, fruit, vegetables, tea, tobacco; cattle, pigs, sheep and goats
Illicit drugs: illicit cultivator of cannabis and opium poppy; mostly for CIS consumption; limited government eradication program; transshipment point for illicit drugs to Western Europe
Economic aid:
recipient: wheat from Turkey
Currency: 1 manat = 100 gopik
Exchange rates: NA
Fiscal year: calendar year

Communications

Railroads: 2,090 km; does not include industrial lines (1990)
Highways:
total: 36,700 km
paved or graveled: 31,800 km
unpaved: earth 4,900 km (1990)
Pipelines: crude oil 1,130 km, petroleum products 630 km, natural gas 1,240 km
Ports: inland—Baku (Baky)
Airports:
total: 65
usable: 33
with permanent-surface runways: 26

Geography

Location: Southwestern Asia, between Armenia and Turkmenistan, bordering the Caspian Sea
Map references: Africa, Asia, Commonwealth of Independent States—Central Asian States, Commonwealth of Independent States—European States, Middle East, Standard Time Zones of the World
Area:
total area: 86,600 sq km
land area: 86,100 sq km
comparative area: slightly larger than Maine
note: includes the Nakhichevan Autonomous Republic and the Nagorno-Karabakh regions; regions' autonomy was abolished by Azerbaijani Supreme Soviet on 26 November 1991
Land boundaries: total 2,013 km, Armenia (west) 566 km, Armenia (southwest) 221 km, Georgia 322 km, Iran (south) 432 km, Iran (southwest) 179 km, Russia 284 km, Turkey 9 km
Coastline: 0 km (landlocked)
note: Azerbaijan borders the Caspian Sea (800 km, est.)
Maritime claims: NA

note: Azerbaijani claims in Caspian Sea unknown; 10-nm fishing zone provided for in 1940 treaty regarding trade and navigation between Soviet Union and Iran
International disputes: violent and longstanding dispute with ethnic Armenians of Nagorno-Karabakh over its status, lesser dispute concerns Nakhichevan; some Azerbaijanis desire absorption of and/or unification with the ethnic Azeri portion of Iran
Climate: dry, semiarid steppe
Terrain: large, flat Kur-Araz Lowland (much of it below sea level) with Great Caucasus Mountains to the north, Qarabag (Karabakh) Upland in west; Baku lies on Abseron (Apsheron) Peninsula that juts into Caspian Sea
Natural resources: petroleum, natural gas, iron ore, nonferrous metals, alumina
Land use:
arable land: 18%
permanent crops: 4%
meadows and pastures: 25%
forest and woodland: 0%
other: 53%
Irrigated land: 14,010 sq km (1990)
Environment:
current issues: local scientists consider the Abseron (Apsheron) Peninsula (including Baku and Sumqayit) and the Caspian Sea to be the ecologically most devastated area in the world because of severe air, water, and soil pollution; soil pollution results from the use of DDT as a pesticide and also from toxic defoliants used in the production of cotton
natural hazards: subject to drought; some coastal areas threatened by rising levels of the Caspian Sea
international agreements: signed, but not ratified—Biodiversity, Climate Change
Note: landlocked

People

Population: 7,684,456 (July 1994 est.)
Population growth rate: 1.41% (1994 est.)
Birth rate: 23.04 births/1,000 population (1994 est.)
Death rate: 6.58 deaths/1,000 population (1994 est.)
Net migration rate: -2.38 migrant(s)/1,000 population (1994 est.)
Infant mortality rate: 34.8 deaths/1,000 live births (1994 est.)
Life expectancy at birth:
total population: 70.85 years
male: 67.08 years
female: 74.8 years (1994 est.)
Total fertility rate: 2.7 children born/woman (1994 est.)
Nationality:
noun: Azerbaijani(s)
adjective: Azerbaijani
Ethnic divisions: Azeri 82.7%, Russian 5.6%, Armenian 5.6%, Dagestani 3.2%, other 2.9% (1989)
note: Armenian share is now approximately 0.3% because most Armenians have fled the ethnic violence since 1989 census; Russian percentage is probably half what it was for the same reason
Religions: Muslim 87%, Russian Orthodox 5.6%, Armenian Orthodox 5.6%, other 1.8%
Languages: Azeri 82%, Russian 7%, Armenian 5%, other 6%
Literacy: age 9-49 can read and write (1970)
total population: 100%
male: 100%
female: 100%
Labor force: 2.789 million
by occupation: agriculture and forestry 32%, industry and construction 26%, other 42% (1990)

Government

Names:
conventional long form: Azerbaijani Republic
conventional short form: Azerbaijan
local long form: Azarbaycan Respublikasi
local short form: none
former: Azerbaijan Soviet Socialist Republic
Digraph: AJ
Type: republic
Capital: Baku (Baky)
Administrative divisions: 1 autonomous republic (avtomnaya respublika); Nakhichevan (administrative center at Nakhichevan)
note: all rayons except for the exclave of

Nakhichevan are under direct republic jurisdiction
Independence: 30 August 1991 (from Soviet Union)
National holiday: Novruz Bayram, 21-22 March
Constitution: adopted NA April 1978; writing a new constitution mid-1993
Legal system: based on civil law system
Suffrage: 18 years of age; universal
Executive branch:
chief of state: President Heydar ALIYEV (since 18 June 1993 after President ELCIBEY left Baku for Nakhichevan); election last held 3 October 1993 (next to be held NA); results—Heydar ALIYEV won 97% of vote
head of government: Prime Minister Surat HUSEYNOV (since 30 June 1993)
cabinet: Council of Ministers; appointed by the president and confirmed by the Mejlas
Legislative branch: unicameral
National Assembly (Milli Mejlis): elections last held 30 September and 14 October 1990 for the Supreme Soviet (next expected to be held NA 1994 for the National Assembly); seats for Supreme Soviet—(360 total) Communists 280, Democratic Bloc 45 (grouping of opposition parties), other 15, vacant 20; note—on 19 May 1992 the Supreme Soviet was prorogued in favor of a Popular Front-dominated National Council; seats—(50 total) Popular Front 25, opposition elements 25
Judicial branch: Supreme Court
Political parties and leaders: Azerbaijan Popular Front (APF), Ebulfez ELCIBEY, chairman; Musavat Party, Isa GAMBAR, chairman; National Independence Party, Etibar MAMEDOV, chairman; Social Democratic Party (SDP), Araz ALIZADE, chairman; Communist Party, Ramiz AKHMEDOV, chairman; People's Freedom Party, Yunus OGUZ, chairman; Independent Social Democratic Party, Arif YUNUSOV and Leila YUNOSOVA, cochairmen; New Azerbaijan Party, Heydar ALIYEV, chairman; Boz Gurd Party, Iskander HAMIDOV, chairman; Azerbaijan Democratic Party, Sardar MAMEDOV, chairman; Azerbaijan Democratic Independence Party, Qabil HUSELNLI, chairman; Islamic Party of Azerbaijan, Ali Akram, chairman
Other political or pressure groups: self-proclaimed Armenian Nagorno-Karabakh Republic; Talysh independence movement
Member of: BSEC, CCC, CIS, CSCE, EBRD, ECE, ECO, ESCAP, IBRD, ICAO, IDB, ILO, IMF, INTELSAT, INTERPOL, IOC, ITU, NACC, OIC, UN, UNCTAD, UNESCO, UPU, WHO
Diplomatic representation in US:
chief of mission: Ambassador Hafiz Mir Jalal Ogly PASHAYEV
chancery: Suite 700, 927 15th Street NW, Washington, DC 20005
telephone: (202) 842-0001
FAX: (202) 842-0004
US diplomatic representation:
chief of mission: Ambassador Richard KAZLAURICH
embassy: Hotel Intourist, Baku
mailing address: use embassy street address
telephone: 7-8922-92-63-06 through 09, extension 441, 442, 446, 447, 448, 450
FAX: Telex 142110 AMEMB SU
Flag: three equal horizontal bands of blue (top), red, and green; a crescent and eight-pointed star in white are centered in red band

U.S. Government Contacts:

U.S. Trade Desk: (202) 482-0988

BELARUS

Economy

Overview: Belarus ranks among the most developed of the former Soviet states, with a relatively modern—by Soviet standards—and diverse machine building sector and a robust agriculture sector. It also serves as a transport link for Russian oil exports to the Baltic states and Eastern and Western Europe. The breakup of the Soviet Union and its command economy has resulted in a sharp economic contraction as traditional trade ties have collapsed. At the same time, the Belarusian Government has lagged behind most other former Soviet states in economic reform; privatization has barely begun; the agriculture sector remains highly subsidized; the state retains control over many prices; and the system of state orders and distribution persists. Meanwhile, the national bank continues to pour credits into inefficient enterprises, fueling inflation and weakening incentives to improve performance. The government is pinning its hopes on reintegration with the Russian economy, but such a path would only partially restore traditional trade ties. Until economic reform is embraced, Belarus will continue in its economic morass.

National product: GDP—purchasing power equivalent—$61 billion (1993 estimate from the UN International Comparison Program, as extended to 1991 and published in the World Bank's World Development Report 1993; and as extrapolated to 1993 using official Belarusian statistics, which are very uncertain because of major economic changes since 1990)

National product real growth rate: -9% (1993 est.)

National product per capita: $5,890 (1993 est.)

Inflation rate (consumer prices): 30% per month (1993)

Unemployment rate: 1.4% officially registered unemployed (December 1993); large numbers of underemployed workers

Budget:
revenues: $NA
expenditures: $NA, including capital expenditures of $NA

Exports: $710 million to outside of the FSU countries (f.o.b., 1993)
commodities: machinery and transport equipment, chemicals, foodstuffs
partners: Russia, Ukraine, Poland, Bulgaria

Imports: $743 million from outside the FSU countries (c.i.f., 1993)
commodities: fuel, industrial raw materials, textiles, sugar
partners: Russia, Ukraine, Poland

External debt: $NA

Industrial production: growth rate -11.0% (1993); accounts for about 40% of GDP (1992)

Electricity:
capacity: 8,025,000 kW
production: 37.6 billion kWh
consumption per capita: 3,626 kWh (1992)

Industries: employ about 40% of labor force and produce a wide variety of products including (in percent share of total output of former Soviet Union): tractors (12%); metal-

cutting machine tools (11%); off-highway dump trucks up to 110-metric-ton load capacity (100%); wheel-type earthmovers for construction and mining (100%); eight-wheel-drive, high-flotation trucks with cargo capacity of 25 metric tons for use in tundra and roadless areas (100%); equipment for animal husbandry and livestock feeding (25%); motorcycles (21.3%); television sets (11%); chemical fibers (28%); fertilizer (18%); linen fabric (11%); wool fabric (7%); radios; refrigerators; and other consumer goods
Agriculture: accounts for almost 25% of GDP and 5.7% of total agricultural output of former Soviet Union; employs 21% of the labor force; in 1988 produced the following (in percent of total Soviet production): grain (3.6%), potatoes (12.2%), vegetables (3.0%), meat (6.0%), milk (7.0%); net exporter of meat, milk, eggs, flour, potatoes
Illicit drugs: illicit cultivator of opium poppy and cannabis; mostly for the domestic market; transshipment point for illicit drugs to Western Europe
Economic aid: $NA
Currency: Belarusian rubel
note: the government signed a framework agreement with Russia for a monetary union in January 1994, but a schedule and mechanism for merging the two monetary systems and replacing Belarusian rubels with Russian rubles have not been worked out
Exchange rates: NA
Fiscal year: calendar year

Communications

Railroads: 5,570 km; does not include industrial lines (1990)
Highways:
total: 98,200 km
paved: 66,100 km
unpaved: earth 32,100 km (1990)
Inland waterways: NA km
Pipelines: crude oil 1,470 km, refined products 1,100 km, natural gas 1,980 km (1992)
Ports: none; landlocked
Merchant marine: claims 5% of former Soviet fleet
Airports:
total: 124
usable: 55
with permanent-surface runways: 31
with runways over 3,659 m: 1
with runways 2,440-3,659 m: 28
with runways 1,060-2,439 m: 20
note: a C-130 can land on a 1,060-m airstrip
Telecommunications: telephone service in Belarus is inadequate for the purposes of either business or the population; total number of telephones 1,849,000 (31 December 1991); telephone density—18 for each 100 persons; about 70% of the telephones are in homes; over 750,000 applications from households for telephones remain unsatisfied (1992); new investment centers on international connections and business needs; the new BelCel NMT 450 cellular system (a joint venture) is now operating in Minsk but progress has been slower in establishing an INTELSAT earth station; international traffic still relies on the Moscow international gateway switch; broadcast receivers—television 3,538,000, radio 3,140,000, radio receivers with multiple speaker systems for program diffusion 5,615,000

Defense Forces

Branches: Army, Air Forces, Air Defense Forces, Security Forces (internal and border troops)
Manpower availability: males age 15-49 2,520,487; fit for military service 1,981,749; reach military age (18) annually 71,922 (1994 est.)
Defense expenditures: 56.5 billion rubles, NA% of GDP (1993 est.); note—conversion of the military budget into US dollars using the current exchange rate could produce misleading results

Geography

Location: Eastern Europe, between Poland and Russia

Map references: Asia, Commonwealth of Independent States—European States, Europe, Standard Time Zones of the World
Area:
total area: 207,600 sq km
land area: 207,600 sq km
comparative area: slightly smaller than Kansas
Land boundaries: total 3,098 km, Latvia 141 km, Lithuania 502 km, Poland 605 km, Russia 959 km, Ukraine 891 km
Coastline: 0 km (landlocked)
Maritime claims: none; landlocked
International disputes: none
Climate: cold winters, cool and moist summers; transitional between continental and maritime
Terrain: generally flat and contains much marshland
Natural resources: forest land, peat deposits
Land use:
arable land: 29%
permanent crops: 1%
meadows and pastures: 15%
forest and woodland: 0%
other: 55%
Irrigated land: 1,490 sq km (1990)
Environment:
current issues: soil pollution from pesticide use; southern part of Belarus contaminated with fallout from 1986 nuclear reactor accident at Chornobyl'
natural hazards: NA
international agreements: party to—Air Pollution, Air Pollution-Nitrogen Oxides, Air Pollution-Sulphur, Biodiversity, Environmental Modification, Marine Dumping, Ozone Layer Protection; signed, but not ratified—Climate Change, Law of the Sea
Note: landlocked

People

Population: 10,404,862 (July 1994 est.)
Population growth rate: 0.32% (1994 est.)
Birth rate: 13.12 births/1,000 population (1994 est.)
Death rate: 11.16 deaths/1,000 population (1994 est.)
Net migration rate: 1.27 migrant(s)/1,000 population (1994 est.)
Infant mortality rate: 18.9 deaths/1,000 live births (1994 est.)
Life expectancy at birth:
total population: 70.88 years
male: 66.2 years
female: 75.79 years (1994 est.)
Total fertility rate: 1.88 children born/woman (1994 est.)
Nationality:
noun: Belarusian(s)
adjective: Belarusian
Ethnic divisions: Byelorussian 77.9%, Russian 13.2%, Polish 4.1%, Ukrainian 2.9%, other 1.9%
Religions: Eastern Orthodox, other
Languages: Byelorussian, Russian, other
Literacy: age 9-49 can read and write (1979)
total population: 100%
male: 100%
female: 100%
Labor force: 4.887 million
by occupation: industry and construction 40%, agriculture and forestry 21%, other 39% (1992)

Government

Names:
conventional long form: Republic of Belarus
conventional short form: Belarus
local long form: Respublika Byelarus'
local short form: none
former: Belorussian (Byelorussian) Soviet Socialist Republic
Digraph: BO
Type: republic
Capital: Minsk
Administrative divisions: 6 voblastsi (singular—voblasts') and one municipality* (harady, singular—horad); Brestskaya (Brest), Homyel'skaya (Homyel'), Horad Minsk*, Hrodzyenskaya (Hrodna), Mahilyowskaya (Mahilyow), Minskaya, Vitsyebskaya (Vitsyebsk)
note: the administrative centers of the voblastsi are included in parentheses
Independence: 25 August 1991 (from Soviet Union)
National holiday: Independence Day, 27 July

(1990)
Constitution: adopted 15 March 1994; replaces constitution of April 1978
Legal system: based on civil law system
Suffrage: 18 years of age; universal
Executive branch:
chief of state: Chairman of the Supreme Soviet Mechislav Ivanovich GRIB (since 28 January 1994)
head of government: Prime Minister Vyacheslav F. KEBICH (since NA April 1990), First Deputy Prime Minister Mikhail MYASNIKOVICH (since NA 1991)
cabinet: Council of Ministers
note: first presidential elections scheduled for 23 June 1994
Legislative branch: unicameral
Supreme Soviet: elections last held 4 April 1990 (next to be held NA); results—Communists 87%; seats—(360 total) number of seats by party NA; note—50 seats are for public bodies; the Communist Party obtained an overwhelming majority
Judicial branch: Supreme Court
Political parties and leaders: Belarusian Popular Front (BPF), Zenon PAZNYAK, chairman; United Democratic Party of Belarus (UDPB), Aleksandr DOBROVOLSKIY, chairman; Social Democratic Party of Belarus (SDBP), Mikhail TKACHEV, chairman; Belarus Workers Union, Mikhail SOBOL, Chairman; Belarus Peasants Party; Party of People's Unity, Gennadiy KARPENKO; Movement for Democracy, Social Progress, and Justice (DSPS; includes the Communist Party), Viktor CHIKIN, chairman
Member of: CBSS (observer), CE (guest), CEI (participating), CIS, CSCE, ECE, IAEA, IBRD, ICAO, IFC, ILO, IMF, INMARSAT, INTELSAT (nonsignatory user), IOC, ITU, NACC, PCA, UN, UNCTAD, UNESCO, UNIDO, UPU, WHO, WIPO, WMO
Diplomatic representation in US:
chief of mission: Ambassador Sergey Nikolayevich MARTYNOV
chancery: 1619 New Hampshire Avenue NW, Washington, DC 20009
telephone: (202) 986-1604
FAX: (202) 986-1805)
US diplomatic representation:
chief of mission: (vacant); Charge d'Affaires George KROL
embassy: Starovilenskaya #46, Minsk
mailing address: use embassy street address
telephone: 7-0172-34-65-37
Flag: three horizontal bands of white (top), red, and white

U.S. Government Contacts:

U.S. Trade Desk: (202) 482-1104

BOSNIA AND HERZEGOVINA

Note: Bosnia and Herzegovina is suffering from interethnic civil strife which began in March 1992 after the Government of Bosnia and Herzegovina held a referendum on independence. Bosnia's Serbs—supported by neighboring Serbia—responded with armed resistance aimed at partitioning the republic along ethnic lines and joining Serb-held areas to a "greater Serbia." Since the onset of the conflict, which has driven approximately half of the pre-war population of 4.4 million from their homes, both the Bosnian Serbs and the Bosnian Croats have asserted control of more than three-quarters of the territory formerly under the control of the Government of Bosnia and Herzegovina. The UN and the EU are continuing to try to mediate a plan for peace. In March 1994 Bosnian Muslims and Bosnian Croats signed an agreement in Washington, DC, creating a Federation of Bosnia and Herzegovina, which is to include territories in which Muslims or Croats predominated, according to the 1991 census. Bosnian Serbs refused to become a part of this Federation.

Economy

Overview: Bosnia and Herzegovina ranked next to The Former Yugoslav Republic of Macedonia as the poorest republic in the old Yugoslav federation. Although agriculture has been almost all in private hands, farms have been small and inefficient, and the republic traditionally has been a net importer of food. Industry has been greatly overstaffed, one reflection of the rigidities of Communist central planning and management. Tito had pushed the development of military industries in the republic with the result that Bosnia hosted a large share of Yugoslavia's defense plants. As of April 1994, Bosnia and Herzegovina was being torn apart by the continued bitter interethnic warfare that has caused production to plummet, unemployment and inflation to soar, and human misery to multiply. No reliable economic statistics for 1992-93 are available, although output clearly has fallen substantially below the levels of earlier years.
National product: GDP—purchasing power equivalent—$NA
National product real growth rate: NA%
National product per capita: $NA
Inflation rate (consumer prices): NA%
Unemployment rate: NA%
Budget:
revenues: $NA
expenditures: $NA, including capital expenditures of $NA
Exports: $NA
commodities: NA
partners: NA
Imports: $NA
commodities: NA
partners: NA
External debt: $NA
Industrial production: growth rate NA%, but production is sharply down because of interethnic and interrepublic warfare (1991-93)
Electricity:

capacity: NA kW
production: NA kWh
consumption per capita: NA kWh
Industries: steel production, mining (coal, iron ore, lead, zinc, manganese, and bauxite), manufacturing (vehicle assembly, textiles, tobacco products, wooden furniture, 40% of former Yugoslavia's armaments including tank and aircraft assembly, domestic appliances), oil refining (1991)
Agriculture: accounted for 9.0% of GDP in 1989; regularly produces less than 50% of food needs; the foothills of northern Bosnia support orchards, vineyards, livestock, and some wheat and corn; long winters and heavy precipitation leach soil fertility reducing agricultural output in the mountains; farms are mostly privately held, small, and not very productive (1991)
Illicit drugs: NA
Economic aid: $NA
Currency: 1 dinar = 100 para; Croatian dinar used in Croat-held area, presumably to be replaced by new Croatian kuna; old and new Serbian dinars used in Serb-held area; hard currencies probably supplanting local currencies in areas held by Bosnian government
Exchange rates: NA
Fiscal year: calendar year

Communications

Railroads: NA km
Highways:
total: 21,168 km
paved: 11,436 km
unpaved: gravel 8,146 km; earth 1,586 km (1991)
Inland waterways: NA km
Pipelines: crude oil 174 km, natural gas 90 km (1992); note—pipelines now disrupted
Ports: coastal—none; inland—Bosanski Brod on the Sava River
Airports:
total: 28
usable: 24
with permanent-surface runways: 5
with runways over 3659: 0
with runways 2440-3659 m: 3
with runways 1220-2439 m: 6
Telecommunications: telephone and telegraph network is in need of modernization and expansion, many urban areas being below average compared with services in other former Yugoslav republics; 727,000 telephones; broadcast stations—9 AM, 2 FM, 6 TV; 840,000 radios; 1,012,094 TVs; satellite ground stations—none

Defense Forces

Branches: Army
Manpower availability: males age 15-49 1,298,102; fit for military service 1,054,068; reach military age (19) annually 38,283 (1994 est.)
Defense expenditures: $NA, NA% of GDP

Geography

Location: Balkan State, Southeastern Europe, on the Balkan Peninsula, between Croatia and Serbia and Montenegro
Map references: Africa, Arctic Region, Ethnic Groups in Eastern Europe, Europe, Standard Time Zones of the World
Area:
total area: 51,233 sq km
land area: 51,233 sq km
comparative area: slightly larger than Tennessee
Land boundaries: total 1,459 km, Croatia 932 km, Serbia and Montenegro 527 km (312 km with Serbia; 215 km with Montenegro)
Coastline: 20 km
Maritime claims:
continental shelf: 200-m depth
exclusive economic zone: 12 nm
exclusive fishing zone: 12 nm
territorial sea: 12 nm

Nationality:
noun: Bosnian(s), Herzegovinian(s)
adjective: Bosnian, Herzegovinian
Ethnic divisions: Muslim 44%, Serb 31%, Croat 17%, other 8%
Religions: Muslim 40%, Orthodox 31%, Catholic 15%, Protestant 4%, other 10%
Languages: Serbo-Croatian 99%
Literacy:

total population: NA%
male: NA%
female: NA%
Labor force: 1,026,254
by occupation: agriculture 2%, industry, mining 45% (1991 est.)

Government

Names:
conventional long form: Republic of Bosnia and Herzegovina
conventional short form: Bosnia and Herzegovina
local long form: Republika Bosna i Hercegovina
local short form: Bosna i Hercegovina
Digraph: BK
Type: emerging democracy
Capital: Sarajevo
Administrative divisions: 109 districts (opstinas, singular—opstina) Banovici, Banja Luka, Bihac, Bijeljina, Bileca, Bosanska Dubica, Bosanska Gradiska, Bosanska Krupa, Bosanski Brod, Bosanski Novi, Bosanski Petrovac, Bosanski Samac, Bosansko Grahovo, Bratunac, Brcko, Breza, Bugojno, Busovaca, Cazin, Cajnice, Capljina, Celinac, Citluk, Derventa, Doboj, Donji Vakuf, Foca, Fojnica, Gacko, Glamoc, Gorazde, Gornji Vakuf, Gracanica, Gradacac, Grude, Han Pijesak, Jablanica, Jajce, Kakanj, Kalesija, Kalinovik, Kiseljak, Kladanj, Kljuc, Konjic, Kotor Varos, Kresevo, Kupres, Laktasi, Listica, Livno, Lopare, Lukavac, Ljubinje, Ljubuski, Maglaj, Modrica, Mostar, Mrkonjic-Grad, Neum, Nevesinje, Odzak, Olovo, Orasje, Posusje, Prijedor, Prnjavor, Prozor, (Pucarevo) Novi Travnik, Rogatica, Rudo, Sanski Most, Sarajevo-Centar, Sarajevo-Hadzici, Sarajevo-Ilidza, Sarajevo-Ilijas, Sarajevo-Novi Grad, Sarajevo-Novo, Sarajevo-Pale, Sarajevo-Stari Grad, Sarajevo-Trnovo, Sarajevo-Vogosca, Skender Vakuf, Sokolac, Srbac, Srebrenica, Srebrenik, Stolac, Sekovici, Sipovo, Teslic, Tesanj, Drvar, Duvno, Travnik, Trebinje, Tuzla, Ugljevik, Vares, Velika Kladusa, Visoko, Visegrad, Vitez, Vlasenica, Zavidovici, Zenica, Zvornik, Zepce, Zivinice
note: currently under negotiation with the assistance of international mediators
Independence: NA April 1992 (from Yugoslavia)
National holiday: NA
Constitution: promulgated in 1974 (under the Communists), amended 1989, 1990, and 1991;
International disputes: as of May 1994, members of the Bosnian Serb armed factions, desirous of establishing a separate state linked with neighboring Serbia, occupied 70% of Bosnia after having killed or driven out non-Serb inhabitants; the Bosnian Croats, occupied and declared an independent state in an additional 10% of Bosnia in 1993, but in March 1994, this faction and the Bosnian Government settled their dispute and entered into a bicommunal Federation; a Bosnian Government army commander who opposes the leadership of Bosnian President IZETBEGOVIC is leading an insurrection in the government-held enclave of Bihac
Climate: hot summers and cold winters; areas of high elevation have short, cool summers and long, severe winters; mild, rainy winters along coast
Terrain: mountains and valleys
Natural resources: coal, iron, bauxite, manganese, timber, wood products, copper, chromium, lead, zinc
Land use:
arable land: 20%
permanent crops: 2%
meadows and pastures: 25%
forest and woodland: 36%
other: 17%
Irrigated land: NA sq km
Environment:
current issues: air pollution from metallurgical plants; water scarce; sites for disposing of urban waste are limited; widespread casualties and destruction of infrastructure because of civil strife
natural hazards: subject to frequent and destructive earthquakes
international agreements: party to—Air Pollution, Marine Life Conservation, Ozone Layer Protection

People

Population: 4,651,485 (July 1994 est.)
note: all data dealing with population is subject to considerable error because of the dislocations caused by military action and ethnic cleansing
Population growth rate: 0.69% (1994 est.)
Birth rate: 13.33 births/1,000 population (1994 est.)
Death rate: 6.39 deaths/1,000 population (1994 est.)
Net migration rate: 0 migrant(s)/1,000 population (1994 est.)
Infant mortality rate: 12.7 deaths/1,000 live births (1994 est.)
Life expectancy at birth:
total population: 75.13 years
male: 72.43 years
female: 78.02 years (1994 est.)
Total fertility rate: 1.61 children born/woman (1994 est.)
the Assembly planned to draft a new constitution in 1991, before conditions deteriorated; constitution of Federation of Bosnia and Herzegovina (including Muslim and Croatian controlled parts of Republic) ratified April 1994
Legal system: based on civil law system
Suffrage: 16 years of age, if employed; 18 years of age, universal
Executive branch:
chief of state: President Alija IZETBEGOVIC (since 20 December 1990), other members of the collective presidency: Ejup GANIC (since NA November 1990), Nijaz DURAKOVIC (since NA October 1993), Stjepan KLJUJIC (since NA October 1993), Ivo KOMSIC (since NA October 1993), Mirko PEJANOVIC (since NA June 1992), Tatjana LJUJIC-MIJATOVIC (since NA December 1992)
head of government: Prime Minister Haris SILAJDZIC (since NA October 1993); Deputy Prime Minister Edib BUKVIC (since NA October 1993)
cabinet: executive body of ministers; members of, and responsible to, the National Assembly
Legislative branch: bicameral National Assembly
Chamber of Municipalities (Vijece Opeina): elections last held November-December 1990 (next to be held NA); seats—(110 total) SDA 43, SDS BiH 38, HDZ BiH 23, Party of Democratic Changes 4, DSS 1, SPO 1
Chamber of Citizens (Vijece Gradanstvo): elections last held November-December 1990 (next to be held NA); seats—(130 total) SDA 43, SDS BiH 34, HDZ BiH 21, Party of Democratic Changes 15, SRSJ BiH 12, MBO 2, DSS 1, DSZ 1, LS 1
note: legislative elections for the Federation of Bosnia and Herzegovina are slated for late 1994
Judicial branch: Supreme Court, Constitutional Court
Political parties and leaders: Party of Democratic Action (SDA), Alija IZETBEGOVIC; Croatian Democratic Union of Bosnia and Herzegovina (HDZ BiH), KresimirZUBAK; Serbian Democratic Party of Bosnia and Herzegovina (SDS BiH), Radovan KARADZIC, president; Muslim-Bosnian Organization (MBO), Adil ZULFIKARPASIC, president; Democratic Party of Socialists (DSS), Nijaz DURAKOVIC, president; Party of Democratic Changes, leader NA; Serbian Movement for Renewal (SPO), Milan TRIVUNCIC; Alliance of Reform Forces of Yugoslavia for Bosnia and Herzegovina (SRSJ BiH), Dr. Nenad KECMANOVIC, president; Democratic League of Greens (DSZ), Drazen PETROVIC; Liberal Party (LS), Rasim KADIC, president
Other political or pressure groups: NA
Member of: CEI, CSCE, ECE, ICAO, ILO, IMO, INTELSAT (nonsignatory user), INTERPOL, IOC, ITU, NAM (guest), UN, UNCTAD, UNESCO, UNIDO, UPU, WHO
Diplomatic representation in US:
chief of mission: (vacant); Minister-Counselor, Charge d'Affaires ad interim Seven ALKALAJ
chancery: Suite 760, 1707 L Street NW, Washington, DC 10036
telephone: (202) 833-3612, 3613, and 3615
FAX: (202) 833-2061
consulate(s) general: New York
US diplomatic representation:
chief of mission: (vacant); Charge d'Affaires Victor JACKOVICH

embassy: American Embassy Bosnia, c/o AmEmbassy Vienna, Boltzmanngasse 16, A-1091, Vienna, Austria
mailing address: (Bosnia) Vienna, Department of State, Washington, D.C. 20521-9900
telephone: [43] (1) 31-339
FAX: [43] (1) 310-0682
note: the US maintains full diplomatic relations with Bosnia and Herzegovina but has not yet established an embassy in Sarajevo
Flag: white with a large blue shield; the shield contains white Roman crosses with a white diagonal band running from the upper hoist corner to the lower fly side

BULGARIA

Economy

Overview: The Bulgarian economy continued its painful adjustment in 1993 from the misdirected development undertaken during four decades of Communist rule. Many aspects of a market economy have been put in place and have begun to function, but much of the economy, especially the industrial sector, has yet to re-establish market links lost with the collapse of other centrally planned Eastern European economies. The prices of many imported industrial inputs, especially energy products, have risen markedly, and falling real wages have not sufficed to restore competitiveness. The trade deficit, exacerbated by UN trade sanctions against neighboring Serbia, grew in late 1993, accelerating the depreciation of the lev. These difficulties in adjusting to the challenges of a more open system, together with a severe drought, caused nonagricultural output to fall by perhaps 8% in 1993. The government plans more extensive privatization in 1994 to improve the management of state enterprises and to encourage foreign investment in ailing state firms. Bulgaria resumed payments on its $10 billion in commercial debt in 1993 following the negotiation of a 50% write-off. An IMF program and second agreement with official creditors on Bulgaria's smaller amount of official debt are required to close the debt deal.

National product: GDP—purchasing power equivalent—$33.9 billion (1993 est.)
National product real growth rate: -4% (1993 est.)
National product per capita: $3,800 (1993 est.)
Inflation rate (consumer prices): 64% (1993)
Unemployment rate: 16% (1993)
Budget:
revenues: $14 billion
expenditures: $17.4 billion, including capital expenditures of $610 million (1993 est.)
Exports: $3.5 billion (f.o.b., 1991)
commodities: machinery and equipment 30.6%; agricultural products 24%; manufactured consumer goods 22.2%; fuels, minerals, raw materials, and metals 10.5%; other 12.7% (1991)
partners: former CEMA countries 57.7% (USSR 48.6%, Poland 2.1%, Czechoslovakia 0.9%); developed countries 26.3% (Germany 4.8%, Greece 2.2%); less developed countries 15.9% (Libya 2.1%, Iran 0.7%) (1991)
Imports: $2.8 billion (f.o.b., 1991)
commodities: fuels, minerals, and raw materials 58.7%; machinery and equipment 15.8%; manufactured consumer goods 4.4%; agricultural products 15.2%; other 5.9%
partners: former CEMA countries 51.0% (former USSR 43.2%, Poland 3.7%); developed countries 32.8% (Germany 7.0%, Austria 4.7%); less developed countries 16.2% (Iran 2.8%, Libya 2.5%)
External debt: $12 billion (1993)
Industrial production: growth rate -10% (1993 est.); accounts for about 37% of GDP (1990)
Electricity:
capacity: 11,500,000 kW
production: 45 billion kWh
consumption per capita: 5,070 kWh (1992)
Industries: machine building and metal working, food processing, chemicals, textiles, building materials, ferrous and nonferrous metals
Agriculture: climate and soil conditions support livestock raising and the growing of various grain crops, oilseeds, vegetables, fruits, and tobacco; more than one-third of the arable

land devoted to grain; world's fourth-largest tobacco exporter; surplus food producer
Illicit drugs: transshipment point for southwest Asian heroin transiting the Balkan route
Economic aid: $NA
Currency: 1 lev (Lv) = 100 stotinki
Exchange rates: leva (Lv) per US$1—32.00 (January 1994), 24.56 (January 1993), 17.18 (January 1992), 16.13 (March 1991), 0.7446 (November 1990), 0.84 (1989); note—floating exchange rate since February 1991
Fiscal year: calendar year

Communications

Railroads: 4,300 km total, all government owned (1987); 4,055 km 1.435-meter standard gauge, 245 km narrow gauge; 917 km double track; 2,640 km electrified
Highways:
total: 36,930 km
paved: 33,902 km (including 276 km expressways)
unpaved: earth 3,028 km (1991)
Inland waterways: 470 km (1987)
Pipelines: crude oil 193 km; petroleum products 525 km; natural gas 1,400 km (1992)
Ports: coastal—Burgas, Varna, Varna West; inland—Ruse, Vidin, and Lom on the Danube
Merchant marine: 111 ships (1,000 GRT and over) totaling 1,225,996 GRT/1,829,642 DWT, short-sea passenger 2, cargo 30, container 2, passenger-cargo 1, roll-on/roll-off cargo 6, oil tanker 16, chemical carrier 4, railcar carrier 2, bulk 48
note: Bulgaria owns 1 ship (1,000 GRT or over) totaling 8,717 DWT operating under Liberian registry
Airports:
total: 487
usable: 85
with permanent-surface runways: 32
with runways over 3659 m: 0
with runways 2,440-3,659 m: 21
with runways 1,060-2,439 m: 36
note: a C-130 can land on a 1,060-m airstrip
Telecommunications: extensive but antiquated transmission system of coaxial cable and microwave radio relay; 2.6 million telephones; direct dialing to 36 countries; phone density is 29 phones per 100 persons (1992); almost two-thirds of the lines are residential; 67% of Sofia households have phones (November 1988); telephone service is available in most villages; broadcast stations—20 AM, 15 FM, and 29 TV, with 1 Soviet TV repeater in Sofia; 2.1 million TV sets (1990); 92% of country receives No. 1 television program (May 1990); 1 satellite ground station using Intersputnik; INTELSAT is used through a Greek earth station

Defense Forces

Branches: Army, Navy, Air and Air Defense Forces, Frontier Troops, Internal Troops
Manpower availability: males age 15-49 2,175,921; fit for military service 1,816,484; reach military age (19) annually 70,306 (1994 est.)
Defense expenditures: 5.77 billion leva, NA% of GDP (1993 est.); note—conversion of defense expenditures into US dollars using the current exchange rate could produce misleading results

Geography

Location: Balkan State, Southeastern Europe, bordering the Black Sea, between Romania and Turkey
Map references: Africa, Arctic Region, Ethnic Groups in Eastern Europe, Europe, Middle East, Standard Time Zones of the World
Area:
total area: 110,910 sq km
land area: 110,550 sq km
comparative area: slightly larger than Tennessee
Land boundaries: total 1,808 km, Greece 494 km, The Former Yugoslav Republic of Macedonia 148 km, Romania 608 km, Serbia and Montenegro 318 km (all with Serbia), Turkey 240 km
Coastline: 354 km
Maritime claims:
contiguous zone: 24 nm
exclusive economic zone: 200 nm

territorial sea: 12 nm
International disputes: none
Climate: temperate; cold, damp winters; hot, dry summers
Terrain: mostly mountains with lowlands in north and south
Natural resources: bauxite, copper, lead, zinc, coal, timber, arable land
Land use:
arable land: 34%
permanent crops: 3%
meadows and pastures: 18%
forest and woodland: 35%
other: 10%
Irrigated land: 10 sq km (1989 est.)
Environment:
current issues: air pollution from industrial emissions; rivers polluted from raw sewage, heavy metals, detergents; deforestation; forest damage from air pollution; soil contamination from heavy metals from metallurgical plants and industrial wastes
natural hazards: subject to earthquakes, landslides
international agreements: party to—Air Pollution, Air Pollution-Nitrogen Oxides, Air Pollution-Sulphur, Antarctic Treaty, Endangered Species, Environmental Modification, Nuclear Test Ban, Ozone Layer Protection, Ship Pollution, Wetlands; signed, but not ratified—Air Pollution-Volatile Organic Compounds, Antarctic-Environmental Protocol, Biodiversity, Climate Change, Law of the Sea
Note: strategic location near Turkish Straits; controls key land routes from Europe to Middle East and Asia

People

Population: 8,799,986 (July 1994 est.)
Population growth rate: -0.32% (1994 est.)
Birth rate: 11.71 births/1,000 population (1994 est.)
Death rate: 11.38 deaths/1,000 population (1994 est.)
Net migration rate: -3.49 migrant(s)/1,000 population (1994 est.)
Infant mortality rate: 12 deaths/1,000 live births (1994 est.)
Life expectancy at birth:
total population: 73.24 years
male: 69.99 years
female: 76.67 years (1994 est.)
Total fertility rate: 1.71 children born/woman (1994 est.)
Nationality:
noun: Bulgarian(s)
adjective: Bulgarian
Ethnic divisions: Bulgarian 85.3%, Turk 8.5%, Gypsy 2.6%, Macedonian 2.5%, Armenian 0.3%, Russian 0.2%, other 0.6%
Religions: Bulgarian Orthodox 85%, Muslim 13%, Jewish 0.8%, Roman Catholic 0.5%, Uniate Catholic 0.2%, Protestant, Gregorian-Armenian, and other 0.5%
Languages: Bulgarian; secondary languages closely correspond to ethnic breakdown
Literacy: age 15 and over can read and write (1970 est.)
total population: 93%
male: NA%
female: NA%
Labor force: 4.3 million
by occupation: industry 33%, agriculture 20%, other 47% (1987)

Government

Names:
conventional long form: Republic of Bulgaria
conventional short form: Bulgaria
Digraph: BU
Type: emerging democracy
Capital: Sofia
Administrative divisions: 9 provinces (oblasti, singular—oblast); Burgas, Grad Sofiya, Khaskovo, Lovech, Montana, Plovdiv, Ruse, Sofiya, Varna
Independence: 22 September 1908 (from Ottoman Empire)
National holiday: Independence Day 3 March (1878)
Constitution: adopted 12 July 1991
Legal system: based on civil law system, with Soviet law influence; has accepted compulsory ICJ jurisdiction
Suffrage: 18 years of age; universal and compulsory

Executive branch:
chief of state: President Zhelyu Mitev ZHELEV (since 1 August 1990); Vice President (vacant); election last held January 1992; results—Zhelyu ZHELEV was elected by popular vote
head of government: Chairman of the Council of Ministers (Prime Minister) Lyuben Borisov BEROV (since 30 December 1992); Deputy Chairman of the Council of Ministers (Deputy Prime Minister) Evgeniy MATINCHEV (since 30 December 1992)
cabinet: Council of Ministers; elected by the National Assembly
Legislative branch: unicameral
National Assembly (Narodno Sobranie): last held 13 October 1991; results—UDF (and breakaway factions) 34%, BSP 33%, MRF 7.5%; seats—(240 total) UDF 110, BSP 106, Movement for Rights and Freedoms 24
note: the UDF split in March 1993 to form the New Union for Democracy (NUD) with 18 seats, and the Union of Democratic Forces (UDF) with 92 seats
Judicial branch: Supreme Court, Constitutional Court
Political parties and leaders: Union of Democratic Forces (UDF), Filip DIMITROV, chairman, an alliance of approximately 20 pro-Democratic parties including United Democratic Center, Democratic Party, Radical Democratic Party, Christian Democratic Union, Alternative Social Liberal Party, Republican Party, Civic Initiative Movement, and about a dozen other groups; Movement for Rights and Freedoms (mainly ethnic Turkish party) (MRF), Ahmed DOGAN, chairman; Bulgarian Socialist Party (BSP), Zhan VIDENOV, chairman; New Union for Democracy (NUD), Dimitar LUDZHEV, chairman
Other political or pressure groups: Ecoglasnost; Podkrepa (Support) Labor Confederation; Fatherland Union; Bulgarian Democratic Youth (formerly Communist Youth Union); Confederation of Independent Trade Unions of Bulgaria (KNSB); Nationwide Committee for Defense of National Interests; Peasant Youth League; Bulgarian Agrarian National Union—United (BZNS); Bulgarian Democratic Center; "Nikola Petkov" Bulgarian Agrarian National Union; Internal Macedonian Revolutionary Organization—Union of Macedonian Societies (IMRO-UMS); numerous regional, ethnic, and national interest groups with various agendas
Member of: ACCT (observer), BIS, BSEC, CCC, CE, CEI (participating), CSCE, EBRD, ECE, FAO, G-9, IAEA, IBRD, ICAO, ICFTU, IDA, IFC, ILO, IMF, IMO, INMARSAT, INTELSAT (nonsignatory user), INTERPOL, IOC, IOM (observer), ISO, ITU, LORCS, NACC, NAM (guest), NSG, PCA, UN, UNCTAD, UNESCO, UNIDO, UNTAC, UPU, WFTU, WHO, WIPO, WMO, WTO, ZC
Diplomatic representation in US:
chief of mission: Ambassador Ognyan Raytchev PISHEV
chancery: 1621 22nd Street NW, Washington, DC 20008
telephone: (202) 387-7969
FAX: (202) 234-7973
US diplomatic representation:
chief of mission: Ambassador William D. MONTGOMERY
embassy: 1 Saborna Street, Sofia
mailing address: Unit 25402, Sofia; APO AE 09213
telephone: [359] (2) 88-48-01 through 05
FAX: [359] (2) 80-19-77
Flag: three equal horizontal bands of white (top), green, and red; the national emblem formerly on the hoist side of the white stripe has been removed—it contained a rampant lion within a wreath of wheat ears below a red five-pointed star and above a ribbon bearing the dates 681 (first Bulgarian state established) and 1944 (liberation from Nazi control)

U.S. Government Contacts:

U.S. Trade Desk: (202) 482-4915

Travel:

International Hotels in Country:
Sofia:
Sheraton Sofia Hotel Balkan, Tel: 3592/87-65-41
Vitosha, Tel: 3592/6-25-11.

CROATIA

Economy

Overview: Before the dissolution of Yugoslavia, the republic of Croatia, after Slovenia, was the most prosperous and industrialized area, with a per capita output roughly comparable to that of Portugal and perhaps one-third above the Yugoslav average. At present, Croatian Serb Nationalists control approximately one third of the Croatian territory, and one of the overriding determinants of Croatia's long-term political and economic prospects will be the resolution of this territorial dispute. Croatia faces monumental economic problems stemming from: the legacy of longtime Communist mismanagement of the economy; large foreign debt; damage during the fighting to bridges, factories, power lines, buildings, and houses; the large refugee population, both Croatian and Bosnian; and the disruption of economic ties to Serbia and the other former Yugoslav republics, as well as within its own territory. At the minimum, extensive Western aid and investment, especially in the tourist and oil industries, would seem necessary to salvage a desperate economic situation. However, peace and political stability must come first; only then will recent government moves toward a "market-friendly" economy reverse the sharp drop in output. As of May 1994, fighting continues among Croats, Serbs, and Muslims, and national boundaries and final political arrangements are still in doubt.

National product: GDP—purchasing power equivalent—$21.8 billion (1992 est.)

National product real growth rate: -19% (1992 est.)

National product per capita: $4,500 (1992 est.)

Inflation rate (consumer prices): 26% monthly average (1993 est.)

Unemployment rate: 21% (December 1993)

Budget:

revenues: $NA

expenditures: $NA, including capital expenditures of $NA

Exports: $3.9 billion (f.o.b., 1993)

commodities: machinery and transport equipment 30%, other manufacturers 37%, chemicals 11%, food and live animals 9%, raw materials 6.5%, fuels and lubricants 5% (1990)

partners: EC countries, Slovenia

Imports: $4.7 billion (c.i.f., 1993)

commodities: machinery and transport equipment 21%, fuels and lubricants 19%, food and live animals 16%, chemicals 14%, manufactured goods 13%, miscellaneous manufactured articles 9%, raw materials 6.5%, beverages and tobacco 1% (1990)

partners: EC countries, Slovenia, FSU countries

External debt: $2.6 billion (December 1993)

Industrial production: growth rate -5.9% (1993 est.)

Electricity:

capacity: 3,570,000 kW

production: 11.5 billion kWh

consumption per capita: 2,400 kWh (1992)

Industries: chemicals and plastics, machine tools, fabricated metal, electronics, pig iron and rolled steel products, aluminum reduction, paper, wood products (including furniture),

building materials (including cement), textiles, shipbuilding, petroleum and petroleum refining, food processing and beverages
Agriculture: Croatia normally produces a food surplus; most agricultural land in private hands and concentrated in Croat-majority districts in Slavonia and Istria; much of Slavonia's land has been put out of production by fighting; wheat, corn, sugar beets, sunflowers, alfalfa, and clover are main crops in Slavonia; central Croatian highlands are less fertile but support cereal production, orchards, vineyards, livestock breeding, and dairy farming; coastal areas and offshore islands grow olives, citrus fruits, and vegetables
Economic aid: $NA
Currency: 1 Croatian dinar (CD) = 100 paras; a new currency, the kuna, replaced the dinar on 30 May 1994
Exchange rates: Croatian dinar per US $1—6,544 (January 1994), 3,637 (15 July 1993), 60.00 (April 1992)
Fiscal year: calendar year

Communications

Railroads: 2,592 km of standard guage (1.435 m) of which 864 km are electrified (1992); note—disrupted by territorial dispute
Highways:
total: 32,071 km
paved: 23,305 km
unpaved: gravel 8,439 km; earth 327 km (1990)
Inland waterways: 785 km perennially navigable
Pipelines: crude oil 670 km, petroleum products 20 km, natural gas 310 km (1992); note—now disrupted because of territorial dispute
Ports: coastal—Omisalj (oil), Ploce, Rijeka, Split; inland—Osijek, Slavonski Samac, Vukovar, Zupanja
Merchant marine: 28 ships (1,000 GRT or over) totaling 108,194 GRT/131,880 DWT, cargo 18, roll-on/roll-off cargo 2, short-sea passenger 3, passenger 2, refrigerated cargo 1, container 1, oil tanker 1
note: also controlled by Croatian shipowners are 151 ships (1,000 GRT or over) under flags of convenience—primarily Malta and St. Vincent—totaling 2,221,931 GRT/3,488,263 DWT; includes cargo 60, roll-on/ roll-off 8, refrigerated cargo 4, container 12, multifunction large load carriers 3, bulk 45, oil tanker 9, liquified gas 1, chemical tanker 4, service vessel 5
Airports:
total: 75
usable: 70
with permanent-surface runways: 16
with runways over 3,659 m: 0
with runways 2,440-3,659 m: 7
with runways 1,220-2,439 m: 5
Telecommunications: 350,000 telephones; broadcast stations—14 AM, 8 FM, 12 (2 repeaters) TV; 1,100,000 radios; 1,027,000 TVs; satellite ground stations—none

Defense Forces

Branches: Ground Forces, Naval Forces, Air and Air Defense Forces
Manpower availability: males age 15-49 1,182,767; fit for military service 946,010; reach military age (19) annually 33,166 (1994 est.)
Defense expenditures: 337-393 billion Croatian dinars, NA% of GDP (1993 est.); note—conversion of defense expenditures into US dollars using the current exchange rate could produce misleading results

Geography

Location: Balkan State, Southeastern Europe, on the Balkan Peninsula, bordering the Adriatic Sea, between Slovenia and Bosnia and Herzegovina
Map references: Africa, Ethnic Groups in Eastern Europe, Europe, Standard Time Zones of the World
Area:
total area: 56,538 sq km
land area: 56,410 sq km
comparative area: slightly smaller than West Virginia
Land boundaries: total 2,028 km, Bosnia and Herzegovina 932 km, Hungary 329 km,

Serbia and Montenegro 266 km (241 km with Serbia; 25 km with Montenego), Slovenia 501 km
Coastline: 5,790 km (mainland 1,778 km, islands 4,012 km)
Maritime claims:
continental shelf: 200-m depth or to depth of exploitation
exclusive economic zone: 12 nm
exclusive fishing zone: 12 nm
territorial sea: 12 nm
International disputes: Serbs have occupied UN protected areas in eastern Croatia and along the western Bosnia and Herzegovinian border; dispute with Slovenia over fishing rights in Adriatic
Climate: Mediterranean and continental; continental climate predominant with hot summers and cold winters; mild winters, dry summers along coast
Terrain: geographically diverse; flat plains along Hungarian border, low mountains and highlands near Adriatic coast, coastline, and islands
Natural resources: oil, some coal, bauxite, low-grade iron ore, calcium, natural asphalt, silica, mica, clays, salt
Land use:
arable land: 32%
permanent crops: 20%
meadows and pastures: 18%
forest and woodland: 15%
other: 15%
Irrigated land: NA sq km
Environment:
current issues: air pollution from metallurgical plants is damaging the forests; coastal pollution from industrial and domestic waste; widespread casualties and destruction of infrastructure in border areas affected by civil strife
natural hazards: subject to frequent and destructive earthquakes
international agreements: party to—Air Pollution, Marine Dumping, Nuclear Test Ban, Ozone Layer Protection, Ship Pollution; signed, but not ratified—Biodiversity, Climate Change
Note: controls most land routes from Western Europe to Aegean Sea and Turkish Straits

People

Population: 4,697,614 (July 1994 est.)
Population growth rate: 0.07% (1994 est.)
Birth rate: 11.27 births/1,000 population (1994 est.)
Death rate: 10.54 deaths/1,000 population (1994 est.)
Net migration rate: 0 migrant(s)/1,000 population (1994 est.)
Infant mortality rate: 8.7 deaths/1,000 live births (1994 est.)
Life expectancy at birth:
total population: 73.6 years
male: 70.14 years
female: 77.26 years (1994 est.)
Total fertility rate: 1.65 children born/woman (1994 est.)
Nationality:
noun: Croat(s)
adjective: Croatian
Ethnic divisions: Croat 78%, Serb 12%, Muslim 0.9%, Hungarian 0.5%, Slovenian 0.5%, others 8.1%
Religions: Catholic 76.5%, Orthodox 11.1%, Slavic Muslim 1.2%, Protestant 0.4%, others and unknown 10.8%
Languages: Serbo-Croatian 96%, other 4%
Literacy:
total population: NA%
male: NA%
female: NA%
Labor force: 1,509,489
by occupation: industry and mining 37%, agriculture 16% (1981 est.), government NA%, other

Government

Names:
conventional long form: Republic of Croatia
conventional short form: Croatia
local long form: Republika Hrvatska
local short form: Hrvatska
Digraph: HR
Type: parliamentary democracy
Capital: Zagreb
Administrative divisions: 21 counties (zupanijas, zupanija—singular): Bjelovar-

Bilogora, City of Zagreb, Dubrovnik-Neretva, Istra, Karlovac, Koprivnica-Krizevci, Krapina-Zagorje, Lika-Senj, Medimurje, Osijek-Baranja, Pozega-Slavonija, Primorje-Gorski Kotar, Sibenik, Sisak-Moslavina, Slavonski Brod-Posavina, Split-Dalmatia, Varazdin, Virovitica-Podravina, Vukovar-Srijem, Zadar-Knin, Zagreb
Independence: NA June 1991 (from Yugoslavia)
National holiday: Statehood Day, 30 May (1990)
Constitution: adopted on 2 December 1990
Legal system: based on civil law system
Suffrage: 16 years of age, if employed; 18 years of age, universal
Executive branch:
chief of state: President Franjo TUDJMAN (since 30 May 1990); election last held 4 August 1992 (next to be held NA 1995); Franjo TUDJMAN reelected with about 56% of the vote; his opponent Dobroslav PARAGA got 5% of the vote
head of government: Prime Minister Nikica VALENTIC (since 3 April 1993); Deputy Prime Ministers Mato GRANIC (since 8 September 1992), Ivica KOSTOVIC (since NA), Vladimir SEKS (since September 1992), Borislav SKEGRO (since NA)
cabinet: Council of Ministers; appointed by the president
Legislative branch: bicameral Assembly (Sabor)
House of Districts (Zupanije Dom): elections last held 7 and 21 February 1993 (next to be held NA February 1997); seats—(68 total; 63 elected, 5 presidentially appointed) HDZ 37, HSLS 16, HSS 5, Istrian Democratic Assembly 3, SPH-SDP 1, HNS 1
House of Representatives (Predstavnicke Dom): elections last held 2 August 1992 (next to be held NA August 1996); seats—(138 total) HDZ 85, HSLS 14, SPH-SDP 11, HNS 6, Dalmatian Action/Istrian Democratic Assembly/ Rijeka Democratic Alliance coalition 6, HSP 5, HSS 3, SNS 3, independents 5
Judicial branch: Supreme Court, Constitutional Court
Political parties and leaders: Croatian Democratic Union (HDZ), Stjepan MESIC, chairman of the executive council; Croatian People's Party (HNS), Savka DABCEVIC-KUCAR, president; Serbian People's Party (SNS), Milan DUKIC; Croatian Party of Rights (HSP), leader NA; Croatian Social Liberal Party (HSLS), Drazen BUDISA, president; Croatian Peasant Party (HSS), leader NA; Dalmatian Action/Istrian Democratic Assembly/Rijecka Democratic Alliance coalition; Social Democratic Party of Croatia-Party of Democratic Changes (SPH-SDP), Ivica RACAN
Other political or pressure groups: NA
Member of: CE (guest), CEI, CSCE, ECE, IAEA, IBRD, ICAO, IDA, IFC, ILO, IMF, IMO, INMARSAT, INTELSAT, INTERPOL, IOC, IOM (observer), ITU, NAM (observer), UN, UNCTAD, UNESCO, UNIDO, UPU, WHO, WIPO, WMO
Diplomatic representation in US:
chief of mission: Ambassador Petr A. SARCEVIC
chancery: (temporary) 236 Massachusetts Avenue NE, Washington, DC 20002
telephone: (202) 543-5580
US diplomatic representation:
chief of mission: Ambassador Peter W. GALBRAITH
embassy: Andrije Hebranga 2, Zagreb
mailing address: Unit 25402, Zagreb; American Embassy APO AE 09213
telephone: [38] (41) 444-800
FAX: [38] (41) 440-235
Flag: red, white, and blue horizontal bands with Croatian coat of arms (red and white checkered)

CZECH REPUBLIC

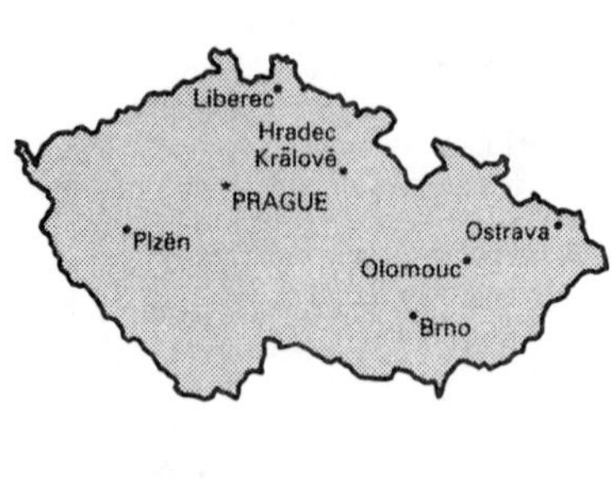

Economy

Overview: The dissolution of Czechoslovakia into two independent nation states—the Czech Republic and Slovakia—on 1 January 1993 has complicated the task of moving toward a more open and decentralized economy. The old Czechoslovakia, even though highly industrialized by East European standards, suffered from an aging capital plant, lagging technology, and a deficiency in energy and many raw materials. In January 1991, approximately one year after the end of communist control of Eastern Europe, the Czech and Slovak Federal Republic launched a sweeping program to convert its almost entirely state-owned and controlled economy to a market system. In 1991-92 these measures resulted in privatization of some medium- and small-scale economic activity and the setting of more than 90% of prices by the market—but at a cost in inflation, unemployment, and lower output. For Czechoslovakia as a whole inflation in 1991 was roughly 50% and output fell 15%. In 1992, in the Czech lands, inflation dropped to an estimated 12.5% and GDP was down a more moderate 5%. In 1993, Czech aggregate output remained unchanged, prices rose about 19%, and unemployment hovered above 3%; exports to Slovakia fell roughly 30%. An estimated 40% of the economy was privately owned. In 1994, Prague expects 2% to 3% growth in GDP, roughly 9% inflation, and 5% unemployment. Economic growth in 1994 is less important than continued economic restructuring; a mere 1% growth would be noteworthy if restructuring is accompanied by rising unemployment and enterprise bankruptcies.

National product: GDP—purchasing power equivalent—$75 billion (1993 est.)

National product real growth rate: 0% (1993 est.)

National product per capita: $7,200 (1993 est.)

Inflation rate (consumer prices): 19% (1993 est.)

Unemployment rate: 3.3% (1993 est.)

Budget:

revenues: $11.9 billion

expenditures: $11.9 billion, including capital expenditures of $NA (1993 est.)

Exports: $12.6 billion (f.o.b., 1993 est.)

commodities: manufactured goods, machinery and transport equipment, chemicals, fuels, minerals, and metals

partners: Germany, Slovakia, Poland, Austria, Hungary, Italy, France, US, UK, CIS republics

Imports: $12.4 billion (f.o.b., 1993 est.)

commodities: machinery and transport equipment, fuels and lubricants, manfactured goods, raw materials, chemicals, agricultural products

partners: Slovakia, CIS republics, Germany, Austria, Poland, Switzerland, Hungary, UK, Italy

External debt: $8.6 billion (October 1993)

Industrial production: growth rate -5.5% (December 1993 over December 1992)

Electricity:

capacity: 16,500,000 kW

production: 62.2 billion kWh

consumption per capita: 6,030 kWh (1992)
Industries: fuels, ferrous metallurgy, machinery and equipment, coal, motor vehicles, glass, armaments
Agriculture: largely self-sufficient in food production; diversified crop and livestock production, including grains, potatoes, sugar beets, hops, fruit, hogs, cattle, and poultry; exporter of forest products
Illicit drugs: transshipment point for Southwest Asian heroin and Latin American cocaine to Western Europe
Economic aid:
donor: the former Czechoslovakia was a donor—$4.2 billion in bilateral aid to non-Communist less developed countries (1954-89)
Currency: 1 koruna (Kc) = 100 haleru
Exchange rates: koruny (Kcs) per US$1—30.122 (January 1994), 29.153 (1993), 28.26 (1992), 29.53 (1991), 17.95 (1990), 15.05 (1989)
note: values before 1993 reflect Czechoslovak exchange rates
Fiscal year: calendar year

Communications

Railroads: 9,434 km total (1988)
Highways:
total: 55,890 km (1988)
paved: NA
unpaved: NA
Inland waterways: NA km; the Elbe (Labe) is the principal river
Pipelines: natural gas 5,400 km
Ports: coastal outlets are in Poland (Gdynia, Gdansk, Szczecin), Croatia (Rijeka), Slovenia (Koper), Germany (Hamburg, Rostock); principal river ports are Prague on the Vltava, Decin on the Elbe (Labe)
Merchant marine: 18 ships (1,000 GRT or over) totaling 225,934 GRT/350,330 DWT, cargo 11, bulk 7
Airports:
total: 155
usable: 123
with permanent-surface runways: 27
with runways over 3,659 m: 1
with runways 2,440-3,659 m: 17
with runways 1,060-2,439 m: 52
note: a C-130 can land on a 1,060-m airstrip
Telecommunications: NA

Defense Forces

Branches: Army, Air and Air Defense Forces, Civil Defense, Railroad Units
Manpower availability: males age 15-49 2,747,126; fit for military service 2,091,532; reach military age (18) annually 93,342 (1994 est.)
Defense expenditures: 23 billion koruny, NA% of GNP (1993 est.); note—conversion of defense expenditures into US dollars using the current exchange rate could produce misleading results

---

Geography

Location: Central Europe, between Germany and Slovakia
Map references: Ethnic Groups in Eastern Europe, Europe, Standard Time Zones of the World
Area:
total area: 78,703 sq km
land area: 78,645 sq km
comparative area: slightly smaller than South Carolina
Land boundaries: total 1,880 km, Austria 362 km, Germany 646 km, Poland 658 km, Slovakia 214 km
Coastline: 0 km (landlocked)
Maritime claims: none; landlocked
International disputes: Liechtenstein claims 1,606 sq km of Czech territory confiscated from its royal family in 1918; Sudeten German claims for restitution of property confiscated in connection with their expulsion after World War II versus the Czech Republic claims that restitution does not proceed before February 1948 when the Communists seized power; unresolved property issues with Slovakia over redistribution of property of the former Czechoslovak federal government
Climate: temperate; cool summers; cold, cloudy, humid winters
Terrain: two main regions: Bohemia in the

west, consisting of rolling plains, hills, and plateaus surrounded by low mountains; and Moravia in the east, consisting of very hilly country
Natural resources: hard coal, soft coal, kaolin, clay, graphite
Land use:
arable land: NA%
permanent crops: NA%
meadows and pastures: NA%
forest and woodland: NA%
other: NA%
Irrigated land: NA sq km
Environment:
current issues: air and water pollution in areas of northwest Bohemia centered around Zeplica and in northern Moravia around Ostrava presents health hazards; acid rain damaging forests
natural hazards: NA
international agreements: party to—Air Pollution, Air Pollution-Nitrogen Oxides, Air Pollution-Sulphur, Antarctic Treaty, Biodiversity, Climate Change, Environmental Modification, Hazardous Wastes, Law of the Sea, Ozone Layer Protection, Ship Pollution, Wetlands; signed, but not ratified—Antarctic-Environmental Protocol
Note: landlocked; strategically located astride some of oldest and most significant land routes in Europe; Moravian Gate is a traditional military corridor between the North European Plain and the Danube in central Europe

People

Population: 10,408,280 (July 1994 est.)
Population growth rate: 0.21% (1994 est.)
Birth rate: 13.23 births/1,000 population (1994 est.)
Death rate: 11.14 deaths/1,000 population (1994 est.)
Net migration rate: 0 migrant(s)/1,000 population (1994 est.)
Infant mortality rate: 9.3 deaths/1,000 live births (1994 est.)
Life expectancy at birth:
total population: 73.08 years
male: 69.38 years
female: 76.99 years (1994 est.)
Total fertility rate: 1.84 children born/woman (1994 est.)
Nationality:
noun: Czech(s)
adjective: Czech
Ethnic divisions: Czech 94.4%, Slovak 3%, Polish 0.6%, German 0.5%, Gypsy 0.3%, Hungarian 0.2%, other 1%
Religions: atheist 39.8%, Roman Catholic 39.2%, Protestant 4.6%, Orthodox 3%, other 13.4%
Languages: Czech, Slovak
Literacy:
total population: NA%
male: NA%
female: NA%
Labor force: 5.389 million
by occupation: industry 37.9%, agriculture 8.1%, construction 8.8%, communications and other 45.2% (1990)

Government

Names:
conventional long form: Czech Republic
conventional short form: Czech Republic
local long form: Ceska Republika
local short form: Cechy
Digraph: EZ
Type: parliamentary democracy
Capital: Prague
Administrative divisions: 8 regions (kraje, kraj—singular); Jihocesky, Jihomoravsky, Praha, Severocesky, Severomoravsky, Stredocesky, Vychodocesky, Zapadocesky
Independence: 1 January 1993 (from Czechoslovakia)
National holiday: National Liberation Day, 9 May; Founding of the Republic, 28 October
Constitution: ratified 16 December 1992; effective 1 January 1993
Legal system: civil law system based on Austro-Hungarian codes; has not accepted compulsory ICJ jurisdiction; legal code modified to bring it in line with Conference on Security and Cooperation in Europe (CSCE) obligations and to expunge Marxist-Leninist legal theory
Suffrage: 18 years of age; universal

Executive branch:
chief of state: President Vaclav HAVEL (since 26 January 1993); election last held 26 January 1993 (next to be held NA January 1998); results—Vaclav HAVEL elected by the National Council
head of government: Prime Minister Vaclav KLAUS (since NA June 1992); Deputy Prime Ministers Ivan KOCARNIK, Josef LUX, Jan KALVODA (since NA June 1992)
cabinet: Cabinet; appointed by the president on recommendation of the prime minister
Legislative branch: bicameral National Council (Narodni rada)
Senate: elections not yet held; seats (81 total)
Chamber of Deputies: elections last held 5-6 June 1992 (next to be held NA 1996); results - percent of vote by party NA; seats—(200 total) Civic Democratic Party/Christian Democratic Party 76, Left Bloc 35, Czech Social Democratic Party 16, Liberal Social Union 16, Christian Democratic Union/Czech People's Party 15, Assembly for the Republic/ Republican Party 14, Civic Democratic Alliance 14, Movement for Self-Governing Democracy for Moravia and Silesia 14
Judicial branch: Supreme Court, Constitutional Court
Political parties and leaders: Civic Democratic Party (ODS), Vaclav KLAUS, chairman; Christian Democratic Union-Czech People's Party (KDU-CSL), Josef LUX, chairman; Civic Democratic Alliance (ODA), Jan KALVODA, chairman; Christian Democratic Party (KDS), Ivan PILIP, chairman; Czech Social Democratic Party, Milos ZEMAN, chairman; Czech-Moravian Center Party, Jan KYCER, chairman; Liberal Social Union (LSU), Frantisek TRNKA; Communist Party of Bohemia/Moravia (KSCM), Miroslav GREBENICEK, chairman; Association for the Republic—Republican Party, Miroslav SLADEK, chairman; Left Bloc, Marie STIBOROVA, chairman
Other political or pressure groups: Left Bloc; Liberal Party; Czech-Moravian Chamber of Trade Unions
Member of: BIS, CCC, CE (guest), CEI, CERN, COCOM (cooperating), CSCE, EBRD, ECE, FAO, GATT, IAEA, IBRD, ICAO, IDA, IFC, IFCTU, ILO, IMF, IMO, INMARSAT, INTELSAT, INTERPOL, IOC, IOM (observer), ISO, ITU, LORCS, NACC, NSG, PCA, UN (as of 8 January 1993), UNAVEM II, UNCTAD, UNESCO, UNIDO, UNOMIG, UNOMOZ, UNPROFOR, UPU, WFTU, WHO, WIPO, WMO, WTO, ZC
Diplomatic representation in US:
chief of mission: Ambassador Michael ZANTOVSKY
chancery: 3900 Spring of Freedom Street NW, Washington, DC 20008
telephone: (202) 363-6315 or 6316
FAX: (202) 966-8540
US diplomatic representation:
chief of mission: Ambassador Adrian A. BASORA
embassy: Trziste 15, 11801, Prague 1
mailing address: Unit 25402; APO AE 09213
telephone: [42] (2) 251-0847
FAX: [42] (2) 531-193
Flag: two equal horizontal bands of white (top) and red with a blue isosceles triangle based on the hoist side (almost identical to the flag of the former Czechoslovakia)

U.S. Government Contacts:

U.S. Trade Desk: (202) 482-4915

Chambers of Commerce & Organizations:

American Chamber of Commerce in the Czech Republic
Karlovo namesti 24
110 00 Prague 1, Czech Republic
Tel: (42) 2 299-887, 296-778
Fax: (42) 2 291-481

Travel:

International Hotels in Country:
Prague:
Diplomat, Tel: 4202/24394111, Fax: 4202/341731
Palace Praha (Interhotel), Tel: 4202/24093111, Fax: 4202/24221240.

ESTONIA

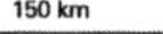

Economy

Overview: Bolstered by a widespread national desire to reintegrate into Western Europe, the Estonian government has pursued a program of market reforms and rough stabilization measures, which is rapidly transforming the economy. Two years after independence—and one year after the introduction of the kroon—Estonians are beginning to reap tangible benefits; inflation is low; production declines appear to have bottomed out; and living standards are rising. Economic restructuring is clearly underway with the once-dominant energy-intensive heavy industrial sectors giving way to labor-intensive light industry and the underdeveloped service sector. The private sector is growing rapidly; the share of the state enterprises in retail trade has steadily declined and by June 1993 accounted for only 12.5% of total turnover, and 70,000 new jobs have reportedly been created as a result of new business start-ups. Estonia's foreign trade has shifted rapidly from East to West with the Western industrialized countries now accounting for two-thirds of foreign trade.

National product: GDP—purchasing power equivalent—$8.8 billion (1993 estimate from the UN International Comparison Program, as extended to 1991 and published in the World Bank's World Development Report 1993; and as extrapolated to 1993 using official Estonian statistics, which are very uncertain because of major economic changes since 1990)
National product real growth rate: -5% (1993 est.)
National product per capita: $5,480 (1993 est.)
Inflation rate (consumer prices): 2.6% per month (1993 average)
Unemployment rate: 3.5% (May 1993); but large number of underemployed workers
Budget:
revenues: $223 million
expenditures: $142 million, including capital expenditures of $NA (1992)
Exports: $765 million (f.o.b., 1993)
commodities: textile 14%, food products 11%, vehicles 11%, metals 11% (1993)
partners: Russia, Finland, Latvia, Germany, Ukraine
Imports: $865 million (c.i.f., 1993)
commodities: machinery 18%, fuels 15%, vehicles 14%, textiles 10% (1993)
partners: Finland, Russia, Sweden, Germany, Netherlands
External debt: $650 million (end of 1991)
Industrial production: growth rate -27% (1993)
Electricity:
capacity: 3,700,000 kW
production: 22.9 billion kWh
consumption per capita: 14,245 kWh (1992)
Industries: accounts for 42% of labor force; oil shale, shipbuilding, phosphates, electric motors, excavators, cement, furniture, clothing, textiles, paper, shoes, apparel
Agriculture: employs 20% of work force; very efficient by Soviet standards; net exports of meat, fish, dairy products, and potatoes; imports of feedgrains for livestock; fruits and vegetables

Illicit drugs: transshipment point for illicit drugs from Central and Southwest Asia and Latin America to Western Europe; limited illicit opium producer; mostly for domestic consumption

Economic aid:
recipient: US commitments, including Ex-Im (1992), $10 million

Currency: 1 Estonian kroon (EEK) = 100 cents (introduced in August 1992)

Exchange rates: kroons (EEK) per US$1—13.9 (January 1994), 13.2 (1993); note—kroons are tied to the German Deutschmark at a fixed rate of 8 to 1

Fiscal year: calendar year

Communications

Railroads: 1,030 km; does not include industrial lines (1990)

Highways:
total: 30,300 km
paved or gravelled: 29,200 km
unpaved: earth 1,100 km (1990)

Inland waterways: 500 km perennially navigable

Pipelines: natural gas 420 km (1992)

Ports: coastal—Tallinn, Novotallin, Parnu; inland—Narva

Merchant marine: 69 ships (1,000 GRT or over) totaling 406,405 GRT/537,016 DWT, cargo 50, roll-on/roll-off cargo 6, short-sea passenger 4, bulk 6, container 2, oil tanker 1

Airports:
total: 29
usable: 18
with permanent-surface runways: 11
with runways over 3,659 m: 0
with runways 2,440-3,659 m: 10
with runways 1,060-2,439 m: 8
note: a C-130 can land on a 1,060-m airstrip

Telecommunications: Estonia's telephone system is antiquated and supports about 400,000 domestic telephone circuits, i.e. 25 telephones for each 100 persons; improvements are being made piecemeal, with emphasis on business needs and international connections; there are still about 150,000 unfulfilled requests for telephone service; broadcast stations—3 TV (provide Estonian programs as well Moscow Ostenkino's first and second programs); international traffic is carried to the other former USSR republics by land line or microwave and to other countries partly by leased connection to the Moscow international gateway switch, and partly by a new Tallinn-Helsinki fiber optic submarine cable which gives Estonia access to international circuits everywhere; substantial investment has been made in cellular systems which are operational throughout Estonia and also Latvia and which have access to the international packet switched digital network via Helsinki

Defense Forces

Branches: Ground Forces, Maritime Border Guard, National Guard (Kaitseliit), Security Forces (internal and border troops), Coast Guard

Manpower availability: males age 15-49 392,135; fit for military service 308,951; reach military age (18) annually 11,789 (1994 est.)

Defense expenditures: 124.4 million kroons, NA% of GDP (forecast for 1993); note—conversion of the military budget into US dollars using the current exchange rate could produce misleading results

Geography

Location: Eastern Europe, bordering the Baltic Sea, between Sweden and Russia

Map references: Arctic Region, Asia, Europe, Standard Time Zones of the World

Area:
total area: 45,100 sq km
land area: 43,200 sq km
comparative area: slightly larger than New Hampshire and Vermont combined
note: includes 1,520 islands in the Baltic Sea

Land boundaries: total 557 km, Latvia 267 km, Russia 290 km

Coastline: 1,393 km

Maritime claims:
territorial sea: 12 nm

International disputes: none

Climate: maritime, wet, moderate winters, cool summers
Terrain: marshy, lowlands
Natural resources: shale oil, peat, phosphorite, amber
Land use:
arable land: 22%
permanent crops: 0%
meadows and pastures: 11%
forest and woodland: 31%
other: 36%
Irrigated land: 110 sq km (1990)
Environment:
current issues: air heavily polluted with sulfur dioxide from oil-shale burning power plants in northeast; contamination of soil and ground water with petroleum products, chemicals at military bases
natural hazards: NA
international agreements: party to—Hazardous Wastes, Ship Pollution; signed, but not ratified—Biodiversity, Climate Change

People

Population: 1,616,882 (July 1994 est.)
Population growth rate: 0.52% (1994 est.)
Birth rate: 13.98 births/1,000 population (1994 est.)
Death rate: 12.04 deaths/1,000 population (1994 est.)
Net migration rate: 3.29 migrant(s)/1,000 population (1994 est.)
Infant mortality rate: 19.1 deaths/1,000 live births (1994 est.)
Life expectancy at birth:
total population: 69.96 years
male: 64.98 years
female: 75.19 years (1994 est.)
Total fertility rate: 2 children born/woman (1994 est.)
Nationality:
noun: Estonian(s)
adjective: Estonian
Ethnic divisions: Estonian 61.5%, Russian 30.3%, Ukrainian 3.17%, Byelorussian 1.8%, Finn 1.1%, other 2.13% (1989)
Religions: Lutheran
Languages: Estonian (official), Latvian, Lithuanian, Russian, other
Literacy: age 9-49 can read and write (1989)
total population: 100%
male: 100%
female: 100%
Labor force: 750,000 (1992)
by occupation: industry and construction 42%, agriculture and forestry 20%, other 38% (1990)

Government

Names:
conventional long form: Republic of Estonia
conventional short form: Estonia
local long form: Eesti Vabariik
local short form: Eesti
former: Estonian Soviet Socialist Republic
Digraph: EN
Type: republic
Capital: Tallinn
Administrative divisions: 15 counties (maakonnad, singular—maakond) and 6 municipalities*: Harju maakond (Tallinn), Hiiu maakond (Kardla), Ida-Viru maakond (Johvi), Jarva maakond (Paide), Jogeva maakond (Jogeva), Kohtla-Jarve*, Laane maakond (Haapsalu), Laane-Viru maakond (Rakvere), Narva*, Parnu*, Parnu maakond (Parnu), Polva maakond (Polva), Rapla maakond (Rapla), Saare maakond (Kuessaare), Sillamae*, Tallinn*, Tartu*, Tartu maakond (Tartu), Valga maakond (Valga), Viljandi maakond (Viljandi), Voru maakond (Voru)
note: county centers are in parentheses
Independence: 6 September 1991 (from Soviet Union)
National holiday: Independence Day, 24 February (1918)
Constitution: adopted 28 June 1992
Legal system: based on civil law system; no judicial review of legislative acts
Suffrage: 18 years of age; universal
Executive branch:
chief of state: President Lennart MERI (since 21 October 1992); election last held 20 September 1992; (next to be held NA 1997); results—no candidate received majority; newly elected Parliament elected Lennart MERI (21 October 1992)
head of government: Prime Minister Mart

LAAR (since 21 October 1992)
cabinet: Council of Ministers; appointed by the prime minister, authorized by the legislature
Legislative branch: unicameral
Parliament (Riigikogu): elections last held 20 September 1992; (next to be held NA); results—Fatherland 21%, Safe Haven 14%, Popular Front 13%, M 10%, ENIP 8%, ERP 7%, ERL 7%, EP 2%, other 18%; seats—(101 total) Fatherland 29, Safe Haven 18, Popular Front 15, M 12, ENIP 10, ERP 8, ERL 8, EP 1
Judicial branch: Supreme Court
Political parties and leaders: National Coalition Party 'Pro Patria' (Isamaa of Fatherland), Mart LAAR, president, made up of 4 parties: Christian Democratic Party (KDE), Aivar KALA, chairman; Christian Democratic Union (KDL), Illar HALLASTE, chairman; Conservative People's Party (KR), Enn TARTO, chairman; Republican Coalition Party (VK), Leo STARKOV, chairman; Moderates (M), made up of two parties: Estonian Social Democratic Party (ESDB), Marju LAURISTIN, chairman; Estonian Rural Center Pary (EMK), Ivar RAIG, chairman; Estonian National Independence Party (ENIP), Tunne KELAM, chairman; Liberal Democratic Party (LDP), Paul-Eerik RUMMO, chairman; Safe Haven, made up of three parties: Estonian Coalition Party (EK), Tiit VAHI, chairman; Estonian Rural Union (EM), Arvo SIRENDI, chairman; Estonian Democratic Justice Union/ Estonian Pensioners' League (EDO/EPU), Harri KARTNER, chairman; Estonian Centrist Party (EK), Edgar SAVISAAR, chairman; Estonian Democratic Labor Party (EDT), Vaino VALJAS, chairman; Estonian Green Party (ERL), Tonu OJA; Estonian Royalist Party (ERP), Kalle KULBOK, chairman; Entrepreneurs' Party (EP), Tiit MADE; Estonian Citizen (EKL), Juri TOOMEPUU, chairman
Member of: BIS, CBSS, CCC, CE, CSCE, EBRD, ECE, FAO, IAEA, IBRD, ICAO, ICFTU, IFC, ILO, IMF, IMO, INTERPOL, IOC, ISO (correspondent), ITU, NACC, UN, UNCTAD, UNESCO, UPU, WHO, WMO
Diplomatic representation in US:
chief of mission: Ambassador Toomas Hendrik ILVES
chancery: 1030 15th Street NW, Washington, DC 20005, Suite 1000
telephone: (202) 789-0320
FAX: (202) 789-0471
consulate(s) general: New York
US diplomatic representation:
chief of mission: Ambassador Robert C. FRASURE
embassy: Kentmanni 20, Tallin EE 0001
mailing address: use embassy street address
telephone: 011-[372] (6) 312-021 through 024
FAX: [372] (6) 312-025
Flag: pre-1940 flag restored by Supreme Soviet in May 1990—three equal horizontal bands of blue (top), black, and white

---

U.S. Government Contacts:

U.S. Trade Desk: (202) 482-4915

FORMER YUGOSLAVA REP. OF MACEDONIA

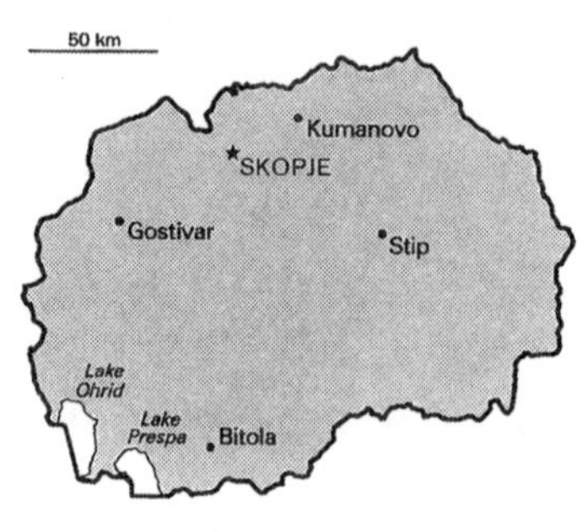

Macedonia has proclaimed indepedent statehood but has not been formally recognized as a state by the United States.

Economy

Overview: The Former Yugoslav Republic of Macedonia, although the poorest republic in the former Yugoslav federation, can meet basic food and energy needs through its own agricultural and coal resources. Its economic decline will continue unless ties are reforged or enlarged with its neighbors Serbia and Montenegro, Albania, Greece, and Bulgaria. The economy depends on outside sources for all of its oil and gas and its modern machinery and parts. Continued political turmoil, both internally and in the region as a whole, prevents any swift readjustments of trade patterns and economic programs. The country's industrial output and GDP are expected to decline further in 1994. The Former Yugoslav Republic of Macedonia's geographical isolation, technological backwardness, and potential political instability place it far down the list of countries of interest to Western investors. Resolution of the dispute with Greece and an internal commitment to economic reform would help to encourage foreign investment over the long run. In the immediate future, the worst scenario for the economy would be the spread of fighting across its borders.

National product: GDP—purchasing power equivalent—$2.2 billion (1993 est.)
National product real growth rate: -14.7% (1992 est.)
National product per capita: $1,000 (1993 est.)
Inflation rate (consumer prices): 13% monthly average (1993 est.)
Unemployment rate: 27% (1993 est.)
Budget:
revenues: $NA
expenditures: $NA, including capital expenditures of $NA
Exports: $889 million (1993)
commodities: manufactured goods 40%, machinery and transport equipment 14%, miscellaneous manufactured articles 23%, raw materials 7.6%, food (rice) and live animals 5.7%, beverages and tobacco 4.5%, chemicals 4.7% (1990)
partners: principally Serbia and Montenegro and the other former Yugoslav republics, Germany, Greece, Albania
Imports: $963 million (1993)
commodities: fuels and lubricants 19%, manufactured goods 18%, machinery and transport equipment 15%, food and live animals 14%, chemicals 11.4%, raw materials 10%, miscellaneous manufactured articles 8.0%, beverages and tobacco 3.5% (1990)
partners: other former Yugoslav republics, Greece, Albania, Germany, Bulgaria
External debt: $840 million (1992)
Industrial production: growth rate -14% (1993 est.)
Electricity:
capacity: 1,600,000 kW
production: 6.3 billion kWh
consumption per capita: 2,900 kWh (1992)
Industries: low levels of technology predominate, such as, oil refining by distillation only; produces basic liquid fuels, coal, metallic chromium, lead, zinc, and

ferronickel; light industry produces basic textiles, wood products, and tobacco
Agriculture: provides 12% of GDP and meets the basic needs for food; principal crops are rice, tobacco, wheat, corn, and millet; also grown are cotton, sesame, mulberry leaves, citrus fruit, and vegetables; The Former Yugoslav Republic of Macedonia is one of the seven legal cultivators of the opium poppy for the world pharmaceutical industry, including some exports to the US; agricultural production is highly labor intensive
Illicit drugs: limited illicit opium cultivation; transshipment point for Asian heroin
Economic aid:
recipient: US $10 million (for humanitarian and technical assistance)
EC promised a 100 ECU million economic aid package (1993)
Currency: the denar, which was adopted by the Macedonian legislature 26 April 1992, was initially issued in the form of a coupon pegged to the German mark; subsequently repegged to a basket of seven currencies
Exchange rates: denar per US$1—865 (October 1992)
Fiscal year: calendar year

Communications

Railroads: NA
Highways:
total: 10,591 km
paved: 5,091 km
unpaved: gravel 1,404 km; earth 4,096 km (1991)
Inland waterways: NA km
Pipelines: none
Ports: none; landlocked
Airports:
total: 16
usable: 16
with permanent-surface runways: 10
with runways over 3,659 m: 0
with runways 2,440-3,659 m: 2
with runways 1,220-2,439 m: 2
Telecommunications: 125,000 telephones; broadcast stations—6 AM, 2 FM, 5 (2 relays) TV; 370,000 radios, 325,000 TV; satellite communications ground stations—none

Defense Forces

Branches: Army, Navy, Air and Air Defense Force, Police Force
Manpower availability: males age 15-49 604,257; fit for military service 489,746; reach military age (19) annually 19,539 (1994 est.)
Defense expenditures: 7 billion denars, NA% of GNP (1993 est.); note—conversion of the military budget into US dollars using the prevailing exchange rate could produce misleading results

Geography

Location: Balkan State, Southeastern Europe, between Serbia and Montenegro and Greece
Map references: Ethnic Groups in Eastern Europe, Europe, Standard Time Zones of the World
Area:
total area: 25,333 sq km
land area: 24,856 sq km
comparative area: slightly larger than Vermont
Land boundaries: total 748 km, Albania 151 km, Bulgaria 148 km, Greece 228 km, Serbia and Montenegro 221 km (all with Serbia)
Coastline: 0 km (landlocked)
Maritime claims: none; landlocked
International disputes: Greece claims republic's name implies territorial claims against Aegean Macedonia
Climate: hot, dry summers and autumns and relatively cold winters with heavy snowfall
Terrain: mountainous territory covered with deep basins and valleys; there are three large lakes, each divided by a frontier line
Natural resources: chromium, lead, zinc, manganese, tungsten, nickel, low-grade iron ore, asbestos, sulphur, timber
Land use:
arable land: 5%
permanent crops: 5%
meadows and pastures: 20%
forest and woodland: 30%
other: 40%
Irrigated land: NA sq km
Environment:
current issues: air pollution from metallurgical

plants
natural hazards: high seismic risks
international agreements: party to—Ozone Layer Protection
Note: landlocked; major transportation corridor from Western and Central Europe to Aegean Sea and Southern Europe to Western Europe

People

Population: 2,213,785 (July 1994 est.)
Population growth rate: 0.89% (1994 est.)
Birth rate: 15.59 births/1,000 population (1994 est.)
Death rate: 6.72 deaths/1,000 population (1994 est.)
Net migration rate: 0 migrant(s)/1,000 population (1994 est.)
Infant mortality rate: 27.8 deaths/1,000 live births (1994 est.)
Life expectancy at birth:
total population: 73.59 years
male: 71.51 years
female: 75.85 years (1994 est.)
Total fertility rate: 1.98 children born/woman (1994 est.)
Nationality:
noun: Macedonian(s)
adjective: Macedonian
Ethnic divisions: Macedonian 65%, Albanian 22%, Turkish 4%, Serb 2%, Gypsies 3%, other 4%
Religions: Eastern Orthodox 67%, Muslim 30%, other 3%
Languages: Macedonian 70%, Albanian 21%, Turkish 3%, Serbo-Croatian 3%, other 3%
Literacy:
total population: NA%
male: NA%
female: NA%
Labor force: 507,324
by occupation: agriculture 8%, manufacturing and mining 40% (1990)

Government

Names:
conventional long form: The Former Yugoslav Republic of Macedonia
conventional short form: none
local long form: Republika Makedonija
local short form: Makedonija
Abbreviation: F.Y.R.O.M.
Digraph: MK
Type: emerging democracy
Capital: Skopje
Administrative divisions: 34 counties (opstinas, singular—opstina) Berovo, Bitola, Brod, Debar, Delcevo, Gevgelija, Gostivar, Kavadarci, Kicevo, Kocani, Kratovo, Kriva Palanka, Krusevo, Kumanovo, Murgasevo, Negotino, Ohrid, Prilep, Probistip, Radovis, Resen, Skopje-Centar, Skopje-Cair, Skopje-Karpos, Skopje-Kisela Voda, Skopje-Gazi Baba, Stip, Struga, Strumica, Sveti Nikole, Tetovo, Titov Veles, Valandovo, Vinica
Independence: 17 September 1991 (from Yugoslavia)
National holiday: NA
Constitution: adopted 17 November 1991, effective 20 November 1991
Legal system: based on civil law system; judicial review of legislative acts
Suffrage: 18 years of age; universal
Executive branch:
chief of state: President Kiro GLIGOROV (since 27 January 1991); election last held 27 January 1991 (next to be held NA); results—Kiro GLIGOROV was elected by the Assembly
head of government: Prime Minister Branko CRVENKOVSKI (since 4 September 1992), Deputy Prime Ministers Jovan ANDONOV (since NA March 1991), Risto IVANOV (since NA), and Becir ZUTA (since NA March 1991)
cabinet: Council of Ministers; elected by the majority vote of all the deputies in the Sobranje
Legislative branch: unicameral
Assembly (Sobranje): elections last held 11 and 25 November and 9 December 1990 (next to be held November 1994); results—percent of vote by party NA; seats—(120 total) VMRO-DPMNE 32, SDSM 29, PDPM 23, SRSM 19, SPM 4, DP 4, SJM 2, others 7
Judicial branch: Constitutional Court, Judicial Court of the Republic
Political parties and leaders: Social-Democratic Alliance of Macedonia (SDSM;

former Communist Party), Branko CRVENKOVSKI, president; Party for Democratic Prosperity (PDPM); National Democratic Party (PDP), Ilijas HALINI, president; Alliance of Reform Forces of Macedonia—Liberal Party (SRSM-LP), Stojan ANDOV, president; Socialist Party of Macedonia (SPM), Kiro POPOVSKI, president; Internal Macedonian Revolutionary Organization—Democratic Party for Macedonian National Unity (VMRO-DPMNE), Ljupco GEORGIEVSKI, president; Party of Yugoslavs in Macedonia (SJM), Milan DURCINOV, president; Democratic Party (DP), Petal GOSEV, president
Other political or pressure groups: Movement for All Macedonian Action (MAAK); Democratic Party of Serbs; Democratic Party of Turks; Party for Democratic Action (Slavic Muslim)
Member of: CE (guest), CSCE (observer), EBRD, ECE, ICAO, ILO, IMF, INTELSAT (nonsignatory user), ITU, UN, UNCTAD, UNESCO, UNIDO, UPU, WHO, WIPO, WMO
Diplomatic representation in US: the US recognized The Former Yugoslav Republic of Macedonia on 9 February 1994
US diplomatic representation: the US recognized The Former Yugoslav Republic of Macedonia on 9 February 1994
Flag: 16-point gold sun (Vergina, Sun) centered on a red field

GEORGIA

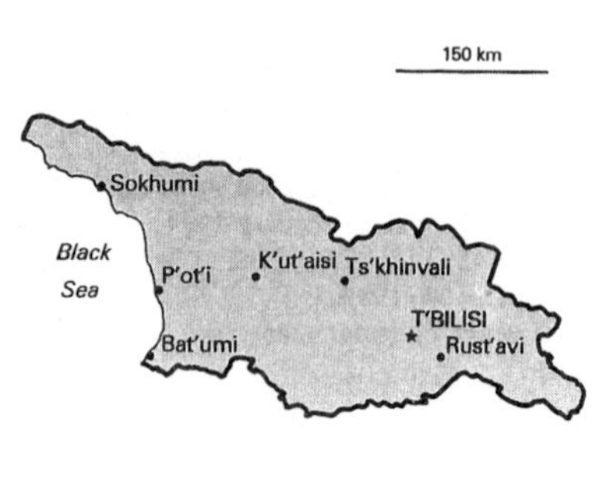

Economy

Overview: Georgia's economy has traditionally revolved around Black Sea tourism; cultivation of citrus fruits, tea, and grapes; mining of manganese and copper; and a small industrial sector producing wine, metals, machinery, chemicals, and textiles. The country imports the bulk of its energy needs, including natural gas and coal. Its only sizable domestic energy resource is hydropower. Since 1990, widespread conflicts, e.g., in Abkhazia, South Ossetia, and Mengrelia, severely aggravated the economic crisis resulting from the disintegration of the Soviet command economy in December 1991. Throughout 1993, much of industry was functioning at only 20% of capacity; heavy disruptions in agricultural cultivation were reported; and tourism was shut down. The country is precariously dependent on US and EU humanitarian grain shipments, as most other foods are priced beyond reach of the average citizen. Georgia is also suffering from an acute energy crisis, as it is having problems paying for even minimal imports. Georgia is pinning its hopes for recovery on reestablishing trade ties with Russia and on developing international transportation through the key Black Sea ports of P'ot'i and Bat'umi.

National product: GDP—purchasing power equivalent—$7.8 billion (1993 estimate from the UN International Comparison Program, as extended to 1991 and published in the World Bank's World Development Report 1993; and as extrapolated to 1993 using official Georgian statistics, which are very uncertain because of major economic changes since 1990)

National product real growth rate: -35% (1993 est.)

National product per capita: $1,390 (1993 est.)

Inflation rate (consumer prices): 40.5% per month (2nd half 1993 est.)

Unemployment rate: officially less than 5% but real unemployment may be up near 20%, with even larger numbers of underemployed workers

Budget:
revenues: $NA
expenditures: $NA, including capital expenditures of $NA

Exports: $NA
commodities: citrus fruits, tea, wine, other agricultural products; diverse types of machinery; ferrous and nonferrous metals; textiles; chemicals; fuel re-exports
partners: Russia, Turkey, Armenia, Azerbaijan (1992)

Imports: $NA
commodities: fuel, grain and other foods, machinery and parts, transport equipment
partners: Russia, Azerbaijan, Turkey (1993)

External debt: $100 million to $200 million (1993 est.)

Industrial production: growth rate -27% (1993); accounts for 36% of GDP

Electricity:
capacity: 4,875,000 kW
production: 15.8 billion kWh
consumption per capita: 2,835 kWh (1992)

Industries: heavy industrial products include raw steel, rolled steel, airplanes; machine tools, foundry equipment, electric locomotives, tower cranes, electric welding equipment, machinery for food preparation and meat packing, electric motors, process control equipment, instruments; trucks, tractors, and other farm machinery; light industrial products, including cloth, hosiery, and shoes; chemicals; wood-working industries; the most important food industry is wine
Agriculture: accounts for 41% of GDP; accounted for 97% of former USSR citrus fruits and 93% of former USSR tea; important producer of grapes; also cultivates vegetables and potatoes; dependent on imports for grain, dairy products, sugar; small livestock sector
Illicit drugs: illicit cultivator of cannabis and opium poppy; mostly for domestic consumption; used as transshipment point for illicit drugs to Western Europe
Economic aid:
recipient: heavily dependent on US for humanitarian grain shipments; EC granted around $70 million in trade credits in 1992 and another $40 million in 1993; Turkey granted $50 million in 1993; smaller scale credits granted by Russia and China
Currency: coupons introduced in April 1993 to be followed by introduction of the lari at undetermined future date; in July 1993 use of the Russian ruble was banned
Exchange rates: NA
Fiscal year: calendar year

Communications

Railroads: 1,570 km, does not include industrial lines (1990)
Highways:
total: 33,900 km
paved and gravelled: 29,500 km
unpaved: earth 4,400 km (1990)
Pipelines: crude oil 370 km, refined products 300 km, natural gas 440 km (1992)
Ports: coastal—Bat'umi, P'ot'i, Sokhumi
Merchant marine: 41 ships (1,000 GRT or over) totaling 575,823 GRT/882,110 DWT, bulk cargo 14, oil tanker 27
Airports:
total: 37
usable: 27
with permanent-surface runways: 14
with runways over 3,659 m: 0
with runways 2,440-3,659 m: 10
with runways 1,060-2,439 m: 4
note: a C-130 can land on a 1,060-m airstrip
Telecommunications: poor telephone service; as of mid-1993, 672,000 telephone lines providing 14 lines per 100 persons; 339,000 unsatisfied applications for telephones (31 December 1990); international links via landline to CIS members and Turkey; low capacity satellite earth station and leased international connections via the Moscow international gateway switch with other countries; international electronic mail and telex service available
Note: transportation network is disrupted by ethnic conflict, criminal activities, and fuel shortages

Defense Forces

Branches: Army, Air Force, Navy, Interior Ministry Troops, Border Guards
Manpower availability: males age 15-49 1,362,818; fit for military service 1,081,624; reach military age (18) annually 42,881 (1994 est.)
Defense expenditures: $NA, NA% of GNP
Note: Georgian forces are poorly organized and not fully under the government's control

Geography

Location: Southwestern Asia, bordering the Black Sea, between Turkey and Russia
Map references: Africa, Asia, Commonwealth of Independent States—European States, Middle East, Standard Time Zones of the World
Area:
total area: 69,700 sq km
land area: 69,700 sq km
comparative area: slightly larger than South Carolina
Land boundaries: total 1,461 km, Armenia

164 km, Azerbaijan 322 km, Russia 723 km, Turkey 252 km
Coastline: 310 km
Maritime claims:
note: 12 nm in 1973 USSR-Turkish Protocol concerning the sea boundary between the two states in the Black Sea; Georgia claims the coastline along the Black Sea as its international waters, although it cannot control this area and the Russian navy and commercial ships transit freely
International disputes: none
Climate: warm and pleasant; Mediterranean-like on Black Sea coast
Terrain: largely mountainous with Great Caucasus Mountains in the north and Lesser Caucasus Mountains in the south; Kolkhida Lowland opens to the Black Sea in the west; Mtkvari River Basin in the east; good soils in river valley flood plains, foothills of Kolkhida Lowland
Natural resources: forest lands, hydropower, manganese deposits, iron ores, copper, minor coal and oil deposits; coastal climate and soils allow for important tea and citrus growth
Land use:
arable land: NA%
permanent crops: NA%
meadows and pastures: NA%
forest and woodland: NA%
other: NA%
Irrigated land: 4,660 sq km (1990)
Environment:
current issues: air pollution, particularly in Rust'avi; heavy pollution of Mtkvari River and the Black Sea; inadequate supplies of safe drinking water; soil pollution from toxic chemicals
natural hazards: NA
international agreements: NA

People

Population: 5,681,025 (July 1994 est.)
Population growth rate: 0.81% (1994 est.)
Birth rate: 16.11 births/1,000 population (1994 est.)
Death rate: 8.69 deaths/1,000 population (1994 est.)
Net migration rate: 0.65 migrant(s)/1,000 population (1994 est.)
Infant mortality rate: 23.4 deaths/1,000 live births (1994 est.)
Life expectancy at birth:
total population: 72.84 years
male: 69.16 years
female: 76.7 years (1994 est.)
Total fertility rate: 2.18 children born/woman (1994 est.)
Nationality:
noun: Georgian(s)
adjective: Georgian
Ethnic divisions: Georgian 70.1%, Armenian 8.1%, Russian 6.3%, Azeri 5.7%, Ossetian 3%, Abkhaz 1.8%, other 5%
Religions: Georgian Orthodox 65%, Russian Orthodox 10%, Muslim 11%, Armenian Orthodox 8%, unknown 6%
Languages: Armenian 7%, Azeri 6%, Georgian 71% (official), Russian 9%, other 7%
Literacy: age 9-49 can read and write (1970)
total population: 100%
male: 100%
female: 100%
Labor force: 2.763 million
by occupation: industry and construction 31%, agriculture and forestry 25%, other 44% (1990)

Government

Names:
conventional long form: Republic of Georgia
conventional short form: Georgia
local long form: Sak'art'velos Respublika
local short form: Sak'art'velo
former: Georgian Soviet Socialist Republic
Digraph: GG
Type: republic
Capital: T'bilisi
Administrative divisions: 2 autonomous republics (avtomnoy respubliki, singular—avtom respublika); Abkhazia (Sokhumi), Ajaria (Bat'umi)
note: the administrative centers of the autonomous republics are included in parentheses; there are no oblasts—the rayons around T'bilisi are under direct republic jurisdiction

Independence: 9 April 1991 (from Soviet Union)
National holiday: Independence Day, 9 April (1991)
Constitution: adopted NA February 1921; currently amending constitution for Parliamentary and popular review by late 1995
Legal system: based on civil law system
Suffrage: 18 years of age; universal
Executive branch:
chief of state: Chairman of Parliament Eduard Amvrosiyevich SHEVARDNADZE (since 10 March 1992); election last held 11 October 1992 (next to be held NA 1995); results—Eduard SHEVARDNADZE 95%
head of government: Prime Minister Otar PATSATSIA (since September 1993); Deputy Prime Ministers Avtandil MARGIANI, Zurab KERVALISHVILI (since NA), Tamaz NADARISHVILI (since September 1993), Teimuraz BASILIA (since NA)
cabinet: Council of Ministers
Legislative branch: unicameral
Georgian Parliament (Supreme Soviet): elections last held 11 October 1992 (next to be held NA 1995); results—percent of vote by party NA; seats—(225 total) number of seats by party NA; note—representatives of 26 parties elected; Peace Bloc, October 11, Unity, National Democratic Party, and the Greens Party won the largest representation
Judicial branch: Supreme Court
Political parties and leaders: Merab Kostava Society, Vazha ADAMIA, chairman; Traditionalists' Union, Akaki ASATIANI, chairman; Georgian Social Democratic Party, Guram MUCHAIDZE, chairman; Green Party, Zurab ZHVANIA, chairman; Georgian Popular Front (GPF), Nodar NATADZE, chairman; National Democratic Party (NDP), Gia CHANTURIA, chairman; National Independence Party (NIP), Irakliy TSERETELI, chairmen; Charter 1991 Party, Tedo PATASHVILI, chairman; Peace Bloc; Unity; October 11
Other political or pressure groups: supporters of ousted President Zuiad GAMSAKHURDIA (deceased 1 January 1994) boycotted the October elections and remain a source of opposition and instability
Member of: BSEC, CIS, CSCE, EBRD, ECE, IBRD, IDA, ILO, IMF, IMO, INMARSAT, IOC, ITU, NACC, UN, UNCTAD, UNESCO, UNIDO, UPU, WHO
Diplomatic representation in US:
chief of mission: Ambassador Petr CHKHEIDZE
chancery: (temporary) Suite 424, 1511 K Street NW, Washington, DC
telephone: (202) 393-6060
US diplomatic representation:
chief of mission: Ambassador Kent N. BROWN
embassy: #25 Antoneli Street, T'bilisi 380026
mailing address: use embassy street address
telephone: (7) 8832-98-99-68
FAX: (7) 8832-93-37-59
Flag: maroon field with small rectangle in upper hoist side corner; rectangle divided horizontally with black on top, white below

---

U.S. Government Contacts:

U.S. Trade Desk: (202) 482-0988

HUNGARY

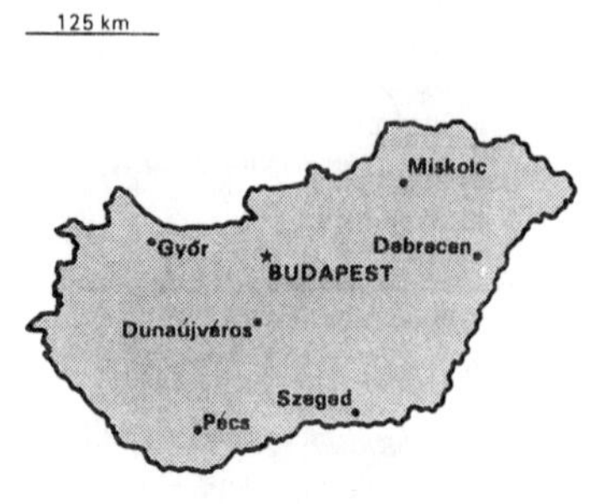

Economy

Overview: Hungary is still in the midst of a difficult transition from a command to a market economy. Its economic reforms during the Communist era gave it a head start on this process, particularly in terms of attracting foreign investors—Hungary has accounted for about half of all foreign direct investment in Eastern Europe since 1989. Nonetheless, the economy continued to contract in 1993, with real GDP falling perhaps 1%. Although the privatization process has lagged, in December 1993 Hungary carried out the largest privatization yet in Eastern Europe, selling a controlling interest in the Matav telecommunications firm to private investors—including a 30% share to a US-German consortium for $875 million. Overall, about half of GDP now originates in the private sector. Unemployment rose to about 13% in 1993 while inflation remained above 20%, and falling exports pushed the trade deficit to about $3 billion. The government hopes that economic recovery in Western Europe in 1994 will boost exports, lower the trade deficit, and help jump-start the economy. The budget, however, is likely to remain a serious concern; depressed tax revenue pushed up the budget deficit in 1993.

National product: GDP—purchasing power equivalent—$57 billion (1993 est.)

National product real growth rate: -1% (1993 est.)

National product per capita: $5,500 (1993 est.)

Inflation rate (consumer prices): 23% (1993 est.)

Unemployment rate: 13% (1993)

Budget:
revenues: $10.2 billion
expenditures: $12.5 billion, including capital expenditures of $NA (1993 est.)

Exports: $8.9 billion (f.o.b., 1993 est.)
commodities: raw materials, semi-finished goods, chemicals 39.6%, machinery 14.5%, consumer goods 22.3%, food and agriculture 20.0%, fuels and energy 3.6% (January-June 1993)
partners: EC 49.8% (Germany 27.8%, Italy 9.5%), Austria 10.7%, the FSU 13.1%, Eastern Europe 9.8% (1992)

Imports: $12.5 billion (f.o.b., 1993 est.)
commodities: fuels and energy 13.9%, raw materials, semi-finished goods, chemicals 35.9%, machinery 22.4%, consumer goods 21.8%, food and agriculture 6.0% (January-June 1993)
partners: EC 42.8% (Germany 23.6%, Italy 6.3%), Austria 14.4%, the FSU 16.8%, Eastern Europe 9.2%

External debt: $24.7 billion (November 1993)

Industrial production: growth rate 4% (1993 est.)

Electricity:
capacity: 7,200,000 kW
production: 30 billion kWh
consumption per capita: 3,000 kWh (1992)

Industries: mining, metallurgy, construction materials, processed foods, textiles, chemicals (especially pharmaceuticals), buses, automobiles

Agriculture: including forestry, accounts for 15% of GDP and 16% of employment; highly diversified crop and livestock farming; principal crops—wheat, corn, sunflowers, potatoes, sugar beets; livestock—hogs, cattle, poultry, dairy products; self-sufficient in food output
Illicit drugs: transshipment point for Southeast Asia heroin transiting the Balkan route
Economic aid:
recipient: assistance pledged by OECD countries since 1989 about $9 billion
Currency: 1 forint (Ft) = 100 filler
Exchange rates: forints per US$1—93.46 (September 1993), 92.5 (1993), 78.99 (1992), 74.74 (1991), 63.21 (1990), 59.07 (1989)
Fiscal year: calendar year

Communications

Railroads: 7,765 km total; 7,508 km 1.435-meter standard gauge, 222 km narrow gauge (mostly 0.760-meter), 35 km 1.520-meter broad gauge; 1,236 km double track, 2,249 km electrified; all government owned (1990)
Highways:
total: 130,224 km
paved: 61,948 km
unpaved: 68,276 km (1988)
Inland waterways: 1,622 km (1988)
Pipelines: crude oil 1,204 km; natural gas 4,387 km (1991)
Ports: Budapest and Dunaujvaros are river ports on the Danube; coastal outlets are Rostock (Germany), Gdansk (Poland), Gdynia (Poland), Szczecin (Poland), Galati (Romania), and Braila (Romania)
Merchant marine: 10 cargo ships (1,000 GRT or over) and 1 bulk totaling 46,121 GRT/ 61,613 DWT
Airports:
total: 126
usable: 65
with permanent-surface runways: 12
with runways over 3,659 m: 1
with runways 2,440-3,659 m: 18
with runways 1,060-2,439 m: 31
note: a C-130 can land on a 1,060-m airstrip
Telecommunications: automatic telephone network based on microwave radio relay system; 1,128,800 phones (1991); telephone density is at 19.4 per 100 inhabitants; 49% of all phones are in Budapest; 608,000 telephones on order (1991); 12-15 year wait for a phone; 14,213 telex lines (1991); broadcast stations—32 AM, 15 FM, 41 TV (8 Soviet TV repeaters); 4.2 million TVs (1990); 1 satellite ground station using INTELSAT and Intersputnik

Defense Forces

Branches: Ground Forces, Air and Air Defense Forces, Border Guard, Territorial Defense
Manpower availability: males age 15-49 2,636,888; fit for military service 2,105,628; reach military age (18) annually 90,134 (1994 est.)
Defense expenditures: 66.5 billion forints, NA% of GNP (1993 est.); note—conversion of defense expenditures into US dollars using the current exchange rate could produce misleading results

Geography

Location: Central Europe, between Slovakia and Romania
Map references: Ethnic Groups in Eastern Europe, Europe
Area:
total area: 93,030 sq km
land area: 92,340 sq km
comparative area: slightly smaller than Indiana
Land boundaries: total 1,989 km, Austria 366 km, Croatia 329 km, Romania 443 km, Serbia and Montenegro 151 km (all with Serbia), Slovakia 515 km, Slovenia 82 km, Ukraine 103 km
Coastline: 0 km (landlocked)
Maritime claims: none; landlocked
International disputes: Gabcikovo Dam dispute with Slovakia
Climate: temperate; cold, cloudy, humid winters; warm summers
Terrain: mostly flat to rolling plains

Natural resources: bauxite, coal, natural gas, fertile soils
Land use:
arable land: 50.7%
permanent crops: 6.1%
meadows and pastures: 12.6%
forest and woodland: 18.3%
other: 12.3%
Irrigated land: 1,750 sq km (1989)
Environment:
current issues: air pollution; industrial and municipal pollution of Lake Balaton
natural hazards: levees are common along many streams, but flooding occurs almost every year
international agreements: party to—Air Pollution, Air Pollution-Nitrogen Oxides, Air Pollution-Sulphur, Antarctic Treaty, Biodiversity, Climate Change, Endangered Species, Environmental Modification, Hazardous Wastes, Marine Dumping, Nuclear Test Ban, Ozone Layer Protection, Ship Pollution, Wetlands; signed, but not ratified—Air Pollution-Volatile Organic Compounds, Antarctic-Environmental Protocol, Law of the Sea
Note: landlocked; strategic location astride main land routes between Western Europe and Balkan Peninsula as well as between Ukraine and Mediterranean basin

People

Population: 10,319,113 (July 1994 est.)
Population growth rate: -0.03% (1994 est.)
Birth rate: 12.46 births/1,000 population (1994 est.)
Death rate: 12.72 deaths/1,000 population (1994 est.)
Net migration rate: 0 migrant(s)/1,000 population (1994 est.)
Infant mortality rate: 12.5 deaths/1,000 live births (1994 est.)
Life expectancy at birth:
total population: 71.37 years
male: 67.37 years
female: 75.58 years (1994 est.)
Total fertility rate: 1.83 children born/woman (1994 est.)
Nationality:
noun: Hungarian(s)
adjective: Hungarian
Ethnic divisions: Hungarian 89.9%, Gypsy 4%, German 2.6%, Serb 2%, Slovak 0.8%, Romanian 0.7%
Religions: Roman Catholic 67.5%, Calvinist 20%, Lutheran 5%, atheist and other 7.5%
Languages: Hungarian 98.2%, other 1.8%
Literacy: age 15 and over can read and write (1980)
total population: 99%
male: 99%
female: 98%
Labor force: 5.4 million
by occupation: services, trade, government, and other 44.8%, industry 29.7%, agriculture 16.1%, construction 7.0% (1991)

Government

Names:
conventional long form: Republic of Hungary
conventional short form: Hungary
local long form: Magyar Koztarsasag
local short form: Magyarorszag
Digraph: HU
Type: republic
Capital: Budapest
Administrative divisions: 38 counties (megyek, singular—megye) and 1 capital city* (fovaros); Bacs-Kiskun, Baranya, Bekes, Bekescsaba, Borsod-Abauj-Zemplen, Budapest*, Csongrad, Debrecen, Dunaujvaros, Eger, Fejer, Gyor, Gyor-Moson-Sopron, Hajdu-Bihar, Heves, Hodmezovasarhely, Jasz-Nagykun-Szolnok, Kaposvar, Kecskemet, Komarom-Esztergom, Miskolc, Nagykanizsa, Nograd, Nyiregyhaza, Pecs, Pest, Somogy, Sopron, Szabolcs-Szatmar-Bereg, Szeged, Szekesfehervar, Szolnok, Szombathely, Tatabanya, Tolna, Vas, Veszprem, Zala, Zalaegerszeg
Independence: 1001 (unification by King Stephen I)
National holiday: St. Stephen's Day (National Day), 20 August (commemorates the founding of Hungarian state circa 1000 A.D.)
Constitution: 18 August 1949, effective 20

August 1949, revised 19 April 1972; 18 October 1989 revision ensured legal rights for individuals and constitutional checks on the authority of the prime minister and also established the principle of parliamentary oversight
Legal system: in process of revision, moving toward rule of law based on Western model
Suffrage: 18 years of age; universal
Executive branch:
chief of state: President Arpad GONCZ (since 3 August 1990; previously interim president from 2 May 1990); election last held 3 August 1990 (next to be held NA 1995); results—President GONCZ elected by parliamentary vote; note—President GONCZ was elected by the National Assembly with a total of 295 votes out of 304 as interim President from 2 May 1990 until elected President
head of government: Prime Minister Peter BOROSS (since 12 December 1993 on the death of Jozsef ANTALL); new prime minister will probably be Gyula HORN
cabinet: Council of Ministers; elected by the National Assembly on recommendation of the president
Legislative branch: unicameral
National Assembly (Orszaggyules): elections last held on 8 and 29 May 1994 (next to be held spring 1998); results—percent of vote by party NA; seats—(386 total) Hungarian Socialist Party 209, Alliance of Free Democrats 70, Hungarian Democratic Forum 37, Independent Smallholders 26, Christian Democratic People's Party 22, Federation of Young Democrats 20, other 2
Judicial branch: Constitutional Court
Political parties and leaders: Democratic Forum, Sandor LESZAK, chairman; Independent Smallholders (FKGP), Jozsef TORGYAN, president; Hungarian Socialist Party (MSZP), Gyula HORN, president; Christian Democratic People's Party (KDNP), Dr. Lazlo SURJAN, president; Federation of Young Democrats (FIDESZ), Viktor ORBAN, chairman; Alliance of Free Democrats (SZDSZ), Ivan PETO, chairman
note: the Hungarian Socialist (Communist) Workers' Party (MSZMP) renounced Communism and became the Hungarian Socialist Party (MSZP) in October 1989; there is still a small MSZMP
Member of: Australian Group, BIS, CCC, CE, CEI, CERN, COCOM (cooperating), CSCE, EBRD, ECE, FAO, G-9, GATT, IAEA, IBRD, ICAO, IDA, IFC, ILO, IMF, IMO, INTELSAT, INTERPOL, IOC, IOM, ISO, ITU, LORCS, MTCR, NACC, NAM (guest), NSG, OAS (observer), PCA, UN, UNAVEM II, UNCTAD, UNESCO, UNHCR, UNIDO, UNIKOM, UNOMOZ, UNOMUR, UNOSOM, UNTAC, UPU, WFTU, WHO, WIPO, WMO, WTO, ZC
Diplomatic representation in US:
chief of mission: Ambassador Pal TAR
chancery: 3910 Shoemaker Street NW, Washington, DC 20008
telephone: (202) 362-6730
FAX: (202) 966-8135
consulate(s) general: Los Angeles and New York
US diplomatic representation:
chief of mission: Ambassador Donald BLINKEN
embassy: V. Szabadsag Ter 12, Budapest
mailing address: Am Embassy, Unit 1320, Budapest; APO AE 09213
telephone: [36] (1) 112-6450
FAX: [36] (1) 132-8934
Flag: three equal horizontal bands of red (top), white, and green

---

U.S. Government Contacts:

U.S. Trade Desk: (202) 482-4915

American Embassy Commercial Section
Baiza Utca 31
H-1062 Budapest, Hungary
APO AE 09213 (BUD)
Tel: 36-1-122-8600
Fax: 36-1-142-2529

Chambers of Commerce

American Chamber of Commerce in Hungary
Dozsa Gyorgy ut. 84/A, Room 222
1068 Budapest, Hungary
Tel: (36 1) 142-7518
Fax: (36 1) 269-6016

KAZAKHSTAN

Economy

Overview: Kazakhstan, the second largest of the former Soviet states in territory, possesses vast oil, coal, rare metals, and agricultural resources. While the economy is gradually making the transition from a Soviet command system to a market system, strong elements of state control persist including government ownership of most economic assets and a continued system of mandatory state procurement for the key products such as grain and energy; likewise, agriculture remains largely collectivized. On the other hand, new businesses are forming rapidly, the economy is opening to foreign investment, and 12% of state-owned commercial enterprises have been privatized. In 1993, a three-year industrial privatization program was launched; an independent currency was successfully introduced; and two large joint ventures were established with western oil companies. These far-reaching structural transformations have resulted in a cumulative decline in national income of more than 30% since 1990. Loose monetary policies have kept the inflation rate high, averaging 28% per month for 1993 and accelerating at the end with the disruption caused by a new currency. Since the introduction of its independent currency in November 1993, the government has renewed its commitment to fiscal discipline and accelerating economic reform. However, growing economic hardship and rising ethnic tensions between Kazakhs and Russians over the division of economic assets will likely lead to strong pressure to backtrack.

National product: GDP—purchasing power equivalent—$60.3 billion (1993 estimate from the UN International Comparison Program, as extended to 1991 and published in the World Bank's World Development Report 1993; and as extrapolated to 1993 using official Kazakhstani statistics, which are very uncertain because of major economic changes since 1990)

National product real growth rate: -13% (1993 est.)

National product per capita: $3,510 (1993 est.)

Inflation rate (consumer prices): 28% per month (1993)

Unemployment rate: 0.6% includes only officially registered unemployed; also large numbers of underemployed workers

Budget:
revenues: $NA
expenditures: $NA, including capital expenditures of $1.76 billion (1991 est.)

Exports: $1.3 billion to outside the FSU countries (1993)
commodities: oil, ferrous and nonferrous metals, chemicals, grain, wool, meat (1992)
partners: Russia, Ukraine, Uzbekistan

Imports: $358.3 million from outside the FSU countries (1993)
commodities: machinery and parts, industrial materials, oil and gas (1992)
partners: Russia and other former Soviet republics, China

External debt: $1.5 billion debt to Russia

Industrial production: growth rate -16% (1993)

Electricity:
capacity: 19,135,000 kW
production: 81.3 billion kWh
consumption per capita: 4,739 kWh (1992)
Industries: extractive industries (oil, coal, iron ore, manganese, chromite, lead, zinc, copper, titanium, bauxite, gold, silver, phosphates, sulfur), iron and steel, nonferrous metal, tractors and other agricultural machinery, electric motors, construction materials
Agriculture: accounts for almost 40% of net material product; employs about 26% of the labor force; grain, mostly spring wheat; meat, cotton, wool
Illicit drugs: illicit cultivation of cannabis and opium poppy; mostly for CIS consumption; limited government eradication program; used as transshipment point for illicit drugs to Western Europe and North America from Central and Southwest Asia
Economic aid:
recipient: approximately $1 billion in foreign credits to become available in 1994
Currency: national currency the tenge introduced on 15 November 1993
Exchange rates: NA
Fiscal year: calendar year

Communications

Railroads: 14,460 km (all 1.520-meter gauge); does not include industrial lines (1990)
Highways:
total: 189,000 km
paved and graveled: 108,100 km
unpaved: earth 80,900 km (1990)
Inland waterways: Syrdariya River, Ertis River
Pipelines: crude oil 2,850 km, refined products 1,500 km, natural gas 3,480 km (1992)
Ports: inland—Atyrau (formerly Gur'yev; on Caspian Sea)
Airports:
total: 365
usable: 152
with permanent-surface runways: 49
with runways over 3,659 m: 8
with runways 2,440-3,659 m: 38
with runways 1,220-2,439 m: 71
Telecommunications: telephone service is poor, with only about 17 telephones for each 100 persons in urban areas and 7.6 telephones per 100 persons in rural areas; of the approximately 2.2 million telephones, Almaty has 184,000; broadcast receivers—TVs 4,750,000, radios 4,088,000, radio receiver systems with multiple speakers for program diffusion 6,082,000; international traffic with other former USSR republics and China carried by landline and microwave, and with other countries by satellite and through 8 international telecommunications circuits at the Moscow international gateway switch; satellite earth stations—INTELSAT and Orbita (TV receive only); new satellite ground station established at Almaty with Turkish financial help (December 1992) with 2500 channel band width

Defense Forces

Branches: Army, National Guard, Security Forces (internal and border troops)
Manpower availability: males age 15-49 4,432,716; fit for military service 3,554,209; reach military age (18) annually 154,989 (1994 est.)
Defense expenditures: 69,326 million rubles, NA% of GDP (forecast for 1993); note—conversion of the military budget into US dollars using the current exchange rate could produce misleading results

Geography

Location: Central Asia, between Russia and Uzbekistan, bordering on the Caspian Sea and the Aral Sea
Map references: Asia, Commonwealth of Independent States—Central Asian States, Standard Time Zones of the World
Area:
total area: 2,717,300 sq km
land area: 2,669,800 sq km
comparative area: slightly less than four times the size of Texas

Land boundaries: total 12,012 km, China 1,533 km, Kyrgyzstan 1,051 km, Russia 6,846 km, Turkmenistan 379 km, Uzbekistan 2,203 km
Coastline: 0 km
note: Kazakhstan borders the Aral Sea (1,015 km) and the Caspian Sea (1,894 km)
Maritime claims: landlocked, but borders with Russia, Azerbaijan, and Turkmenistan in the Caspian Sea are under negotiation at present
International disputes: Russia may dispute current de facto maritime border to midpoint of Caspian Sea from shore
Climate: continental, cold winters and hot summers, arid and semiarid
Terrain: extends from the Volga to the Altai Mountains and from the plains in western Siberia to oasis and desert in Central Asia
Natural resources: major deposits of petroleum, coal, iron ore, manganese, chrome ore, nickel, cobalt, copper, molybdenum, lead, zinc, bauxite, gold, uranium
Land use:
arable land: 15%
permanent crops: NEGL%
meadows and pastures: 57%
forest and woodland: 4%
other: 24%
Irrigated land: 23,080 sq km (1990)
Environment:
current issues: radioactive or toxic chemical sites associated with its former defense industries and test ranges are found throughout the country and pose health risks for humans and animals; industrial pollution is severe in some cities; because the two main rivers which flowed into the Aral Sea have been diverted for irrigation, it is drying up and leaving behind a harmful layer of chemical pesticides and natural salts; these substances are then picked up by the wind and blown into noxious dust storms; pollution in the Caspian Sea; soil pollution from overuse of agricultural chemicals and salinization from faulty irrigation practices
natural hazards: NA
international agreements: signed, but not ratified—Biodiversity, Climate Change
Note: landlocked

People

Population: 17,267,554 (July 1994 est.)
Population growth rate: 0.64% (1994 est.)
Birth rate: 19.4 births/1,000 population (1994 est.)
Death rate: 7.93 deaths/1,000 population (1994 est.)
Net migration rate: -5.09 migrant(s)/1,000 population (1994 est.)
Infant mortality rate: 40.9 deaths/1,000 live births (1994 est.)
Life expectancy at birth:
total population: 68.04 years
male: 63.39 years
female: 72.93 years (1994 est.)
Total fertility rate: 2.44 children born/woman (1994 est.)
Nationality:
noun: Kazakhstani(s)
adjective: Kazakhstani
Ethnic divisions: Kazakh (Qazaq) 41.9%, Russian 37%, Ukrainian 5.2%, German 4.7%, Uzbek 2.1%, Tatar 2%, other 7.1% (1991 official data)
Religions: Muslim 47%, Russian Orthodox 44%, Protestant 2%, other 7%
Languages: Kazakh (Qazaqz) official language spoken by over 40% of population, Russian (language of interethnic communication) spoken by two-thirds of population and used in everyday business
Literacy: age 9-49 can read and write (1970)
total population: 100%
male: 100%
female: 100%
Labor force: 7.356 million
by occupation: industry and construction 31%, agriculture and forestry 26%, other 43% (1992)

Government

Names:
conventional long form: Republic of Kazakhstan
conventional short form: Kazakhstan
local long form: Kazakhstan Respublikasy
local short form: none
former: Kazakh Soviet Socialist Republic

Digraph: KZ
Type: republic
Capital: Almaty
Administrative divisions: 19 oblystar (singular—oblys) and 1 city (qalalar, singular—qala)*; Almaty*, Almaty Oblysy, Aqmola Oblysy, Aqtobe Oblysy, Atyrau Oblysy, Batys Qazaqstan Oblysy (Oral), Kokshetau Oblysy, Mangghystau Oblysy, Ongtustik Qazaqstan Oblysy (Shymkent), Qaraghandy Oblysy, Qostanay Oblysy, Qyzylorda Oblysy, Pavlodar Oblysy, Semey Oblysy, Shyghys Qazaqstan Oblysy (Oskemen; formerly Ust'-Kamenogorsk), Soltustik Qazaqstan Oblysy (Petropavl), Taldyqorghan Oblysy, Torghay Oblysy, Zhambyl Oblysy, Zhezqazghan Oblysy
note: names in parentheses are administrative centers when name differs from oblys name
Independence: 16 December 1991 (from the Soviet Union)
National holiday: Independence Day, 16 December (1991)
Constitution: adopted 28 January 1993
Legal system: based on civil law system
Suffrage: 18 years of age; universal
Executive branch:
chief of state: President Nursultan A. NAZARBAYEV (since NA April 1990); Vice President Yerik ASANBAYEV (since 1 December 1991); election last held 1 December 1991 (next to be held NA 1995); percent of vote by party NA; Nursultan A. NAZARBAYEV ran unopposed
head of government: Prime Minister Sergey TERESHCHENKO (since 14 October 1991); First Deputy Prime Minister Arkezhan KAZHEGELDIN (since NA November 1993)
cabinet: Council of Ministers; appointed by the prime minister
Legislative branch: unicameral
Supreme Council: elections last held 7 March 1994 (next to be held NA 1999); results—percent of vote by party NA; seats—(177 total) Union Peoples' Unity of Kazakhstan 33, Federation of Trade Unions of the Republic of Kazakhstan 11, People's Congress of Kazakhstan Party 9, Socialist Party of Kazakhstan 8, Peasant Union of the Republic Kazakhstan 4, Social Movement "LAD" 4, Organization of Veterans 1, Union of Youth of Kazakhstan 1, Democratic Committee for Human Rights 1, Association of Lawyers of Kazakhstan 1, International Public Committee "Aral-Asia-Kazakhstan" 1, Congress of Entrepreneurs of Kazakhstan 1, Deputies of the 12th Supreme Soviet 40, independents 62
Judicial branch: Supreme Court
Political parties and leaders: Peoples Unity Movement (PUU), Kuanysh SULTANOV, chairman; Peoples Congress, Olzhas SULEYMENOV, chairman; Kazakhstan Socialist Party (SPK; former Communist Party), Piotr SVOIK, co-chairman; Republican Party (Azat), Kamal ORMANTAYEV, chairman; Democratic Progress (Russian) Party, Alexandra DOKUCHAYEVA, chairman; Union Peoples' Unity of Kazakhstan (SNEK); Federation of Trade Unions of the Republic of Kazakhstan; Peasant Union of the Republic Kazakhstan; Social Movement LAD (Slavic Rebirth Society), V. MIKHAYLOV, chairman; Union of Youth of Kazakhstan; Democratic Committee for Human Rights; Association of Lawyers of Kazakhstan; International Public Committee "Aral-Asia-Kazakhstan"; Congress of Entrepreneurs of Kazakhstan; Deputies of the 12th Supreme Soviet
Other political or pressure groups: Independent Trade Union Center (Birlesu; an association of independent trade union and business associations), Leonid SOLOMIN, president
Member of: CCC, CIS, CSCE, EBRD, ECO, ESCAP, IBRD, ICAO, IDA, IFC, ILO, IMF, INTELSAT (nonsignatory user), INTERPOL, IOD, NACC, OIC (observer), UN, UNCTAD, UNESCO, UPU, WHO, WMO
Diplomatic representation in US:
chief of mission: Ambassador Tuleutai SULEYMENOV
chancery: 3421 Massachusetts Avenue, NW, Washington, DC 20007
telephone: (202) 333-4504/7
FAX: (202) 333-4509
US diplomatic representation:
chief of mission: Ambassador William H. COURTNEY

embassy: 99/97 Furmanova Street, Almaty, Republic of Kazakhstan 480012
mailing address: American Embassy Almaty, c/o Department of State, Washington, DC, 20521-7030
telephone: (7) (3272) 63-17-70, 63-24-26, 63-28-80, 63-34-05
FAX: (7) (3272) 63-38-83
Flag: sky blue background representing the endless sky and a gold sun with 32 rays soaring above a golden steppe eagle in the center; on the hoist side is a "national ornamentation" in yellow

KAZAKHSTAN

U.S. Government Contacts:

U.S. Trade Desk: (202) 482-0360

KYRGYZSTAN

Economy

Overview: Kyrgyzstan is one of the smallest and poorest states of the former Soviet Union. Its economy is heavily agricultural, producing cotton and tobacco on irrigated land in the south, grain in the foothills of the north, and sheep and goats on mountain pastures. Its small and obsolescent industrial sector, concentrated around Bishkek, is heavily dependent on Russia and other CIS countries for customers and for inputs, including most of its fuel. Since 1990, the economy has contracted by almost 40%. Kyrgyzstan's inflation was high in 1993, about 23% per month, but rates were declining at the end of the year. Kyrgyzstan introduced its national currency, the som, in May 1993, it has privatized 28% of its former state assets, and plans call for a massive voucher privatization in 1994. Although Kyrgyzstan will receive relatively large flows of foreign aid, ongoing economic restructuring will continue to be painful with an anticipated increase in unemployment as uneconomic enterprises close. President AKAYEV will be under strong political pressure to backtrack on some reform measures.

National product: GDP—purchasing power equivalent—$11.3 billion (1993 estimate from the UN International Comparison Program, as extended to 1991 and published in the World Bank's World Development Report 1993; and as extrapolated to 1993 using official Kirghiz statistics, which are very uncertain because of major economic changes since 1990)
National product real growth rate: -13.4% (1993 est.)
National product per capita: $2,440 (1993 est.)
Inflation rate (consumer prices): 23% per month (1993 est.)
Unemployment rate: 0.2% includes officially registered unemployed; also large numbers of unregistered unemployed and underemployed workers
Budget:
revenues: $NA
expenditures: $NA, including capital expenditures of $NA
Exports: $100.4 million to countries outside the FSU (1993 est.)
commodities: wool, chemicals, cotton, ferrous and nonferrous metals, shoes, machinery, tobacco
partners: Russia 70%, Ukraine, Uzbekistan, Kazakhstan, and others
Imports: $105.8 million from countries outside the FSU (1993 est.)
commodities: grain, lumber, industrial products, ferrous metals, fuel, machinery, textiles, footwear
partners: other CIS republics
External debt: $NA
Industrial production: growth rate -27% (1993 est.)
Electricity:
capacity: 4,100,000 kW
production: 11.8 billion kWh
consumption per capita: 2,551 kWh (1992)
Industries: small machinery, textiles, food-processing industries, cement, shoes, sawn logs, refrigerators, furniture, electric motors, gold, and rare earth metals

Agriculture: wool, tobacco, cotton, livestock (sheep, goats, cattle), vegetables, meat, grapes, fruits and berries, eggs, milk, potatoes
Illicit drugs: illicit cultivator of cannabis and opium poppy; mostly for CIS consumption; limited government eradication program; used as transshipment point for illicit drugs to Western Europe and North America from Central and Southwest Asia
Economic aid:
recipient: $80 million in 1993 and an anticipated $400 million in 1994
Currency: introduced national currency, the som (10 May 1993)
Exchange rates: NA
Fiscal year: calendar year

Communications

Railroads: 370 km; does not include industrial lines (1990)
Highways:
total: 30,300 km
paved and graveled: 22,600 km
unpaved: earth 7,700 km (1990)
Pipelines: natural gas 200 km
Ports: none; landlocked
Airports:
total: 52
usable: 27
with permanent-surface runways: 12
with runways over 3,659 m: 1
with runways 2,440-3,659 m: 4
with runways 1,060-2,439 m: 13
note: a C-130 can land on a 1,060-m airstrip
Telecommunications: poorly developed; 342,000 telephones in 1991 (also about 100,000 unsatisfied applications for household telephones); 76 telephones per 1,000 persons (31 December 1991); microwave radio relay is principal means of intercity telephone links; connections with other CIS countries by landline or microwave and with other countries by leased connections with Moscow international gateway switch and by satellite; 2 satellite earth stations—1 GORIZONT and 1 INTELSAT (links through Ankara to 200 other countries and receives Turkish broadcasts); broadcast receivers—radios 825,000, TVs 875,000, radio receiver systems with multiple speakers for program diffusion 748,000

Defense Forces

Branches: National Guard, Security Forces (internal and border troops), Civil Defense
Manpower availability: males age 15-49 1,123,959; fit for military service 912,516; reach military age (18) annually 44,528 (1994 est.)
Defense expenditures: $NA, NA% of GDP

Geography

Location: Central Asia, between China and Kazakhstan
Map references: Asia, Commonwealth of Independent States—Central Asian States, Standard Time Zones of the World
Area:
total area: 198,500 sq km
land area: 191,300 sq km
comparative area: slightly smaller than South Dakota
Land boundaries: total 3,878 km, China 858 km, Kazakhstan 1,051 km, Tajikistan 870 km, Uzbekistan 1,099 km
Coastline: 0 km (landlocked)
Maritime claims: none; landlocked
International disputes: territorial dispute with Tajikistan on southwestern boundary in Isfara Valley area
Climate: dry continental to polar in high Tien Shan; subtropical in southwest (Fergana Valley); temperate in northern foothill zone
Terrain: peaks of Tien Shan rise to 7,000 meters, and associated valleys and basins encompass entire nation
Natural resources: small amounts of coal abundant hydroelectric potential; significant deposits of gold and rare earth metals; locally exploitable coal, oil and natural gas; other deposits of nepheline, mercury, bismuth, lead, and zinc, natural gas, oil, nepheline, rare earth metals, mercury, bismuth, gold, lead, zinc, hydroelectric power
Land use:
arable land: 7%

permanent crops: NEGL%
meadows and pastures: 42%
forest and woodland: 0%
other: 51%
Irrigated land: 10,320 sq km (1990)
Environment:
current issues: water pollution; many people get their water directly from contaminated streams and wells and as a result, water-borne diseases are prevalent; increasing soil salinity from faulty irrigation practices
natural hazards: NA
international agreements: NA
Note: landlocked

People

Population: 4,698,108 (July 1994 est.)
Population growth rate: 1.53% (1994 est.)
Birth rate: 26.33 births/1,000 population (1994 est.)
Death rate: 7.36 deaths/1,000 population (1994 est.)
Net migration rate: -3.64 migrant(s)/1,000 population (1994 est.)
Infant mortality rate: 46.8 deaths/1,000 live births (1994 est.)
Life expectancy at birth:
total population: 67.92 years
male: 63.69 years
female: 72.35 years (1994 est.)
Total fertility rate: 3.35 children born/woman (1994 est.)
Nationality:
noun: Kyrgyz(s)
adjective: Kyrgyz
Ethnic divisions: Kirghiz 52.4%, Russian 21.5%, Uzbek 12.9%, Ukrainian 2.5%, German 2.4%, other 8.3%
Religions: Muslim 70%, Russian Orthodox NA%
Languages: Kirghiz (Kyrgyz)—official language, Russian widely used
Literacy: age 9-49 can read and write (1970)
total population: 100%
male: 100%
female: 100%
Labor force: 1.836 million
by occupation: agriculture and forestry 38%, industry and construction 21%, other 41% (1990)

Government

Names:
conventional long form: Kyrgyz Republic
conventional short form: Kyrgyzstan
local long form: Kyrgyz Respublikasy
local short form: none
former: Kirghiz Soviet Socialist Republic
Digraph: KG
Type: republic
Capital: Bishkek
Administrative divisions: 6 oblasttar (singular—oblast); Chuy Oblasty, Jalal-Abad Oblasty, Naryn Oblasty, Osh Oblasty, Talas Oblasty, Ysyk-Kol Oblasty
note: the administrative center for Chuy Oblasty is Bishkek; the administrative center for Ysyk-Kol Oblasty may be Ksyk-Kol or Karakol; all other oblasttar have administrative centers of the same name as the oblast
Independence: 31 August 1991 (from Soviet Union)
National holiday: National Day, 2 December; Independence Day, 31 August (1991)
Constitution: adopted 5 May 1993
Legal system: based on civil law system
Suffrage: 18 years of age; universal
Executive branch:
chief of state: President Askar AKAYEV (since 28 October 1990); election last held 12 October 1991 (next to be held NA 1996); results—Askar AKAYEV won in uncontested election with 95% of vote and with 90% of electorate voting; note—president elected by Supreme Soviet 28 October 1990, then by popular vote 12 October 1991; note—AKAYEV won 96% of the vote in a referendum on his status as president on 30 January 1993
head of government: Prime Minister Apas DZHUMAGULOV (since NA December 1993); First Deputy Prime Minister Almambet MATURBRAIMOV (since NA)
cabinet: Cabinet of Ministers; subordinate to the president
Legislative branch: unicameral
Zhogorku Keneshom: elections last held 25 February 1990 for the Supreme Soviet (next to

be held no later than NA November 1994 for the Zhogorku Keneshom); results—Communists 90%; seats—(350 total) Communists 310
Judicial branch: Supreme Court
Political parties and leaders: Social Democrats, Ishenbai KADYRBEKOV, chairman; Kyrgyzstan Democratic Movement (KDM), Kazat AKHMATOV, chairman; National Unity, German KUZNETSOV; Communist Party, Dzhumalbek AMANBAYEV, chairman; Erkin (Free) Kyrgyzstan Party, Topchubek TURGUNALIYEV, chairman
Other political or pressure groups: National Unity Democratic Movement; Peasant Party; Council of Free Trade Unions; Union of Entrepreneurs; Agrarian Party
Member of: CIS, CSCE, EBRD, ECE, ECO, ESCAP, IBRD, ICAO, IDA, IDB, IFAD, IFC, ILO, IMF, IOC, NACC, OIC, PCA, UN, UNCTAD, UNESCO, UNIDO, UPU, WHO
Diplomatic representation in US:
chief of mission: (vacant)
chancery: (temporary) Suite 705, 1511 K Street NW, Washington, DC 20005
telephone: (202) 347-3732/3
FAX: (202) 347-3718
US diplomatic representation:
chief of mission: Ambassador Edward HURWITZ
embassy: Erkindik Prospekt #66, Bishkek 720002
mailing address: use embassy street address
telephone: 7-3312 22-29-20, 22-26-93, 22-29-89
FAX: 7-3312 22-35-51
Flag: red field with a yellow sun in the center having 40 rays representing the 40 Krygyz tribes; on the obverse side the rays run counterclockwise, on the reverse, clockwise; in the center of the sun is a red ring crossed by

---

U.S. Government Contacts:

U.S. Trade Desk: (202) 482-0360

LATVIA

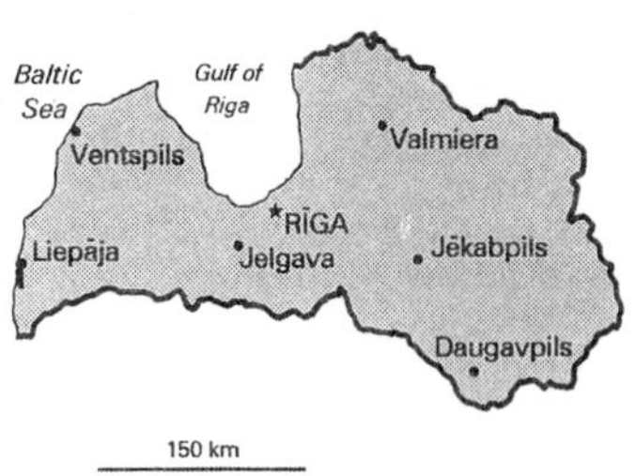

Economy

Overview: Latvia is rapidly becoming a dynamic market economy, rivaled only by Estonia among the former Soviet states in the speed of its transformation. The transition has been painful with GDP falling over 45% in 1992-93, according to official statistics, and industrial production experiencing even steeper declines. Nevertheless, the government's tough monetary policies and reform program, which foster the development of the private sector and market mechanisms, have kept inflation low, created a dynamic private sector—much of which is not captured in official statistics—and expanded trade ties with the West. Much of agriculture is already privatized and the government plans to step up the pace of privatization of state enterprises. The economy is now poised for recovery and will benefit from the country's strategic location on the Baltic Sea, its well-educated population, and its diverse—albeit largely obsolete—industrial structure.
National product: GDP—purchasing power equivalent—$13.2 billion (1993 estimate from the UN International Comparison Program, as extended to 1991 and published in the World Bank's World Development Report 1993; and as extrapolated to 1993 using official Latvian statistics, which are very uncertain because of major economic changes since 1990)
National product real growth rate: -5% (1993 est.)
National product per capita: $4,810 (1993 est.)
Inflation rate (consumer prices): 2% per month (1993 average)
Unemployment rate: 5.6% (December 1993)
Budget:
revenues: $NA
expenditures: $NA, including capital expenditures of $NA
Exports: $429 million from non-FSU countries (f.o.b., 1992)
commodities: oil products, timber, ferrous metals, dairy products, furniture, textiles
partners: Russia, other CIS countries, Western Europe
Imports: $NA
commodities: fuels, cars, ferrous metals, chemicals
partners: Russia, other CIS countries, Western Europe
External debt: $NA
Industrial production: growth rate -38% (1992 est.)
Electricity:
capacity: 2,140,000 kW
production: 5.8 billion kWh
consumption per capita: 2,125 kWh (1992)
Industries: employs 41% of labor force; highly diversified; dependent on imports for energy, raw materials, and intermediate products; produces buses, vans, street and railroad cars, synthetic fibers, agricultural machinery, fertilizers, washing machines, radios, electronics, pharmaceuticals, processed foods, textiles
Agriculture: employs 16% of labor force; principally dairy farming and livestock feeding; products—meat, milk, eggs, grain,

sugar beets, potatoes, vegetables; fishing and fish packing
Illicit drugs: transshipment point for illicit drugs from Central and Southwest Asia and Latin America to Western Europe; limited producer of illicit opium; mostly for domestic consumption; also produces illicit amphetamines for export
Economic aid: $NA
Currency: 1 lat = 100 cents; introduced NA March 1993
Exchange rates: lats per US$1—0.5917 (January 1994), 1.32 (March 1993)
Fiscal year: calendar year

Communications

Railroads: 2,400 km (1,524-mm gauge); 270 km electrified
Highways:
total: 59,500 km
paved and graveled: 33,000 km
unpaved: earth 26,500 km (1990)
Inland waterways: 300 km perennially navigable
Pipelines: crude oil 750 km, refined products 780 km, natural gas 560 km (1992)
Ports: coastal—Riga, Ventspils, Liepaja; inland—Daugavpils
Merchant marine: 93 ships (1,000 GRT or over) totaling 850,840 GRT/1,107,403 DWT, cargo 15, refrigerated cargo 27, container 2, roll-on/roll-off cargo 8, oil tanker 41
Airports:
total: 50
usable: 15
with permanent-surface runways: 11
with runways over 3,659 m: 0
with runways 2,440-3,659 m: 7
with runways 1,060-2,439 m: 7
note: a C-130 can land on a 1,060-m airstrip
Telecommunications: Latvia is better provided with telephone service than most of the other former Soviet republics; subscriber circuits 660,000; subscriber density 240 per 1,000 persons (1993); an NMT-450 analog cellular telephone network covers 75% of Latvia's population; international traffic carried by leased connection to the Moscow international gateway switch and through the new Ericsson AXE local/transit digital telephone exchange in Riga and through the Finnish cellular net; electronic mail capability by Sprint data network; broadcasting services NA

Defense Forces

Branches: Ground Forces, Navy, Air Force, Security Forces (internal and border troops), Border Guard, Home Guard (Zemessardze)
Manpower availability: males age 15-49 652,444; fit for military service 514,055; reach military age (18) annually 18,803 (1994 est.)
Defense expenditures: 176 million rubles, 3%-5% of GDP; note—conversion of the military budget into US dollars using the prevailing exchange rate could produce misleading results

---

Geography

Location: Eastern Europe, bordering on the Baltic Sea, between Sweden and Russia
Map references: Arctic Region, Asia, Europe, Standard Time Zones of the World
Area:
total area: 64,100 sq km
land area: 64,100 sq km
comparative area: slightly larger than West Virginia
Land boundaries: total 1,078 km, Belarus 141 km, Estonia 267 km, Lithuania 453 km, Russia 217 km
Coastline: 531 km
Maritime claims:
exclusive economic zone: 200 nm
territorial sea: 12 nm
International disputes: the Abrene section of border ceded by the Latvian Soviet Socialist Republic to Russia in 1944
Climate: maritime; wet, moderate winters
Terrain: low plain
Natural resources: minimal; amber, peat, limestone, dolomite
Land use:
arable land: 27%
permanent crops: 0%

meadows and pastures: 13%
forest and woodland: 39%
other: 21%
Irrigated land: 160 sq km (1990)
Environment:
current issues: air and water pollution because of a lack of waste conversion equipment; Gulf of Riga and Daugava River heavily polluted; contamination of soil and groundwater with chemicals and petroleum products at military bases
natural hazards: NA
international agreements: party to—Hazardous Wastes, Ship Pollution; signed, but not ratified—Biodiversity, Climate Change

---

People

Population: 2,749,211 (July 1994 est.)
Population growth rate: 0.5% (1994 est.)
Birth rate: 13.84 births/1,000 population (1994 est.)
Death rate: 12.61 deaths/1,000 population (1994 est.)
Net migration rate: 3.74 migrant(s)/1,000 population (1994 est.)
Infant mortality rate: 21.5 deaths/1,000 live births (1994 est.)
Life expectancy at birth:
total population: 69.44 years
male: 64.37 years
female: 74.75 years (1994 est.)
Total fertility rate: 1.98 children born/woman (1994 est.)
Nationality:
noun: Latvian(s)
adjective: Latvian
Ethnic divisions: Latvian 51.8%, Russian 33.8%, Byelorussian 4.5%, Ukrainian 3.4%, Polish 2.3%, other 4.2%
Religions: Lutheran, Roman Catholic, Russian Orthodox
Languages: Lettish (official), Lithuanian, Russian, other
Literacy: age 9-49 can read and write (1970)
total population: 100%
male: 100%
female: 100%
Labor force: 1.407 million
by occupation: industry and construction 41%, agriculture and forestry 16%, other 43% (1990)

Government

Names:
conventional long form: Republic of Latvia
conventional short form: Latvia
local long form: Latvijas Republika
local short form: Latvija
former: Latvian Soviet Socialist Republic
Digraph: LG
Type: republic
Capital: Riga
Administrative divisions: 26 counties (singular—rajons) and 7 municipalities*: Aizkraukles Rajons, Aluksnes Rajons, Balvu Rajons, Bauskas Rajons, Cesu Rajons, Daugavpils*, Daugavpils Rajons, Dobeles Rajons, Gulbenes Rajons, Jekabpils Rajons, Jelgava*, Jelgavas Rajons, Jurmala*, Kraslavas Rajons, Kuldigas Rajons, Leipaja*, Liepajas Rajons, Limbazu Rajons, Ludzas Rajons, Madonas Rajons, Ogres Rajons, Preiju Rajons, Rezekne*, Rezeknes Rajons, Riga*, Rigas Rajons, Saldus Rajons, Talsu Rajons, Tukuma Rajons, Valkas Rajons, Valmieras Rajons, Ventspils*, Ventspils Rajons
Independence: 6 September 1991 (from Soviet Union)
National holiday: Independence Day, 18 November (1918)
Constitution: newly elected Parliament in 1993 restored the 1933 constitution
Legal system: based on civil law system
Suffrage: 18 years of age; universal
Executive branch:
chief of state: President Guntis ULMANIS (since 7 July 1993); Saeima elected President ULMANIS in the third round of balloting on 7 July 1993
head of government: Prime Minister Valdis BIRKAVS (since 20 July 1993)
cabinet: Council of Ministers; appointed by the Supreme Council
Legislative branch: unicameral
Parliament (Saeima): elections last held 5-6 June 1993 (next to be held NA June 1996); results—percent of vote by party NA; seats—

(100 total) LC 36, LNNK 15, Concord for Latvia 13, LZS 12, Equal Rights 7, LKDS 6, TUB 6, DCP 5
Judicial branch: Supreme Court
Political parties and leaders: Latvian Way Union (LC), Valdis BIRKAVS; Latvian Farmers Union (LZS), Alvars BERKIS; Latvian National Independence Movement (LNNK), Andrejs KRASTINS, Aristids LAMBERGS, cochairmen; Concord for Latvia, Janis JURKANS; Equal Rights, Sergejs DIMANIS; Christian Democrat Union (LKDS), Peteris CIMDINS, Andris SAULITIS, Janis RUSKO; Fatherland and Freedom (TUB), Maris GRINBLATS, Roberts MILBERGS, Oigerts DZENTIS; Democratic Center (DCP), Ints CALITIS; Popular Front of Latvia (LTF), Uldis AUGSTKALNS
Member of: BIS, CBSS, CCC, CE (guest), CSCE, EBRD, ECE, FAO, IBRD, ICAO, IDA, IFC, ILO, IMF, IMO, INTELSAT (nonsignatory user), INTERPOL, IOC, IOM (observer), ITU, LORCS, NACC, UN, UNCTAD, UNESCO, UNIDO, UPU, WHO, WIPO, WMO
Diplomatic representation in US:
chief of mission: Ambassador Ojars Eriks KALNINS
chancery: 4325 17th Street NW, Washington, DC 20011
telephone: (202) 726-8213 and 8214
US diplomatic representation:
chief of mission: Ambassador Ints M. SILINS
embassy: Raina Boulevard 7, Riga 226050
mailing address: use embassy street address
telephone: 46-9-882-0046
FAX: 46-9-882-0047
Flag: two horizontal bands of maroon (top and bottom), white (middle, narrower than other two bands)

Chambers of Commerce & Organizations:

American Chamber of Commerce in Latvia
Jauniela 24, Room 205
Riga, Republic of Latvia
Tel: 371-2-215-205
Fax: 371-882-0090

LITHUANIA

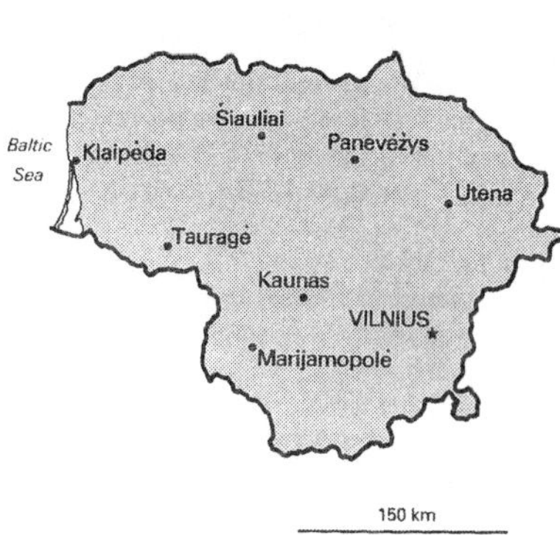

Economy

Overview: Since independence in September 1991, Lithuania has made steady progress in developing a market economy. Over 40% of state property has been privatized and trade is diversifying with a gradual shift away from the former Soviet Union to Western markets. Nevertheless, the process has been painful with industrial output in 1993 less than half the 1991 level. Inflation, while lower than in most ex-Soviet states, has exceeded rates in the other Baltic states. Full monetary stability and economic recovery are likely to be impeded by periodic government backtracking on key elements of its reform and stabilization program as it seeks to ease the economic pain of restructuring. Recovery will build on Lithuanian's strategic location with its ice-free port at Klaipeda and its rail and highway hub in Vilnius connecting it with Eastern Europe, Belarus, Russia, and Ukraine, and on its agriculture potential, highly skilled labor force, and diversified industrial sector. Lacking important natural resources, it will remain dependent on imports of fuels and raw materials.

National product: GDP—purchasing power equivalent—$12.4 billion (1993 estimate from the UN International Comparison Program, as extended to 1991 and published in the World Bank's World Development Report 1993; and as extrapolated to 1993 using official Lithuanian statistics, which are very uncertain because of major economic changes since 1990)
National product real growth rate: -10% (1993 est.)
National product per capita: $3,240 (1993 est.)
Inflation rate (consumer prices): 188% (1993)
Unemployment rate: 1.8% (July 1993)
Budget:
revenues: $258.5 million
expenditures: $270.2 million, including capital expenditures of $NA (1992 est.)
Exports: $NA
commodities: electronics 18%, petroleum products 5%, food 10%, chemicals 6% (1989)
partners: Russia 40%, Ukraine 16%, other FSU countries 32%, West 12%
Imports: $NA
commodities: oil 24%, machinery 14%, chemicals 8%, grain NA% (1989)
partners: Russia 62%, Belarus 18%, other FSU countries 10%, West 10%
External debt: $NA
Industrial production: growth rate -52% (1992)
Electricity:
capacity: 5,925,000 kW
production: 25 billion kWh
consumption per capita: 6,600 kWh (1992)
Industries: employs 42% of the labor force; accounts for 23% of GOP shares in the total production of the former USSR are: metal-cutting machine tools 6.6%; electric motors 4.6%; television sets 6.2%; refrigerators and freezers 5.4%; other branches: petroleum refining, shipbuilding (small ships), furniture making, textiles, food processing, fertilizers,

agricultural machinery, optical equipment, electronic components, computers, and amber
Agriculture: employs around 18% of labor force; accounts for 25% of GDP; sugar, grain, potatoes, sugar beets, vegetables, meat, milk, dairy products, eggs, fish; most developed are the livestock and dairy branches, which depend on imported grain; net exporter of meat, milk, and eggs
Illicit drugs: transshipment point for illicit drugs from Central and Southwest Asia and Latin America to Western Europe; limited producer of illicit opium; mostly for domestic consumption
Economic aid:
recipient: US commitments, including Ex-Im (1992), $10 million; Western (non-US) countries, ODA and OOF bilateral commitments (1970-86), $NA million; Communist countries (1971-86), $NA million
Currency: introduced the convertible litas in June 1993
Exchange rates: litai per US$1—4 (fixed rate 1 May 1994); 3.9 (late January 1994)
Fiscal year: calendar year

Communications

Railroads: 2,000 km (1,524-mm gauge); 120 km electrified
Highways:
total: 44,200 km
paved: 35,500 km
unpaved: earth 8,700 km (1990)
Inland waterways: 600 km perennially navigable
Pipelines: crude oil 105 km, natural gas 760 km (1992)
Ports: coastal—Klaipeda; inland—Kaunas
Merchant marine: 44 ships (1,000 GRT or over) totaling 276,265 GRT/323,505 DWT, cargo 29, railcar carrier 3, roll-on/roll-off cargo 1, combination bulk 11
Airports:
total: 96
usable: 18
with permanent-surface runways: 12
with runways over 3,659 m: 0
with runways 2,440-3,659 m: 5
with runways 1,060-2,439 m: 11
note: a C-130 can land on a 1,060-m airstrip
Telecommunications: Lithuania ranks among the most modern of the former Soviet republics in respect to its telecommunications system; telephone subscriber circuits 900,000; subscriber density 240 per 1,000 persons; land lines or microwave to former USSR republics; international connections no longer depend on the Moscow gateway switch, but are established by satellite through Oslo from Vilnius and through Copenhagen from Kaunas; 2 satellite earth stations—1 EUTELSAT and 1 INTELSAT; an NMT-450 analog cellular network operates in Vilnius and other cities and is linked internationally through Copenhagen by EUTELSAT; international electronic mail is available;
broadcast stations —13 AM, 26 FM, 1 SW, 1 LW, 3 TV

Defense Forces

Branches: Ground Forces, Navy, Air Force, Security Forces (internal and border troops), National Guard (Skat)
Manpower availability: males age 15-49 941,273; fit for military service 744,867; reach military age (18) annually 27,375 (1994 est.)
Defense expenditures: exchange rate conversion—$NA, 5.5% of GDP (1993 est.)

Geography

Location: Eastern Europe, bordering the Baltic Sea, between Sweden and Russia
Map references: Asia, Europe, Standard Time Zones of the World
Area:
total area: 65,200 sq km
land area: 65,200 sq km
comparative area: slightly larger than West Virginia
Land boundaries: total 1,273 km, Belarus 502 km, Latvia 453 km, Poland 91 km, Russia (Kaliningrad) 227 km
Coastline: 108 km
Maritime claims:
territorial sea: 12 nm

International disputes: dispute with Russia (Kaliningrad Oblast) over the position of the Nemunas (Nemen) River border presently located on the Lithuanian bank and not in midriver as by international standards
Climate: maritime; wet, moderate winters and summers
Terrain: lowland, many scattered small lakes, fertile soil
Natural resources: peat
Land use:
arable land: 49.1%
permanent crops: 0%
meadows and pastures: 22.2%
forest and woodland: 16.3%
other: 12.4%
Irrigated land: 430 sq km (1990)
Environment:
current issues: contamination of soil and groundwater with petroleum products and chemicals at military bases
natural hazards: NA
international agreements: party to—Ship Pollution; signed, but not ratified—Biodiversity, Climate Change

People

Population: 3,848,389 (July 1994 est.)
Population growth rate: 0.74% (1994 est.)
Birth rate: 14.71 births/1,000 population (1994 est.)
Death rate: 10.95 deaths/1,000 population (1994 est.)
Net migration rate: 3.62 migrant(s)/1,000 population (1994 est.)
Infant mortality rate: 16.7 deaths/1,000 live births (1994 est.)
Life expectancy at birth:
total population: 71.24 years
male: 66.53 years
female: 76.19 years (1994 est.)
Total fertility rate: 2.01 children born/woman (1994 est.)
Nationality:
noun: Lithuanian(s)
adjective: Lithuanian
Ethnic divisions: Lithuanian 80.1%, Russian 8.6%, Polish 7.7%, Byelorussian 1.5%, other 2.1%
Religions: Roman Catholic, Lutheran, other
Languages: Lithuanian (official), Polish, Russian
Literacy: age 9-49 can read and write (1989)
total population: 98%
male: 99%
female: 98%
Labor force: 1.836 million
by occupation: industry and construction 42%, agriculture and forestry 18%, other 40% (1990)

Government

Names:
conventional long form: Republic of Lithuania
conventional short form: Lithuania
local long form: Lietuvos Respublika
local short form: Lietuva
former: Lithuanian Soviet Socialist Republic
Digraph: LH
Type: republic
Capital: Vilnius
Administrative divisions: 44 regions (rajonai, singular—rajonas) and 11 municipalities*: Akmenes Rajonas, Alytaus Rajonas, Alytus*, Anyksciu Rajonas, Birsionas*, Birzu Rajonas, Druskininkai*, Ignalinos Rajonas, Jonavos Rajonas, Joniskio Rajonas, Jurbarko Rajonas, Kaisiadoriu Rajonas, Marijampoles Rajonas, Kaunas*, Kauno Rajonas, Kedainiu Rajonas, Kelmes Rajonas, Klaipeda*, Klaipedos Rajonas, Kretingos Ragonas, Kupiskio Rajonas, Lazdiju Rajonas, Marijampole*, Mazeikiu Ragonas, Moletu Rajonas, Neringa* Pakruojo Rajonas, Palanga*, Panevezio Rajonas, Panevezys*, Pasvalio Rajonas, Plunges Rajonas, Prienu Rajonas, Radviliskio Rajonas, Raseiniu Rajonas, Rokiskio Rajonas, Sakiu Rajonas, Salcininky Rajonas, Siauliai*, Siauliu Rajonas, Silales Rajonas, Siltues Rajonas, Sirvinty Rajonas, Skuodo Rajonas, Svencioniu Rajonas, Taurages Rajonas, Telsiu Rajonas, Traky Rajonas, Ukmerges Rajonas, Utenos Rajonas, Varenos Rajonas, Vilkaviskio Rajonas, Vilniaus Rajonas, Vilnius*, Zarasu Rajonas
Independence: 6 September 1991 (from Soviet Union)

National holiday: Independence Day, 16 February (1918)
Constitution: adopted 25 October 1992
Legal system: based on civil law system; no judicial review of legislative acts
Suffrage: 18 years of age; universal
Executive branch:
chief of state: President Algirdas Mykolas BRAZAUSKAS (since 25 November 1992; elected acting president by Parliament 25 November 1992 and elected by direct vote 15 February 1993); election last held 14 February 1993 (next to be held NA 1997); results—Algirdas BRAZAUSKAS was elected; note—on 25 November 1992 BRAZAUSKAS was elected chairman of Parliament and, as such, acting president of the Republic; he was confirmed in office by direct balloting 15 February 1993
head of government: Premier Adolfas SLEZEVICIUS (since 10 March 1993)
cabinet: Council of Ministers; appointed by the president on the nomination of the prime minister
Legislative branch: unicameral
Seimas (parliament): elections last held 26 October and 25 November 1992 (next to be held NA); results—LDDP 51%; seats—(141 total) LDDP 73, Conservative Party 30, LKDP 17, LTS 8, Farmers' Union 4, LLS 4, Center Union 2, others 3
Judicial branch: Supreme Court, Court of Appeals
Political parties and leaders: Christian Democratic Party (LKDP), Povilas KATILIUS, chairman; Democratic Labor Party of Lithuania (LDDP), Adolfas SLEZEVICIUS, chairman; Lithuanian Nationalist Union (LTS), Rimantas SMETONA, chairman; Lithuanian Social Democratic Party (LSDP), Aloyzas SAKALAS, chairman; Farmers' Union, Jonas CIULEVICIUS, chairman; Center Union, Romualdas OZOLAS, chairman; Conservative Party, Vytautas LANDSBERGIS, chairman; Lithuanian Polish Union (LLS), Rytardas MACIKIANEC, chairman
Other political or pressure groups: Homeland Union; Lithuanian Future Forum; Farmers Union
Member of: BIS, CBSS, CCC, CE, CSCE, EBRD, ECE, FAO, IBRD, ICAO, ILO, IMF, INTELSAT (nonsignatory user), INTERPOL, IOC, ISO (correspondent), ITU, LORCS, NACC, UN, UNCTAD, UNESCO, UNIDO, UPU, WHO, WIPO, WMO
Diplomatic representation in US:
chief of mission: Ambassador Alfonsas EIDINTAS
chancery: 2622 16th Street NW, Washington, DC 20009
telephone: (202) 234-5860, 2639
FAX: (202) 328-0466
consulate(s) general: New York
US diplomatic representation:
chief of mission: Ambassador Darryl N. JOHNSON
embassy: Akmenu 6, Vilnius 232600
mailing address: APO AE 09723
telephone: 370-2-223-031
FAX: 370-2-222-779
Flag: three equal horizontal bands of yellow (top), green, and red

---

U.S. Government Contacts:

U.S. Trade Desk: (202) 482-4915

MOLDOVA

Economy

Overview: Moldova has pushed ahead boldly on economic reform since gaining its independence from the Soviet Union in 1991. It introduced a convertible currency—the leu—in late 1993 that has remained stable against the dollar, removed price controls on most products, eliminated licenses and quotas on most imports and exports, and freed interest rates. In 1994, Moldova aims to privatize at least one-third of state enterprises, lower inflation to 1% per month, and reduce the budget deficit to 3.5% of GDP. Moldova enjoys a favorable climate and good farmland but has no major mineral deposits. As a result, Moldova's economy is primarily based on agriculture, featuring fruits, vegetables, wine, and tobacco. Moldova, however, must import all of its supplies of oil, coal, and natural gas, and energy shortages have contributed to sharp production declines since the break-up of the Soviet Union. Activities by separatist groups in the Dniester region have held back economic development in that area. Foreign economic assistance has been a tangible plus for Moldova, whereas direct foreign investment has been lacking.

National product: GDP—purchasing power equivalent—$16.3 billion (1993 estimate from the UN International Comparison Program, as extended to 1991 and published in the World Bank's World Development Report 1993; and as extrapolated to 1993 using official Moldovan statistics, which are very uncertain because of major economic changes since 1990)

National product real growth rate: -4% (1993 est.)
National product per capita: $3,650 (1993 est.)
Inflation rate (consumer prices): 30% per month (1993)
Unemployment rate: less than 1% (includes only officially registered unemployed; large numbers of underemployed workers)
Budget:
revenues: $NA
expenditures: $NA, including capital expenditures of $NA
note: budget deficit for 1993 approximately 6% of GDP
Exports: $108 million to outside the FSU countries (January-September 1993); over 70% of exports go to FSU countries
commodities: foodstuffs, wine, tobacco, textiles and footwear, machinery, chemicals (1991)
partners: Russia, Kazakhstan, Ukraine, Romania, Germany
Imports: $145 million from outside the FSU countries (January-September 1993); over 70% of imports are from FSU countries
commodities: oil, gas, coal, steel machinery, foodstuffs, automobiles, and other consumer durables
partners: Russia, Ukraine, Uzbekistan, Romania, Germany
External debt: $325 million (end of 1993)
Industrial production: growth rate -10% (1993)
Electricity:
capacity: 3,115,000 kW

production: 11.1 billion kWh
consumption per capita: 2,491 kWh (1992)
Industries: key products are canned food, agricultural machinery, foundry equipment, refrigerators and freezers, washing machines, hosiery, refined sugar, vegetable oil, shoes, textiles
Agriculture: Moldova's principal economic activity; products are vegetables, fruits, wine, grain, sugar beets, sunflower seed, meat, milk, tobacco
Illicit drugs: illicit cultivator of opium poppy and cannabis; mostly for CIS consumption; transshipment point for illicit drugs to Western Europe
Economic aid:
recipient: Joint EC-US loan (1993), $127 million; IMF STF credit (1993), $64 million; IMF stand-by loan (1993), $72 million; US commitments (1992-93), $61 million in humanitarian aid, $11 million in technical assistance; World Bank loan (1993), $60 million; Russia (1993), 50 billion ruble credit; Romania (1993), 20 billion lei credit
Currency: the leu (plural lei) was introduced in late 1993
Exchange rates: NA
Fiscal year: calendar year

Communications

Railroads: 1,150 km; does not include industrial lines (1990)
Highways:
total: 20,000 km
paved or gravelled: 13,900 km
unpaved: earth 6,100 km (1990)
Pipelines: natural gas 310 km (1992)
Ports: none; landlocked
Airports:
total: 26
usable: 15
with permanent-surface runways: 6
with runways over 3,659 m: 0
with runways 2,440-3,659 m: 5
with runways 1,060-2,439 m: 8
note: a C-130 can land on a 1,060-m airstrip
Telecommunications: The telecommunication system of Moldova is not well developed; number of telephone subscribers 577,000 (1991); number of subscribers per 1,000 persons 134 (1991); number of unsuccessful requests for telephone service 215,000 (1991); international connections to the other former Soviet republics by land line and microwave radio relay through Ukraine, and to other countries by leased connections to the Moscow international gateway switch; 2 satellite earth stations—1 EUTELSAT and 1 INTELSAT; broadcast services NA

Defense Forces

Branches: Ground Forces, Air and Air Defence Force, Security Forces (internal and border troops)
Manpower availability: males age 15-49 1,098,156; fit for military service 869,866; reach military age (18) annually 35,814 (1994 est.)
Defense expenditures: exchange rate conversion—$NA, NA% of GDP

Geography

Location: Eastern Europe, between Ukraine and Romania
Map references: Asia, Europe, Standard Time Zones of the World
Area:
total area: 33,700 sq km
land area: 33,700 sq km
comparative area: slightly more than twice the size of Hawaii
Land boundaries: total 1,389 km, Romania 450 km, Ukraine 939 km
Coastline: 0 km (landlocked)
Maritime claims: none; landlocked
International disputes: no official territorial claims by either Moldova or Romania, but nationalists in Romania seek the merger of Moldova into Romania; potential future dispute by Moldova and Romania against Ukraine over former southern and northern Bessarabian areas and Northern Bukovina ceded to Ukraine upon Moldova's incorporation into USSR

Climate: moderate winters, warm summers
Terrain: rolling steppe, gradual slope south to Black Sea
Natural resources: lignite, phosphorites, gypsum
Land use:
arable land: 50%
permanent crops: 13%
meadows and pastures: 9%
forest and woodland: 0%
other: 28%
Irrigated land: 2,920 sq km (1990)
Environment:
current issues: heavy use of agricultural chemicals, including banned pesticides such as DDT, has contaminated soil and groundwater; extensive soil erosion from poor farming methods
natural hazards: NA
international agreements: signed, but not ratified—Biodiversity, Climate Change
Note: landlocked

People

Population: 4,473,033 (July 1994 est.)
Population growth rate: 0.38% (1994 est.)
Birth rate: 16.02 births/1,000 population (1994 est.)
Death rate: 10.02 deaths/1,000 population (1994 est.)
Net migration rate: -2.2 migrant(s)/1,000 population (1994 est.)
Infant mortality rate: 30.3 deaths/1,000 live births (1994 est.)
Life expectancy at birth:
total population: 68.07 years
male: 64.65 years
female: 71.67 years (1994 est.)
Total fertility rate: 2.18 children born/woman (1994 est.)
Nationality:
noun: Moldovan(s)
adjective: Moldovan
Ethnic divisions: Moldavian/Romanian 64.5%, Ukrainian 13.8%, Russian 13%, Gagauz 3.5%, Jewish 1.5%, Bulgarian 2%, other 1.7% (1989 figures)
note: internal disputes with ethnic Russians and Ukrainians in the Dniester region and Gagauz Turks in the south
Religions: Eastern Orthodox 98.5%, Jewish 1.5%, Baptist (only about 1,000 members) (1991)
note: the large majority of churchgoers are ethnic Moldavian
Languages: Moldovan (official; virtually the same as the Romanian language), Russian, Gagauz (a Turkish dialect)
Literacy: age 9-49 can read and write (1970)
total population: 100%
male: 100%
female: 99%
Labor force: 2.05 million (1992)
by occupation: agriculture 34.4%, industry 20.1%, other 45.5% (1985 figures)

Government

Names:
conventional long form: Republic of Moldova
conventional short form: Moldova
local long form: Republica Moldoveneasca
local short form: none
former: Soviet Socialist Republic of Moldova; Moldavia
Digraph: MD
Type: republic
Capital: Chisinau
Administrative divisions: previously divided into 40 rayons; new districts possible under new constitution in 1994
Independence: 27 August 1991 (from Soviet Union)
National holiday: Independence Day, 27 August 1991
Constitution: old Soviet constitution (adopted NA 1979) is still in effect but has been heavily amended during the past few years; a new constitution is expected in 1994
Legal system: based on civil law system; no judicial review of legislative acts; does not accept compulsory ICJ jurisdiction but accepts many UN and CSCE documents
Suffrage: 18 years of age; universal
Executive branch:
chief of state: President Mircea SNEGUR

(since 3 September 1990); election last held 8 December 1991 (next to be held NA 1996); results—Mircea SNEGUR ran unopposed and won 98.17% of vote; note—President SNEGUR was named executive president by the Supreme Soviet on 3 September 1990 and was confirmed by popular election on 8 December 1991
head of government: Prime Minister Andrei SANGHALI (since 1 July 1992; reappointed 5 April 1994 after elections for new legislature)
cabinet: Council of Ministers; appointed by the president on recommendation of the prime minister
Legislative branch: unicameral
Parliament: elections last held 27 February 1994 (next to be held NA 1999); results—percent by party NA; seats—(104 total) Agrarian-Democratic Party 56, Socialist/Yedinstvo Bloc 28, Peasants and Intellectual Bloc 11, Christian Democratic Popular Front 9
Judicial branch: Supreme Court
Political parties and leaders: Christian Democratic Popular Front (formerly Moldovan Popular Front), Iurie ROSCA, chairman; Yedinstvo Intermovement, V. YAKOVLEV, chairman; Social Democratic Party, Oazu NANTOI, chairman, two other chairmen; Agrarian-Democratic Party, Dumitru MOTPAN, chairman; Democratic Party, Gheorghe GHIMPU, chairman; Democratic Labor Party, Alexandru ARSENI, chairman; Reform Party, Anatol SELARU; Republican Party, Victor PUSCAS; Socialist Party, Valeriu SENIC, chairman; Communist Party, Vladimir VORONIN
Other political or pressure groups: United Council of Labor Collectives (UCLC), Igor SMIRNOV, chairman; Congress of Intellectuals, Alexandru MOSANU; The Ecology Movement of Moldova (EMM), G. MALARCHUK, chairman; The Christian Democratic League of Women of Moldova (CDLWM), L. LARI, chairman; National Christian Party of Moldova (NCPM), D. TODIKE, M. BARAGA, V. NIKU, leaders; The Peoples Movement Gagauz Khalky (GKh), S. GULGAR, leader; The Democratic Party of Gagauzia (DPG), G. SAVOSTIN, chairman; The Alliance of Working People of Moldova (AWPM), G. POLOGOV, president; Christian Alliance for Greater Romania; Stefan the Great Movement; Liberal Convention of Moldova; Association of Victims of Repression; Christian Democratic Youth League
Member of: BSEC, CE (guest), CIS, CSCE, EBRD, ECE, IBRD, ICAO, ILO, IMF, INTELSAT (nonsignatory user), IOC, ITU, NACC, UN, UNCTAD, UNESCO, UNIDO, UPU, WHO, WIPO
Diplomatic representation in US:
chief of mission: Ambassador Nicolae TIU
chancery: 1511 K Street NW, Room 329, Washington, DC
telephone: (202) 783-3012 or -2807
US diplomatic representation:
chief of mission: Ambassador Mary C. PENDLETON
embassy: Strada Alexei Mateevich #103, Chisinau
mailing address: use embassy street address
telephone: 373 (2) 23-37-72 or 23-34-76
FAX: 7-0422-23-30-44
Flag: same color scheme as Romania—3 equal vertical bands of blue (hoist side), yellow, and red; emblem in center of flag is of a Roman eagle of gold outlined in black with a red beak and talons carrying a yellow cross in its beak and a green olive branch in its right talons and a yellow scepter in its left talons; on its breast is a shield divided horizontally red over blue with a stylized ox head, star, rose, and crescent all in black-outlined yellow

MONGOLIA

Economy

Overview: Mongolia's severe climate, scattered population, and wide expanses of unproductive land have constrained economic development. Economic activity traditionally has been based on agriculture and the breeding of livestock—Mongolia has the highest number of livestock per person in the world. In past years extensive mineral resources had been developed with Soviet support; total Soviet assistance at its height amounted to 30% of GDP. The mining and processing of coal, copper, molybdenum, tin, tungsten, and gold account for a large part of industrial production. Timber and fishing are also important sectors. The Mongolian leadership is trying to make the transition from Soviet-style central planning to a market economy through privatization and price reform, and is soliciting support from international financial agencies and foreign investors. The economy, however, has still not recovered from the loss of Soviet aid, and the country continues to suffer substantial economic hardships.
National product: GDP—purchasing power equivalent—$2.8 billion (1993 est.)
National product real growth rate: -1.3% (1993 est.)
National product per capita: $1,200 (1993 est.)
Inflation rate (consumer prices): 325% (1992 est.)
Unemployment rate: 15% (1991 est.)
Budget:
revenues: $NA
expenditures: $NA, including capital expenditures of $NA (1991 est.)
note: deficit of $67 million
Exports: $355 million (f.o.b., 1992 est.)
commodities: copper, livestock, animal products, cashmere, wool, hides, fluorspar, other nonferrous metals
partners: former CMEA countries 62%, China 17%, EC 8% (1992)
Imports: $501 million (f.o.b., 1991 est.)
commodities: machinery and equipment, fuels, food products, industrial consumer goods, chemicals, building materials, sugar, tea
partners: USSR 75%, Austria 5%, China 5%
External debt: $16.8 billion (yearend 1990); 98.6% with USSR
Industrial production: growth rate -15% (1992 est.); accounts for about 42% of GDP
Electricity:
capacity: 1,248,000 kW
production: 3,740 kWh
consumption per capita: 1,622 kWh (1992)
Industries: copper, processing of animal products, building materials, food and beverage, mining (particularly coal)
Agriculture: accounts for about 35% of GDP and provides livelihood for about 50% of the population; livestock raising predominates (primarily sheep and goats, but also cattle, camels, and horses); crops—wheat, barley, potatoes, forage
Economic aid: NA
Currency: 1 tughrik (Tug) = 100 mongos
Exchange rates: tughriks (Tug) per US$1—150 (1 January 1993), 40 (1992), 7.1 (1991), 5.63 (1990), 3.00 (1989)
note: the exchange rate 40 tughriks = 1US$ was introduced June 1991 and was in force to the end of 1992

Fiscal year: calendar year

Communications

Railroads: 1,750 km 1.524-meter broad gauge (1988)
Highways:
total: 46,700 km
paved: 1,000 km
unpaved: 45,700 km (1988)
Inland waterways: 397 km of principal routes (1988)
Ports: none; landlocked
Airports:
total: 81
usable: 31
with permanent-surface runways: 11
with runways over 3,659 m: fewer than 5
with runways 2,440-3,659 m: fewer than 20
with runways 1,220-2,439 m: 12
Telecommunications: 63,000 telephones (1989); broadcast stations—12 AM, 1 FM, 1 TV (with 18 provincial repeaters); repeat of Russian TV; 120,000 TVs; 220,000 radios; at least 1 earth station

Defense Forces

Branches: Mongolian People's Army (includes Internal Security Forces and Frontier Guards), Air Force
Manpower availability: males age 15-49 587,113; fit for military service 382,633; reach military age (18) annually 25,261 (1994 est.)
Defense expenditures: exchange rate conversion—$22.8 million of GDP, 1% of GDP (1992)
embassy: address NA, Ulaanbaatar
mailing address: Ulaanbaatar, c/o American Embassy Beijing, Micro Region II, Big Ring Road; PSC 461, Box 300, FPO AP 96521-0002
telephone: [976] (1) 329095 through 329606
FAX: [976] (1) 320-776
Flag: three equal, vertical bands of red (hoist side), blue, and red, centered on the hoist-side red band in yellow is the national emblem ("soyombo"—a columnar arrangement of abstract and geometric representation for fire, sun, moon, earth, water, and the yin-yang symbol)

Geography

Location: Northern Asia, between China and Russia
Map references: Asia, Standard Time Zones of the World
Area:
total area: 1.565 million sq km
land area: 1.565 million sq km
comparative area: slightly larger than Alaska
Land boundaries: total 8,114 km, China 4,673 km, Russia 3,441 km
Coastline: 0 km (landlocked)
Maritime claims: none; landlocked
International disputes: none
Climate: desert; continental (large daily and seasonal temperature ranges)
Terrain: vast semidesert and desert plains; mountains in west and southwest; Gobi Desert in southeast
Natural resources: oil, coal, copper, molybdenum, tungsten, phosphates, tin, nickel, zinc, wolfram, fluorspar, gold
Land use:
arable land: 1%
permanent crops: 0%
meadows and pastures: 79%
forest and woodland: 10%
other: 10%
Irrigated land: 770 sq km (1989)
Environment:
current issues: limited water resources; policies of the former communist regime promoting rapid urbanization and industrial growth have raised concerns about their negative effects on the environment; the burning of soft coal and the concentration of factories in Ulaanbaatar have severely polluted the air; deforestation, overgrazing, the converting of virgin land to agricultural production have increased soil erosion from wind and rain; desertification
natural hazards: NA
international agreements: party to—Biodiversity, Climate Change, Environmental Modification, Nuclear Test Ban; signed, but not ratified—Law of the Sea

Note: landlocked; strategic location between China and Russia

People

Population: 2,429,762 (July 1994 est.)
Population growth rate: 2.61% (1994 est.)
Birth rate: 33.04 births/1,000 population (1994 est.)
Death rate: 6.99 deaths/1,000 population (1994 est.)
Net migration rate: 0 migrant(s)/1,000 population (1994 est.)
Infant mortality rate: 43.4 deaths/1,000 live births (1994 est.)
Life expectancy at birth:
total population: 66.16 years
male: 63.9 years
female: 68.52 years (1994 est.)
Total fertility rate: 4.33 children born/woman (1994 est.)
Nationality:
noun: Mongolian(s)
adjective: Mongolian
Ethnic divisions: Mongol 90%, Kazakh 4%, Chinese 2%, Russian 2%, other 2%
Religions: predominantly Tibetan Buddhist, Muslim 4%
note: previously limited religious activity because of Communist regime
Languages: Khalkha Mongol 90%, Turkic, Russian, Chinese
Literacy:
total population: NA%
male: NA%
female: NA%
Labor force: NA
by occupation: primarily herding/agricultural
note: over half the adult population is in the labor force, including a large percentage of women; shortage of skilled labor

Government

Names:
conventional long form: none
conventional short form: Mongolia
local long form: none
local short form: Mongol Uls
former: Outer Mongolia
Digraph: MG
Type: republic
Capital: Ulaanbaatar
Administrative divisions: 18 provinces (aymguud, singular—aymag) and 3 municipalities* (hotuud, singular—hot); Arhangay, Bayanhongor, Bayan-Olgiy, Bulgan, Darhan*, Dornod, Dornogovi, Dundgovi, Dzavhan, Erdenet*, Govi-Altay, Hentiy, Hovd, Hovsgol, Omnogovi, Ovorhangay, Selenge, Suhbaatar, Tov, Ulaanbaatar*, Uvs
Independence: 13 March 1921 (from China)
National holiday: National Day, 11 July (1921)
Constitution: adopted 13 January 1992
Legal system: blend of Russian, Chinese, and Turkish systems of law; no constitutional provision for judicial review of legislative acts; has not accepted compulsory ICJ jurisdiction
Suffrage: 18 years of age; universal
Executive branch:
chief of state: President Punsalmaagiyn OCHIRBAT (since 3 September 1990); election last held 6 June 1993 (next to be held NA 1997); results—Punsalmaagiyn OCHIRBAT (MNDP and MSDP) elected directly with 57.8% of the vote; other candidate Lodongiyn TUDEV (MPRP)
head of government: Prime Minister Putsagiyn JASRAY (since 3 August 1992); Deputy Prime Ministers Lhamsuren ENEBISH and Choijilsurengiyn PUREVDORJ (since NA)
cabinet: Cabinet; appointed by the Great Hural
Legislative branch: unicameral
State Great Hural: elections first time held 28 June 1992 (next to be held NA); results—percent of vote by party NA; seats—(76 total) MPRP 71, United Party 4, MSDP 1
note: the People's Small Hural no longer exists
Judicial branch: Supreme Court serves as appeals court for people's and provincial courts, but to date rarely overturns verdicts of lower courts
Political parties and leaders: Mongolian People's Revolutionary Party (MPRP), Budragchagiin DASH-YONDON, secretary general; Mongolian Democratic Party (MDP), Erdenijiyn BAT-UUL, general coordinator; National Progress Party (NPP), S. BYAMBAA and Luusandambyn DASHNYAM, leaders; Social Democratic Party (SDP), BATBAYAR

and Tsohiogyyn ADYASUREN, leaders; Mongolian Independence Party (MIP), D. ZORIGT, leader; United Party of Mongolia (made up of the MDP, SDP, and NPP); Mongolian National Democratic Party (MNDP), D. GANBOLD, chairman; Mongolian Social Democratic Party (MSDP), B. BATBAYAR, chairman; Mongolian Conservative Party, O. ZOYA; Mongolian Green Party (MGP), M. GANBAT
note: opposition parties were legalized in May 1990
Member of: AsDB, CCC, ESCAP, FAO, G-77, IAEA, IBRD, ICAO, IDA, IFC, ILO, IMF, INTELSAT (nonsignatory user), INTERPOL, IOC, ISO, ITU, LORCS, NAM (observer), UN, UNCTAD, UNESCO, UNIDO, UPU, WFTU, WHO, WIPO, WMO, WTO
Diplomatic representation in US:
chief of mission: Ambassador Luvsandorj DAWAGIV
chancery: 2833 M Street NW, Washington, DC 20007
telephone: (202) 333-7117
FAX: (202) 298-9227
consulate(s) general: New York
US diplomatic representation:
chief of mission: Ambassador Donald C. JOHNSON

U.S. Government Contacts:

U.S. Trade Desk: (202) 482-3932

PAKISTAN

Economy

Overview: Pakistan is a poor Third World country faced with the usual problems of rapidly increasing population, sizable government deficits, and heavy dependence on foreign aid. In addition, the economy must support a large military establishment. Rapid economic growth, averaging 5%-6% over the past decade has helped Pakistan cope with these problems. However, growth slumped to 3% in FY93 because of severe flooding, which damaged the key export crop, cotton. Almost all agriculture and small-scale industry is in private hands. In 1990, Pakistan embarked on a sweeping economic liberalization program to boost foreign and domestic private investment and lower foreign aid dependence. The SHARIF government denationalized several state-owned firms and attracted some foreign investment. Pakistan likely will have difficulty raising living standards because of its rapidly expanding population. At the current rate of growth, population would double in 25 years.
National product: GNP—purchasing power equivalent—$239 billion (1993 est.)
National product real growth rate: 3% (FY93 est.)
National product per capita: $1,900 (1993 est.)
Inflation rate (consumer prices): 12.7% (FY91)
Unemployment rate: 10% (FY91 est.)
Budget:
revenues: $9.4 billion
expenditures: $10.9 billion, including capital expenditures of $3.1 billion (1993 est.)
Exports: $6.8 billion (f.o.b., FY92)
commodities: cotton, textiles, clothing, rice, leather, carpets
partners: US, Japan, Hong Kong, Germany, UK
Imports: $9.1 billion (f.o.b., FY92)
commodities: petroleum, petroleum products, machinery, transportation equipment, vegetable oils, animal fats, chemicals
partners: Japan, US, Germany, UK, Saudi Arabia
External debt: $24 billion (1993 est.)
Industrial production: growth rate 7.3% (FY92); accounts for 23% of GDP
Electricity:
capacity: 10,000,000 kW
production: 43 billion kWh
consumption per capita: 350 kWh (1992)
Industries: textiles, food processing, beverages, construction materials, clothing, paper products, shrimp
Agriculture: 22% of GDP, over 50% of labor force; world's largest contiguous irrigation system; major crops—cotton, wheat, rice, sugarcane, fruits, vegetables; livestock products—milk, beef, mutton, eggs; self-sufficient in food grain
Illicit drugs: major illicit producer of opium and hashish for the international drug trade; despite some success in reducing cultivation, remains world's fourth largest opium producer (140 metric tons in 1993)
Economic aid:
recipient: US commitments, including Ex-Im

(FY70-89), $4.5 billion; Western (non-US) countries, ODA and OOF bilateral commitments (1980-89), $91 billion; OPEC bilateral aid (1979-89), $2.3 billion; Communist countries (1970-89), $3.2 billion
note: including Bangladesh prior to 1972
Currency: 1 Pakistani rupee (PRe) = 100 paisa
Exchange rates: Pakistani rupees (PRs) per US$1—30.214 (January 1994), 28.107 (1993), 25.083 (1992), 23.801 (1991), 21.707 (1990), 20.541 (1989)
Fiscal year: 1 July—30 June

Communications

Railroads: 8,773 km total; 7,718 km broad gauge, 445 km 1-meter gauge, and 610 km less than 1-meter gauge; 1,037 km broad-gauge double track; 286 km electrified; all government owned (1985)
Highways:
total: 110,677 km
paved: 58,677 km
unpaved: gravel 23,000 km; improved earth 29,000 km (1988)
Pipelines: crude oil 250 km; natural gas 4,044 km; petroleum products 885 km (1987)
Ports: Gwadar, Karachi, Port Muhammad bin Qasim
Merchant marine: 30 ships (1,000 GRT or over) totaling 352,189 GRT/532,782 DWT, passenger-cargo 3, cargo 25, oil tanker 1, bulk 1
Airports:
total: 110
usable: 104
with permanent-surface runways: 75
with runways over 3,659 m: 1
with runways 2,440-3,659 m: 30
with runways 1,220-2,439 m: 43
Telecommunications: the domestic telephone system is poor, adequate only for government and business use; about 7 telephones per 1,000 persons; the system for international traffic is better and employs both microwave radio relay and satellites; satellite ground stations—1 Atlantic Ocean INTELSAT and 2 Indian Ocean INTELSAT; broadcast stations—19 AM, 8 FM, 29 TV

Defense Forces

Branches: Army, Navy, Air Force, Civil Armed Forces, National Guard, paramilitary/security forces
Manpower availability: males age 15-49 29,548,746; fit for military service 18,134,013; reach military age (17) annually 1,391,258 (1994 est.)
Defense expenditures: exchange rate conversion—$3.2 billion, 6% of GNP (FY91/92)

Geography

Location: Southern Asia, along the Arabian Sea, between India and Afghanistan
Map references: Asia, Standard Time Zones of the World
Area:
total area: 803,940 sq km
land area: 778,720 sq km
comparative area: slightly less than twice the size of California
Land boundaries: total 6,774 km, Afghanistan 2,430 km, China 523 km, India 2,912 km, Iran 909 km
Coastline: 1,046 km
Maritime claims:
contiguous zone: 24 nm
continental shelf: 200 nm or the edge of continental margin
exclusive economic zone: 200 nm
territorial sea: 12 nm
International disputes: status of Kashmir with India; border question with Afghanistan (Durand Line); water-sharing problems (Wular Barrage) over the Indus with upstream riparian India
Climate: mostly hot, dry desert; temperate in northwest; arctic in north
Terrain: flat Indus plain in east; mountains in north and northwest; Balochistan plateau in west
Natural resources: land, extensive natural gas reserves, limited petroleum, poor quality coal, iron ore, copper, salt, limestone
Land use:
arable land: 26%
permanent crops: 0%

meadows and pastures: 6%
forest and woodland: 4%
other: 64%
Irrigated land: 162,200 sq km (1989)
Environment:
current issues: water pollution from untreated sewage, industrial wastes, and agricultural runoff; water scarcity; a majority of the population does not have access to safe drinking water; deforestation; soil erosion; desertification
natural hazards: frequent earthquakes, occasionally severe especially in north and west; flooding along the Indus after heavy rains (July and August)
international agreements: party to—Endangered Species, Environmental Modification, Nuclear Test Ban, Wetlands; signed, but not ratified—Biodiversity, Climate Change, Law of the Sea, Marine Life Conservation
Note: controls Khyber Pass and Bolan Pass, traditional invasion routes between Central Asia and the Indian Subcontinent

People

Population: 128,855,965 (July 1994 est.)
Population growth rate: 2.86% (1994 est.)
Birth rate: 42.22 births/1,000 population (1994 est.)
Death rate: 12.38 deaths/1,000 population (1994 est.)
Net migration rate: -1.21 migrant(s)/1,000 population (1994 est.)
Infant mortality rate: 101.9 deaths/1,000 live births (1994 est.)
Life expectancy at birth:
total population: 57.41 years
male: 56.79 years
female: 58.06 years (1994 est.)
Total fertility rate: 6.43 children born/woman (1994 est.)
Nationality:
noun: Pakistani(s)
adjective: Pakistani
Ethnic divisions: Punjabi, Sindhi, Pashtun (Pathan), Baloch, Muhajir (immigrants from India and their descendents)
Religions: Muslim 97% (Sunni 77%, Shi'a 20%), Christian, Hindu, and other 3%
Languages: Urdu (official), English (official; lingua franca of Pakistani elite and most government ministries), Punjabi 64%, Sindhi 12%, Pashtu 8%, Urdu 7%, Balochi and other 9%
Literacy: age 15 and over can read and write (1990 est.)
total population: 35%
male: 47%
female: 21%
Labor force: 28.9 million
by occupation: agriculture 54%, mining and manufacturing 13%, services 33%, extensive export of labor (1987 est.)

Government

Names:
conventional long form: Islamic Republic of Pakistan
conventional short form: Pakistan
former: West Pakistan
Digraph: PK
Type: republic
Capital: Islamabad
Administrative divisions: 4 provinces, 1 territory*, and 1 capital territory**; Balochistan, Federally Administered Tribal Areas*, Islamabad Capital Territory**, North-West Frontier, Punjab, Sindh
note: the Pakistani-administered portion of the disputed Jammu and Kashmir region includes Azad Kashmir and the Northern Areas
Independence: 14 August 1947 (from UK)
National holiday: Pakistan Day, 23 March (1956) (proclamation of the republic)
Constitution: 10 April 1973, suspended 5 July 1977 restored with amendments, 30 December 1985
Legal system: based on English common law with provisions to accommodate Pakistan's stature as an Islamic state; accepts compulsory ICJ jurisdiction, with reservations
Suffrage: 21 years of age; universal; separate electorates and reserved parliamentary seats for non-Muslims

Executive branch:
chief of state: President Sardar Farooq LEGHARI election last held on 13 November 1993 (next to be held no later than 14 October 1998); results—LEGHARI was elected by Parliament and the four provincial assemblies
head of government: Prime Minister Benazir BHUTTO
cabinet: Cabinet
Legislative branch: bicameral Parliament (Majlis-e-Shoora)
Senate: elections last held NA March 1994 (next to be held NA March 1997); seats—(87 total) Pakistan People's Party (PPP) 22, Pakistan Muslim League, Nawaz Sharif faction (PML/N) 17; Tribal Area Representatives (nonparty) 8, Awami National Party (ANP) 6, Pakistan Muslim League, Junejo faction (PML/J) 5, Jamhoori Watan Party (JWP) 5, Mohajir Quami Movement, Altaf faction (MQM/A) 5, Jamiat Ulema-i-Islam, Fazlur Rehman group (JUI/F) 2, Pakhtun Khwa Milli Awami Party (PKMAP) 2, Jamaat-i-Islami (JI) 2, National People's Party (NPP) 2, Balochistan National Movement, Hayee Group (BNM/H) 1, Balochistan National Movement, Mengal Group (BNM/M) 1, Jamiat Ulema-i-Pakistan, Niazi faction (JUP/NI) 1, Jamiat Ulema-i-Pakistan, Noorani faction (JUP/NO) 1, Jamiat-al-Hadith (JAH) 1, Jamiat Ulema-i-Islam, Sami-ul-Haq faction (JUI/S) 1, Pakistan Muslim League, Functional Group (PML/F) 1, Pakistan National Party (PNP) 1, Independents 2, vacant 1
National Assembly: elections last held 6 October 1993 (next to be held by October 1998); seats—(217 total); Pakistan People's Party (PPP) 92; Pakistan Muslim League, Nawaz Sharif faction (PML/N) 75; Pakistan Muslim League, Junejo faction (PML/J) 6; Islami-Jamhoori-Mahaz (IJM-Islamic Democratic Front) 4; Awami National Party (ANP) 3; Pakhtun Khwa Milli Awami Party (PKMAP) 4; Pakistan Islamic Front (PIF) 3; Jamhoori Watan Party (JWP) 2; Mutaheda Deeni Mahaz (MDM) 2; Balochistan National Movement, Hayee Group (BNM/H) 1; Balochistan National Movement, Mengal Group (BNM/M) 1; National Democratic Alliance (NDA) 1; National People's Party (NPP) 1; Pakhtun Quami Party (PKQP) 1; Religious minorities 10 reserved seats; independents, 9; results pending, 2
Judicial branch: Supreme Court, Federal Islamic (Shari'at) Court
Political parties and leaders:
government: Pakistan People's Party (PPP), Benazir BHUTTO; Pakistan Muslim League, Junejo faction (PML/J), Hamid Nasir CHATTHA; National People's Party (NPP), Ghulam Mustapha JATOI; Pakhtun Khwa Milli Awami Party (PKMAP), Mahmood Khan ACHAKZAI; Balochistan National Movement, Hayee Group (BNM/H), Dr. HAYEE Baluch; National Democratic Alliance (NDA), Maulana Kausar NIAZI; Pakhtun Quami Party (PKQP), Mohammed AFZAL Khan; Jamhoori Watan Party (JWP), Akbar Khan BUGTI
opposition: Pakistan Muslim League, Nawaz Sharif faction (PML/N), Nawaz SHARIF; Awami National Party (ANP), Khan Abdul WALI KHAN; Pakistan Islamic Front (PIF), Qazi Hussain AHMED; Balochistan National Movement, Mengal Group (BNM/M), Sardar Akhtar MENGAL; Mohajir Quami Movement, Altaf faction (MQM/A); Jamaat-i-Islami (JI); Jamiat-al-Hadith (JAH)
frequently shifting: Mutaheda Deeni Mahaz (MDM), Maulana Sami-ul-HAQ, the MDM includes Jamiat Ulema-i-Pakistan, Niazi faction (JUP/NI) and Anjuman Sepah-i-Sahaba Pakistan (ASSP); Islami-Jamhoori-Mahaz (IJM-Islamic Democratic Party), the IJM includes Jamiat Ulema-i-Islami, Fazlur Rehman group (JUI/F); Jamiat Ulema-i-Pakistan, Noorani faction (JUP/NO); Jamiat Ulema-i-Islam, Sami-ul-Haq faction (JUI/S); Pakistan Muslim League, Functional Group (PML/F); Pakistan National Party (PNP)
note: most Pakistani political groups are motivated primarily by opportunism and political alliances can shift frequently
Other political or pressure groups: military remains important political force; ulema (clergy), landowners, industrialists, and small merchants also influential
Member of: AsDB, C, CCC, CP, ECO, ESCAP, FAO, G-19, G-24, G-77, GATT, IAEA, IBRD, ICAO, ICC, ICFTU, IDA, IDB,

IFAD, IFC, ILO, IMF, IMO, INMARSAT, INTELSAT, INTERPOL, IOC, IOM, ISO, ITU, LORCS, MINURSO, NAM, OAS (observer), OIC, PCA, SAARC, UN, UNCTAD, UNESCO, UNHCR, UNIDO, UNIKOM, UNOSOM, UNTAC, UPU, WCL, WFTU, WHO, WIPO, WMO, WTO
Diplomatic representation in US:
chief of mission: Ambassador Maleeha LODHI
chancery: 2315 Massachusetts Avenue NW, Washington, DC 20008
telephone: (202) 939-6205
FAX: (202) 387-0484
consulate(s) general: Los Angeles and New York
US diplomatic representation:
chief of mission: Ambassador John MONJO
embassy: Diplomatic Enclave, Ramna 5, Islamabad
mailing address: P. O. Box 1048, PSC 1212, Box 2000, Unit 6220,Islamabad or APO AE 09812-2000
telephone: [92] (51) 826161 through 79
FAX: [92] (51) 214222
consulate(s) general: Karachi, Lahore
consulate(s): Peshawar
Flag: green with a vertical white band (symbolizing the role of religious minorities) on the hoist side; a large white crescent and star are centered in the green field; the crescent, star, and color green are traditional symbols of Islam

---

U.S. Government Contacts:

U.S. Trade Desk: (202) 482-2954

American Consulate General - Karachi, Pakistan
8 Abdullah Harroon Road
Karachi, Pakistan
APO AE 09814
Tel: 92-21-518-180
Fax: 92-21-511-381

American Embassy Econ/Commercial Section
Diplomatic Enclave, Ramna 5
P.O. Box 1048
Islamabad, Pakistan
Tel: 92-51-826-161

American Consulate General - Lahore Commercial Section
50 Zafar Ali Road
Gulberg 5
Lahore, Pakistan
APO AE 09812
Tel: 92-42-871-406

Pakistan Government Contacts:

Embassy of Pakistan Commercial Section
2315 Massachusetts Avenue, N.W.
Washington, DC 20008
Tel: (202) 939-6200

Chambers of Commerce & Organizations:

American Chamber of Commerce in Pakistan
3rd Floor, Shaheen Commercial Complex
G.P.O. 1322
M.R. Kayani Road
Karachi, Pakistan
Tel: 92-21-526-436

POLAND

Boundary representation is not necessarily authoritative.

Economy

Overview: Poland is continuing the difficult transition to a market economy that began on 1 January 1990, when the new democratic government instituted "shock therapy" by decontrolling prices, slashing subsidies, and drastically reducing import barriers. The economy contracted sharply in 1990 and 1991, but in 1992 real GDP grew 1% despite a severe drought. Real GDP expanded about 4% in 1993, the highest rate in Europe except for Albania. About half of GDP now comes from the private sector even though privatization of the large state-owned enterprises is proceeding slowly and most industry remains in state hands. The pattern of industrial production is changing rapidly; output of textiles and construction materials is well above 1990 levels, while output of basic metals remains depressed. Inflation, which had exceeded 50% monthly in late 1989, was down to about 37% for all of 1993, as the government held the budget deficit below 3% of GDP. Unemployment has risen steadily, however, to about 16%. The trade deficit is also a problem, in part due to recession in Western Europe, Poland's main customer. The new government elected in September 1993 is politically to the left of its predecessor but is continuing the reform process.
National product: GDP—purchasing power equivalent—$180.4 billion (1993 est.)
National product real growth rate: 4.1% (1993 est.)
National product per capita: $4,680 (1993 est.)
Inflation rate (consumer prices): 37% (1993)
Unemployment rate: 15.7% (December 1993)
Budget:
revenues: $24.3 billion
expenditures: $27.1 billion, including capital expenditures of $1.5 billion (1993 est.)
Exports: $13.5 billion (f.o.b., 1993 est.)
commodities: machinery 24%, metals 17%, chemicals 12%, fuels and power 11%, food 10% (1992)
partners: Germany 31.4%, Netherlands 6.0%, Italy 5.6%, Russia 5.5% (1992)
Imports: $15.6 billion (f.o.b., 1993 est.)
commodities: fuels and power 17%, machinery 36%, chemicals 17%, food 8% (1992)
partners: Germany 23.9%, Russia 8.5%, Italy 6.9%, UK 6.7% (1992)
External debt: $47 billion (1993); note—Poland's Western government creditors promised in 1991 to forgive 30% of Warsaw's $35 billion official debt immediately and to forgive another 20% in 1994; foreign banks agreed in early 1994 to forgive 45% of their $12 billion debt claim
Industrial production: growth rate 7% (1993)
Electricity:
capacity: 31,530,000 kW
production: 137 billion kWh
consumption per capita: 3,570 kWh (1992)
Industries: machine building, iron and steel, extractive industries, chemicals, shipbuilding, food processing, glass, beverages, textiles

Agriculture: accounts for 7% of GDP and a much larger share of labor force; 75% of output from private farms, 25% from state farms; productivity remains low by European standards; leading European producer of rye, rapeseed, and potatoes; wide variety of other crops and livestock; major exporter of pork products; normally self-sufficient in food
Illicit drugs: illicit producers of opium for domestic consumption and amphetamines for the international market; transshipment point for Asian and Latin American illicit drugs to Western Europe
Economic aid:
donor: bilateral aid to non-Communist less developed countries (1954-89), $2.2 billion
recipient: Western governments and institutions have pledged $8 billion in grants and loans since 1989, but most of the money has not been disbursed
Currency: 1 zloty (Zl) = 100 groszy
Exchange rates: zlotych (Zl) per US$1—21,080 (January 1994), 18,115 (1993), 13,626 (1992), 10,576 (1991), 9,500 (1990), 1,439.18 (1989)
Fiscal year: calendar year

Communications

Railroads: 26,250 km total; 23,857 km 1.435-meter gauge, 397 km 1.520-meter gauge, 1,996 km narrow gauge; 8,987 km double track; 11,510 km electrified; government owned (1991)
Highways:
total: 360,629 km (excluding farm, factory and forest roads)
paved: 220,000 km (220 km of which are limited access expressways)
unpaved: 140,629 km (1988)
Inland waterways: 3,997 km navigable rivers and canals (1991)
Pipelines: natural gas 4,600 km, crude oil 1,986 km, petroleum products 360 km (1992)
Ports: Gdansk, Gdynia, Szczecin, Swinoujscie; principal inland ports are Gliwice on Kanal Gliwicki, Wrocaw on the Oder, and Warsaw on the Vistula
Merchant marine: 173 ships (1,000 GRT or over) totaling 2,327,855 GRT/3,458,445 DWT, short-sea passenger 5, cargo 57, roll-on/roll-off cargo 8, container 8, oil tanker 1, chemical tanker 4, bulk 89, passenger 1
note: Poland owns 3 ships operating under Liberian registry
Airports:
total: 209
usable: 167
with permanent-surface runways: 70
with runway over 3,659 m: 1
with runways 2,440-3,659 m: 47
with runways 1,060-2,439 m: 78
note: a C-130 can land on a 1,060-m airstrip
Telecommunications: severely underdeveloped and outmoded system; cable, open wire and microwave; phone density is 10.5 phones per 100 residents (October 1990); 3.6 million telephone subscribers; exchanges are 86% automatic (1991); broadcast stations—27 AM, 27 FM, 40 (5 Soviet repeaters) TV; 9.6 million TVs; 1 satellite earth station using INTELSAT, EUTELSAT, INMARSAT and Intersputnik

Defense Forces

Branches: Army, Navy, Air and Air Defense Force
Manpower availability: males age 15-49 10,046,993; fit for military service 7,856,680; reach military age (19) annually 316,339 (1994 est.)
Defense expenditures: 30.8 trillion zlotych, 1.8% of GNP (1993 est.); note—conversion of defense expenditures into US dollars using the current exchange rate could produce misleading results

Geography

Location: Central Europe, between Germany and Belarus
Map references: Asia, Ethnic Groups in Eastern Europe, Europe, Standard Time Zones of the World
Area:
total area: 312,680 sq km

land area: 304,510 sq km
comparative area: slightly smaller than New Mexico
Land boundaries: total 3,114 km, Belarus 605 km, Czech Republic 658 km, Germany 456 km, Lithuania 91 km, Russia (Kaliningrad Oblast) 432 km, Slovakia 444 km, Ukraine 428 km
Coastline: 491 km
Maritime claims:
exclusive economic zone: 200 nm
territorial sea: 12 nm
International disputes: none
Climate: temperate with cold, cloudy, moderately severe winters with frequent precipitation; mild summers with frequent showers and thundershowers
Terrain: mostly flat plain; mountains along southern border
Natural resources: coal, sulfur, copper, natural gas, silver, lead, salt
Land use:
arable land: 46%
permanent crops: 1%
meadows and pastures: 13%
forest and woodland: 28%
other: 12%
Irrigated land: 1,000 sq km (1989 est.)
Environment:
current issues: forest damage due to air pollution; improper means for disposal of large amounts of hazardous and industrial waste; severe water pollution from industrial and municipal sources; severe air pollution results from emissions of sulfur dioxide from coal-fired power plants
natural hazards: NA
international agreements: party to—Air Pollution, Antarctic Treaty, Endangered Species, Environmental Modification, Hazardous Wastes, Marine Dumping, Nuclear Test Ban, Ozone Layer Protection, Ship Pollution, Wetlands; signed, but not ratified—Air Pollution-Nitrogen Oxides, Antarctic-Environmental Protocol, Biodiversity, Climate Change, Law of the Sea
Note: historically, an area of conflict because of flat terrain and the lack of natural barriers on the North European Plain

People

Population: 38,654,561 (July 1994 est.)
Population growth rate: 0.35% (1994 est.)
Birth rate: 13.44 births/1,000 population (1994 est.)
Death rate: 9.4 deaths/1,000 population (1994 est.)
Net migration rate: -0.52 migrant(s)/1,000 population (1994 est.)
Infant mortality rate: 13.1 deaths/1,000 live births (1994 est.)
Life expectancy at birth:
total population: 72.66 years
male: 68.64 years
female: 76.91 years (1994 est.)
Total fertility rate: 1.94 children born/woman (1994 est.)
Nationality:
noun: Pole(s)
adjective: Polish
Ethnic divisions: Polish 97.6%, German 1.3%, Ukrainian 0.6%, Byelorussian 0.5% (1990 est.)
Religions: Roman Catholic 95% (about 75% practicing), Eastern Orthodox, Protestant, and other 5%
Languages: Polish
Literacy: age 15 and over can read and write (1978)
total population: 98%
male: 99%
female: 98%
Labor force: 17.329 million
by occupation: industry and construction 32.0%, agriculture 27.6%, trade, transport, and communications 14.7%, government and other 24.6% (1992)

Government

Names:
conventional long form: Republic of Poland
conventional short form: Poland
local long form: Rzeczpospolita Polska
local short form: Polska
Digraph: PL
Type: democratic state
Capital: Warsaw

Administrative divisions: 49 provinces (wojewodztwa, singular—wojewodztwo); Biala Podlaska, Bialystok, Bielsko Biala, Bydgoszcz, Chelm, Ciechanow, Czestochowa, Elblag, Gdansk, Gorzow, Jelenia Gora, Kalisz, Katowice, Kielce, Konin, Koszalin, Krakow, Krosno, Legnica, Leszno, Lodz, Lomza, Lublin, Nowy Sacz, Olsztyn, Opole, Ostroleka, Pila, Piotrkow, Plock, Poznan, Przemysl, Radom, Rzeszow, Siedlce, Sieradz, Skierniewice, Slupsk, Suwalki, Szczecin, Tarnobrzeg, Tarnow, Torun, Walbrzych, Warszawa, Wloclawek, Wroclaw, Zamosc, Zielona Gora
Independence: 11 November 1918 (independent republic proclaimed)
National holiday: Constitution Day, 3 May (1791)
Constitution: interim "small constitution" came into effect in December 1992 replacing the Communist-imposed Constitution of 22 July 1952; new democratic Constitution being drafted
Legal system: mixture of Continental (Napoleonic) civil law and holdover Communist legal theory; changes being gradually introduced as part of broader democratization process; limited judicial review of legislative acts; has not accepted compulsory ICJ jurisdiction
Suffrage: 18 years of age; universal
Executive branch:
chief of state: President Lech WALESA (since 22 December 1990); election first round held 25 November 1990, second round held 9 December 1990 (next to be held NA November 1995); results—second round Lech WALESA 74.7%, Stanislaw TYMINSKI 25.3%
head of government: Prime Minister Waldemar PAWLAK (since 26 October 1993)
cabinet: Council of Ministers; responsible to the president and the Sejm
Legislative branch: bicameral National Assembly (Zgromadzenie Narodowe)
Senate (Senat): elections last held 19 September 1993 (next to be held no later than NA October 1997); seats—(100 total)
post-Solidarity bloc: UW 6, NSZZ 12, BBWR 2
non-Communist, non-Solidarity: independents 7, unaffiliated 1, vacant 1 (to be filled in a 19 June election)
Communist origin or linked: PSL 34, SLD 37
Diet (Sejm): elections last held 19 September 1993 (next to be held no later than NA October 1997); seats—(460 total)
post-Solidarity bloc: UW 74, UP 41, BBWR 16
non-Communist, non-Solidarity: KPN 22
Communist origin or linked: SLD 171, PSL 132
note: 4 seats were won by ethnic Germans
Judicial branch: Supreme Court
Political parties and leaders:
post-Solidarity parties: Freedom Union (WD; UD and Liberal Democratic Congress merged to form Freedom Union), Tadeusz MAZOWIECKI; Christian-National Union (ZCHN), Wieslaw CHRZANOWSKI; Centrum (PC), Jaroslaw KACZYNSKI; Peasant Alliance (PL), Gabriel JANOWSKI; Solidarity Trade Union (NSZZ), Marian KRZAKLEWSKI; Union of Labor (UP), Ryszard BUGAJ; Christian-Democratic Party (PCHD), Pawel LACZKOWSKI; Conservative Party, Alexander HALL; Nonparty Bloc for the Support of the Reforms (BBWR)
non-Communist, non-Solidarity: Confederation for an Independent Poland (KPN), Leszek MOCZULSKI; Polish Economic Program (PPG), Janusz REWINSKI; Christian Democrats (CHD), Andrzej OWSINSKI; German Minority (MN), Henryk KROL; Union of Real Politics (UPR), Janusz KORWIN-MIKKE; Democratic Party (SD), Antoni MACKIEWICZ; Party X, Stanislaw Tyminski
Communist origin or linked: Social Democracy (SDRP, party of Poland), Aleksander KWASNIEWSKI; Polish Peasants' Party (PSL), Waldemar PAWLAK; Democratic Left Alliance, Aleksander KWASNIEWSKI
Other political or pressure groups: powerful Roman Catholic Church; Solidarity (trade union); All Poland Trade Union Alliance (OPZZ), populist program
Member of: BIS, BSEC (observer), CBSS, CCC, CE, CEI, CERN, COCOM

(cooperating), CSCE, EBRD, ECE, FAO, GATT, IAEA, IBRD, ICAO, ICFTU, IDA, IFC, ILO, IMF, IMO, INMARSAT, INTELSAT (nonsignatory user), INTERPOL, IOC, IOM, ISO, ITU, LORCS, MINURSO, NACC, NAM (guest), NSG, OAS (observer), PCA, UN, UNCTAD, UNESCO, UNDOF, UNIDO, UNIFIL, UNIKOM, UNOMIG, UNPROFOR, UNTAC, UPU, WCL, WFTU, WHO, WIPO, WMO, WTO, ZC

Diplomatic representation in US:
chief of mission: Ambassador Jerzy KOZMINSKI
chancery: 2640 16th Street NW, Washington, DC 20009
telephone: (202) 234-3800 through 3802
FAX: (202) 328-6271
consulate(s) general: Chicago, Los Angeles, and New York

US diplomatic representation:
chief of mission: Ambassador Nicholas A. REY
embassy: Aleje Ujazdowskie 29/31, Warsaw
mailing address: American Embassy Warsaw, Unit 1340, or APO AE 09213-1340
telephone: [48] (2) 628-3041
FAX: [48] (2) 628-8298
consulate(s) general: Krakow, Poznan

Flag: two equal horizontal bands of white (top) and red; similar to the flags of Indonesia and Monaco which are red (top) and white

---

U.S. Government Contacts:

U.S. Trade Desk: (202) 482-4915

American Embassy Commercial Section
Ulica Wiejska 20
Warsaw, Poland
APO AE 09213 (WAW)
Tel: 48-22-21-45-15
Fax: 48-22-21-63-27

Poland Government Contacts:

Ministry of Foreign Economic Relations
Pl. Trzech Krzyzy 5
00-950 Warszawa
Tel: 693-50-00

Ploand Foreign Investment Agency (PAIZ)
Al. Roz 2
00-556 Warszawa, Poland
Tel: 48 2 621-6261
Fax: 48-2 621-8427

Chambers of Commerce & Organizations:

American Chamber of Commerce in Poland
Swietokrzyska 36 m 6, Entrance I
00-116 Warsaw, Poland
Tel: (48 22) 209-867, 209-962 Ext. 222, 223
Fax: (48 22) 622-5525

Travel:

International Hotels in Country:
Warsaw:
Bristol, Tel: 4822 02/625-25-25, Fax: 4822 02/625-25-77
Marriott, Tel: 4822 02/630-63-06, Fax: 4822 022/30-52-39
Holiday Inn, Tel: 4822/20-03-41, Fax: 4822/30-05-69.

ROMANIA

Economy

Overview: Despite the continuing difficulties in moving away from the former command system, the Romanian economy seems to have bottomed out in 1993. Market oriented reforms have been introduced fitfully since the downfall of CEAUSESCU in December 1989, with the result a growing private sector, especially in services. The slow pace of structural reform, however, has exacerbated Romania's high inflation rate and eroded real wages. Agricultural production rebounded in 1993 from the previous year's drought-reduced harvest; food supplies are adequate, but expensive. Bucharest resisted pressure to devalue its currency despite a $638 million trade deficit in the first half of 1993 and the emergence of a black market for hard currency. Unable to support the currency, the national bank, nonetheless, was forced to depreciate the currency 65% over the course of the year. The return of winter revealed that much of Romania's infrastructure had deteriorated over the last four years due to reduced levels of public investment. Residents of the capital reported frequent disruptions of heating and water services.

National product: GDP—purchasing power equivalent—$63.7 billion (1993 est.)
National product real growth rate: 1% (1993)
National product per capita: $2,700 (1993 est.)
Inflation rate (consumer prices): 6% per month (March 1994)
Unemployment rate: 11% (March 1994)
Budget:
revenues: $19 billion
expenditures: $20 billion, including capital expenditures of $2.1 billion (1991 est.)
Exports: $4 billion (f.o.b., 1993)
commodities: metals and metal products 24%, mineral products 14%, textiles 10.7%, electric machines and equipment 9.3%, transport materials 9.2% (1993)
partners: EC 36.1%, developing countries 27.4%, East and Central Europe 14.9%, EFTA 5.1%, Russia 5%, Japan 1.4%, US 1.3% (1993)
Imports: $5.4 billion (f.o.b., 1993)
commodities: minerals 29%, machinery and equipment 17.2%, textiles 10%, agricultural goods 9% (1993)
partners: EC 45.8%, East and Central Europe 8.6%, developing countries 22.6%, Russia 11%, EFTA 6.2%, US 5.0%, Japan 0.8% (1993)
External debt: $4 billion (1993)
Industrial production: growth rate -1% (1993 est.); accounts for 45% of GDP
Electricity:
capacity: 22,500,000 kW
production: 59 billion kWh
consumption per capita: 2,540 kWh (1992)
Industries: mining, timber, construction materials, metallurgy, chemicals, machine building, food processing, petroleum production and refining
Agriculture: accounts for 18% of GDP and 28% of labor force; major wheat and corn producer; other products—sugar beets, sunflower seed, potatoes, milk, eggs, meat, grapes

Illicit drugs: transshipment point for southwest Asian heroin and Latin American cocaine transiting the Balkan route
Economic aid: $NA
Currency: 1 leu (L) = 100 bani
Exchange rates: lei (L) per US$1—1,387.16 (January 1994), 760.05 (1993), 307.95 (1992), 76.39 (1991), 22.432 (1990), 14.922 (1989)
Fiscal year: calendar year

Communications

Railroads: 11,275 km total; 10,860 km 1.435-meter gauge, 370 km narrow gauge, 45 km broad gauge; 3,411 km electrified, 3,060 km double track; government owned (1987)
Highways:
total: 72,799 km
paved: 35,970 km
unpaved: gravel, crushed stone, stabilized earth 27,729 km; unsurfaced earth 9,100 km (1985)
Inland waterways: 1,724 km (1984)
Pipelines: crude oil 2,800 km, petroleum products 1,429 km, natural gas 6,400 km (1992)
Ports: Constanta, Galati, Braila, Mangalia; inland ports are Giurgiu, Drobeta-Turnu Severin, Orsova
Merchant marine: 241 ships (1,000 GRT or over) totaling 2,626,421 GRT/4,017,380 DWT, passenger-cargo 1, cargo 167, container 2, rail-car carrier 1, roll-on/roll-off cargo 7, oil tanker 14, bulk 49
Airports:
total: 234
usable: 74
with permanent-surface runways: 26
with runways over 3,659 m: 0
with runways 2,440-3,659 m: 21
with runways 1,060-2,439 m: 24
note: a C-130 can land on a 1,060-m airstrip
Telecommunications: poor service; about 2.3 million telephone customers; 89% of phone network is automatic; cable and open wire; trunk network is microwave; present phone density is 9.85 per 100 residents; roughly 3,300 villages with no service (February 1990); new digital international direct dial exchanges are in Bucharest (1993); broadcast stations—12 AM, 5 FM, 13 TV (1990); 1 satellite ground station using INTELSAT

Defense Forces

Branches: Army, Navy, Air and Air Defense Forces, Paramilitary Forces, Civil Defense
Manpower availability: males age 15-49 5,888,452; fit for military service 4,972,834; reach military age (20) annually 193,901 (1994 est.)
Defense expenditures: 137 billion lei, 3% of GDP (1993); note—conversion of defense expenditures into US dollars using the current exchange rate could produce misleading results

Geography

Location: Balkan State, Southeastern Europe, bordering the Black Sea between Bulgaria and Ukraine
Map references: Ethnic Groups in Eastern Europe, Europe, Standard Time Zones of the World
Area:
total area: 237,500 sq km
land area: 230,340 sq km
comparative area: slightly smaller than Oregon
Land boundaries: total 2,508 km, Bulgaria 608 km, Hungary 443 km, Moldova 450 km, Serbia and Montenegro 476 km (all with Serbia), Ukraine (north) 362 km, Ukraine (south) 169 km
Coastline: 225 km
Maritime claims:
contiguous zone: 24 nm
continental shelf: 200-m depth or to depth of exploitation
exclusive economic zone: 200 nm
territorial sea: 12 nm
International disputes: no official territorial claim by either Moldova or Romania, but nationalists in Romania seek the merger of Moldova with Romania; potential future dispute by Moldova and Romania against

Ukraine over former southern and northern Bessarabian areas
Climate: temperate; cold, cloudy winters with frequent snow and fog; sunny summers with frequent showers and thunderstorms
Terrain: central Transylvanian Basin is separated from the Plain of Moldavia on the east by the Carpathian Mountains and separated from the Walachian Plain on the south by the Transylvanian Alps
Natural resources: petroleum (reserves declining), timber, natural gas, coal, iron ore, salt
Land use:
arable land: 43%
permanent crops: 3%
meadows and pastures: 19%
forest and woodland: 28%
other: 7%
Irrigated land: 34,500 sq km (1989 est.)
Environment:
current issues: soil erosion and degradation; water pollution; air pollution in south from industrial effluents; contamination of Danube delta wetlands
natural hazards: earthquakes most severe in south and southwest; geologic structure and climate promote landslides
international agreements: party to—Air Pollution, Antarctic Treaty, Environmental Modification, Hazardous Wastes, Nuclear Test Ban, Ozone Layer Protection, Ship Pollution, Wetlands; signed, but not ratified—Antarctic-Environmental Protocol, Biodiversity, Climate Change, Law of the Sea
Note: controls most easily traversable land route between the Balkans, Moldova, and Ukraine

---

People

Population: 23,181,415 (July 1994 est.)
note: the Romanian census of January 1992 gives the population for that date as 22.749 million; the government estimates that population declined in 1993 by 0.3%
Population growth rate: 0.06% (1994 est.)
Birth rate: 13.66 births/1,000 population (1994 est.)
Death rate: 10.02 deaths/1,000 population (1994 est.)
Net migration rate: -3.07 migrant(s)/1,000 population (1994 est.)
Infant mortality rate: 19.9 deaths/1,000 live births (1994 est.)
Life expectancy at birth:
total population: 71.74 years
male: 68.81 years
female: 74.84 years (1994 est.)
Total fertility rate: 1.82 children born/woman (1994 est.)
Nationality:
noun: Romanian(s)
adjective: Romanian
Ethnic divisions: Romanian 89.1%, Hungarian 8.9%, German 0.4%, Ukrainian, Serb, Croat, Russian, Turk, and Gypsy 1.6%
Religions: Romanian Orthodox 70%, Roman Catholic 6% (of which 3% are Uniate), Protestant 6%, unaffiliated 18%
Languages: Romanian, Hungarian, German
Literacy: age 15 and over can read and write (1978 est.)
total population: 98%
male: NA%
female: NA%
Labor force: 10,945,700
by occupation: industry 38%, agriculture 28%, other 34% (1989)

Government

Names:
conventional long form: none
conventional short form: Romania
local long form: none
local short form: Romania
Digraph: RO
Type: republic
Capital: Bucharest
Administrative divisions: 40 counties (judete, singular—judet) and 1 municipality* (municipiu); Alba, Arad, Arges, Bacau, Bihor, Bistrita-Nasaud, Botosani, Braila, Brasov, Bucuresti*, Buzau, Calarasi, Caras-Severin, Cluj, Constanta, Covasna, Dimbovita, Dolj, Galati, Gorj, Giurgiu, Harghita, Hunedoara,

Ialomita, Iasi, Maramures, Mehedinti, Mures, Neamt, Olt, Prahova, Salaj, Satu Mare, Sibiu, Suceava, Teleorman, Timis, Tulcea, Vaslui, Vilcea, Vrancea
Independence: 1881 (from Turkey; republic proclaimed 30 December 1947)
National holiday: National Day of Romania, 1 December (1990)
Constitution: 8 December 1991
Legal system: former mixture of civil law system and Communist legal theory is being revised to conform with European norms
Suffrage: 18 years of age; universal
Executive branch:
chief of state: President Ion ILIESCU (since 20 June 1990, previously President of Provisional Council of National Unity since 23 December 1989); election last held 27 September 1992—with runoff between top two candidates on 11 October 1992 (next to be held NA 1996); results—Ion ILIESCU 61.4%, Emil CONSTANTINESCU 38.6%
head of government: Prime Minister Nicolae VACAROIU (since November 1992)
cabinet: Council of Ministers; appointed by the prime minister
Legislative branch: bicameral Parliament
Senate (Senat): elections last held 27 September 1992 (next to be held NA 1996); results—PDSR 27.5%, CDR 22.5%, PP-(FSN) 11%, others 39%; seats—(143 total) PDSR 49, CDR 34, PP-(FSN) 18, PUNR 14, UDMR 12, PRM 6, PDAR 5, PSM 5
House of Deputies (Adunarea Deputatilor): elections last held 27 September 1992 (next to be held NA 1996); results—PDSR 27.5%, CDR 22.5%, PP-(FSN) 11%, others 39%; seats—(341 total) PDSR 117, CDR 82, PP-(FSN) 43, PUNR 30, UDMR 27, PRM 16, PSM 13, other 13
Judicial branch: Supreme Court of Justice, Constitutional Court
Political parties and leaders: Democratic Party (PD-(FSN)), Petre ROMAN; Party of Social Democracy in Romania (PDSR), Adrian NASTASE; Democratic Union of Hungarians in Romania (UDMR), Bela MARKO; National Liberal Party (PNL), Mircea IONESCU-QUINTUS; National Peasants' Christian and Democratic Party (PNTCD), Corneliu COPOSU; Romanian National Unity Party (PUNR), Gheorghe FUNAR; Socialist Labor Party (PSM), Ilie VERDET; Agrarian Democratic Party of Romania (PDAR), Victor SURDU; The Democratic Convention (CDR), Emil CONSTANTINESCU; Romania Mare Party (PRM), Corneliu Vadim TUDOR
note: numerous other small parties exist but almost all failed to gain representation in the most recent election
Other political or pressure groups: various human rights and professional associations
Member of: ACCT (observer), BIS, BSEC, CCC, CE, CEI (participating), CSCE, EBRD, ECE, FAO, G-9, G-77, GATT, IAEA, IBRD, ICAO, ICFTU, IFAD, IFC, ILO, IMF, IMO, INMARSAT, INTELSAT, INTERPOL, IOC, IOM (observer), ISO, ITU, LORCS, NACC, NAM (guest), NSG, OAS (observer), PCA, UN, UNCTAD, UNESCO, UNIDO, UNIKOM, UNOSOM, UPU, WCL, WFTU, WHO, WIPO, WMO, WTO, ZC
Diplomatic representation in US:
chief of mission: (vacant)
chancery: 1607 23rd Street NW, Washington, DC 20008
telephone: (202) 332-4846, 4848, 4851
FAX: (202) 232-4748
consulate(s) general: New York
US diplomatic representation:
chief of mission: Ambassador John R. DAVIS, Jr.
embassy: Strada Tudor Arghezi 7-9, Bucharest
mailing address: AmEmbassy (Buch), Unit 1315, Bucharest; APO AE 09213-1315
telephone: [40] (1) 210-4042
FAX: [40] (1) 210-0395
Flag: three equal vertical bands of blue (hoist side), yellow, and red; the national coat of arms that used to be centered in the yellow band has been removed; now similar to the flags of Andorra and Chad

---

U.S. Government Contacts:

U.S. Trade Desk: (202) 482-4915

American Embassy Commercial Section
Strada Tudor Arghezi 7-9
Bucharest, Romania
APO AE 09213 (BUCH)
Tel: 40-010-40-40
Fax: 40-0-11-84-47

Chambers of Commerce & Organizations:

American Chamber of Commerce in Romania
Str. Gh. Manu nr. 9
71 106 Bucharest 1, Romania
Tel: (40 1) 659-3600 Ext. 127
Fax: (40 1) 650-6684

Travel:

International Hotels in Country:
Bucharest:
Helvetia, Tel: 40 01/3110566, Fax: 40 01/3110567
Intercontinental, Tel: 40 01/6140400, Fax: 40 01/3120486
Continental, Tel: 40 01/6145348, Fax: 40 01/3120134.

RUSSIA

Economy

Overview: Russia, a vast country with a wealth of natural resources, a well-educated population, and a diverse industrial base, continues to experience severe difficulties in moving from its old centrally planned economy to a modern market economy. President YEL'TSIN's government has made some progress toward a market economy by freeing most prices, slashing defense spending, unifying foreign exchange rates, and launching an ambitious privatization program. Yet much of the old order persists and YEL'TSIN faces formidable opposition to further measures such as the reduction of subsidies to old-line industries. Output continues to fall although the mix is gradually becoming more responsive to Russia's needs. According to Russian official data, GDP declined by 12% in 1993 compared with 19% in 1992. Industrial output in 1993 fell 16% with all major sectors taking a hit. Agricultural production, meanwhile, was down 6%. The grain harvest totalled 99 million tons—some 8 million tons less than in 1992. Unemployment climbed in 1993 but remained low by Western standards. The official number of unemployed rose from 578,000 at the beginning of 1993 to about 1 million—or roughly 1.4% of the work force—by yearend. According to the Russian labor minister, the actual number of unemployed probably was closer to 4 million. Government fears of large-scale unemployment continued to hamper industrial restructuring efforts. According to official statistics, average real wages remained flat. Nonetheless, a substantial portion of the population, particularly the elderly and people in remote areas, finds its well-being steadily shrinking. The disparity in incomes between the rich and poor continued to rise in 1993, primarily reflecting the high earnings of enterprise managers and persons employed in the emerging private sector. The government tried to narrow the income gap by raising the wages of budget-funded workers—mainly teachers and health care specialists. Official data may overstate hardships, because many Russians supplement their income by moonlighting or by bartering goods and services, activities that often go unreported. Russia made good progress on privatization in 1993 despite active opposition from key cabinet members, hard-line legislators, and antireform regional leaders. By yearend, for example, roughly 35% of Russia's medium and large state enterprises had been auctioned, while the number of private farms in Russia increased by 86,000, reaching a total of 170,000. As a result, about 6% of agricultural land now has been privatized. Financial stabilization continued to remain a challenge for the government. Moscow tightened financial policies in early 1993—including postponing planned budget spending—and succeeded in reducing monthly inflation from 27% in January to 20% in May and June. In the summer, however, the government relaxed austerity measures in the face of mounting pressure from industry and agriculture, sparking a new round of inflation; the monthly inflation rate jumped to 25% in August. In response, Moscow announced a package of measures designed to curb government spending and inflation. It included eliminating bread subsidies, delaying payment obligations, raising interest rates, and phasing out concessionary Central Bank credits to enterprises and regions. The measures met with some success; the monthly inflation rate declined to 13% in December. According to official statistics, Russia's 1993 trade with nations outside the former Soviet Union produced a $16 billion surplus, up from $6 billion in 1992. Moscow arrested the steep drop in exports that it had been suffering as a result of ruptured ties with former trading partners, output declines, and erratic efforts to move to world prices. Foreign sales—comprised largely of oil, natural gas, and other raw materials—grew slightly. Imports were down by 15% or so as a result of new import taxes and Moscow's reluctance to increase its debt burden by purchasing grain and other goods with foreign credits. Russian trade with other former Soviet republics continued to decline and yielded a surplus of some $5 billion. At the same time, Russia paid only a fraction of the roughly $20 billion in debt coming due in 1993, and by mid-year, Russia's foreign debt had amounted to $81.5 billion. While Moscow reached agreement to restructure debts with Paris Club official creditors in April 1993, Moscow's refusal to waive its right to sovereign immunity kept Russia and its bank creditors from agreeing to restructure Moscow's commercial loans. Capital flight continued to be a serious problem in 1993, with billions of dollars in assets owned by Russians being parked abroad at yearend. Russia's capital stock continues to deteriorate because of insufficient maintenance and new construction. The capital stock on average is twice the age of capital stock in the West. Many years will pass before Russia can take full advantage of its natural resources and its human assets.

National product: GDP—purchasing power equivalent—$775.4 billion (1993 estimate from the UN International Comparison Program, as extended to 1991 and published in the World Bank's World Development Report 1993; and as extrapolated to 1993 using official Russian statistics, which are very uncertain because of major economic changes since 1990)

National product real growth rate: -12% (1993 est.)

National product per capita: $5,190 (1993 est.)

Inflation rate (consumer prices): 21% per month (average 1993); 13% per month (December 1993)

Unemployment rate: 1.4% (1 January 1994; official data)

Budget:

revenues: $NA

expenditures: $NA, including capital expenditures of $NA

Exports: $43 billion (f.o.b., 1993)

commodities: petroleum and petroleum products, natural gas, wood and wood products, metals, chemicals, and a wide variety of civilian and military manufactures

partners: Europe, North America, Japan, Third World countries, Cuba

Imports: $27 billion (f.o.b., 1993)

commodities: machinery and equipment, chemicals, consumer goods, grain, meat, sugar, semifinished metal products

partners: Europe, North America, Japan, Third World countries, Cuba

External debt: $81.5 billion (mid-year 1993 est.)

Industrial production: growth rate -16% (1993 est.)

Electricity:

capacity: 213,000,000 KW

production: 956 billion kWh

consumption per capita: 6,782 kWh (1 January 1992)

Industries: complete range of mining and extractive industries producing coal, oil, gas, chemicals, and metals; all forms of machine building from rolling mills to high-performance aircraft and space vehicles; ship-building; road and rail transportation equipment; communications equipment; agricultural machinery, tractors, and construction equipment; electric power

generating and transmitting equipment; medical and scientific instruments; consumer durables
Agriculture: grain, sugar beet, sunflower seeds, meat, milk, vegetables, fruits; because of its northern location does not grow citrus, cotton, tea, and other warm climate products
Illicit drugs: illicit cultivator of cannabis and opium poppy; mostly for domestic consumption; government has active eradication program; used as transshipment point for Asian and Latin American illicit drugs to Western Europe and Latin America
Economic aid:
recipient: US commitments, including Ex-Im (1990-93), $13 billion; other countries, ODA and OOF bilateral commitments (1988-93), $115 billion
Currency: 1 ruble (R) = 100 kopeks
Exchange rates: rubles per US$1—1,247 (27 December 1993), 415 (24 December 1992); nominal exchange rate still deteriorating but real exchange rate strengthening
Fiscal year: calendar year

Communications

Railroads: 158,100 km all 1.520-meter broad gauge; 86,800 km in common carrier service, of which 48,900 km are diesel traction and 37,900 km are electric traction; 71,300 km serves specific industry and is not available for common carrier use (30 June 1993)
Highways:
total: 893,000 km
paved and gravel: 677,000 km
unpaved: 216,000 km
Inland waterways: total navigable routes in general use 100,000 km; routes with navigation guides serving the Russian River Fleet 95,900 km; of which routes with night navigational aids 60,400 km; man-made navigable routes 16,900 km (30 June 1993)
Pipelines: crude oil 48,000 km, petroleum products 15,000 km, natural gas 140,000 km (30 June 1993)
Ports: coastal—St. Petersburg, Kaliningrad, Murmansk, Petropavlovsk, Arkhangel'sk, Novorossiysk, Vladivostok, Nakhodka, Kholmsk, Korsakov, Magadan, Tiksi, Tuapse, Vanino, Vostochnyy, Vyborg; inland—Astrakhan', Nizhniy Novgorod, Kazan', Khabarovsk, Krasnoyarsk, Samara, Moscow, Rostov, Volgograd
Merchant marine: 867 ships (1,000 GRT or over) totaling 8,084,988 GRT/11,124,929 DWT, cargo 454, container 82, multi-function large load carrier 3, barge carrier 2, roll-on/roll-off cargo 74, oil tanker 125, bulk cargo 26, chemical tanker 9, specialized tanker 2, combination ore/oil 16, passenger cargo 5, short-sea passenger 18, passenger 6, combination bulk 28, refrigerated cargo 17
Airports:
total: 2,550
usable: 964
with permanent-surface runways: 565
with runways over 3,659 m: 19
with runways 2,440-3,659 m: 275
with runways 1,220-2,439 m: 426
Telecommunications: Russia is enlisting foreign help, by means of joint ventures, to speed up the modernization of its telecommunications system; NMT-450 analog cellular telephone networks are operational and growing in Moscow and St. Petersburg; expanded access to international E-mail service available via Sprint network; intercity fiberoptic cable installation remains limited; the inadequacy of Russian telecommunications is a severe handicap to the economy, especially with respect to international connections; total installed telephones 24,400,000, of which in urban areas 20,900,000 and in rural areas 3,500,000; of these, total installed in homes 15,400,000; total pay phones for long distant calls 34,100; telephone density is about 164 telephones per 1,000 persons (in 1992, only 661,000 new telephones were installed compared with 855,000 in 1991 and in 1992 the number of unsatisfied applications for telephones reached 11,000,000); international traffic is handled by an inadequate system of satellites, land lines, microwave radio relay and outdated submarine cables; this traffic passes through the international gateway switch in Moscow which carries most of the international traffic for the other countries of the Commonwealth of Independent States; a new Russian Raduga satellite will link

Moscow and St. Petersburg with Rome from whence calls will be relayed to destinations in Europe and overseas; satellite ground stations—INTELSAT, Intersputnik, Eutelsat (Moscow), INMARSAT, Orbita; broadcast stations—1,050 AM/FM/SW (reach 98.6% of population), 7,183 TV; receiving sets—54,200,000 TVs, 48,800,000 radio receivers, 74,300,000 radio receivers with multiple speaker systems for program diffusion

Defense Forces

Branches: Ground Forces, Navy, Air Forces, Air Defense Forces, Strategic Rocket Forces, Command and General Support, Security Forces
Manpower availability: males age 15-49 37,706,825; fit for military service 29,623,429; reach military age (18) annually 1,098,307 (1994 est.)
Defense expenditures: $NA, NA% of GDP

Geography

Location: Northern Asia (that part west of the Urals is sometimes included with Europe), between Europe and the North Pacific Ocean
Map references: Asia, Commonwealth of Independent States—Central Asian States, Commonwealth of Independent States—European States, Standard Time Zones of the World
Area:
total area: 17,075,200 sq km
land area: 16,995,800 sq km
comparative area: slightly more than 1.8 times the size of the US
Land boundaries: total 20,139 km, Azerbaijan 284 km, Belarus 959 km, China (southeast) 3,605 km, China (south) 40 km, Estonia 290 km, Finland 1,313 km, Georgia 723 km, Kazakhstan 6,846 km, North Korea 19 km, Latvia 217 km, Lithuania (Kaliningrad Oblast) 227 km, Mongolia 3,441 km, Norway 167 km, Poland (Kaliningrad Oblast) 432 km, Ukraine 1,576 km
Coastline: 37,653 km
Maritime claims:
continental shelf: 200-m depth or to depth of exploitation
exclusive economic zone: 200 nm
territorial sea: 12 nm
International disputes: inherited disputes from former USSR including: sections of the boundary with China; islands of Etorofu, Kunashiri, and Shikotan and the Habomai group occupied by the Soviet Union in 1945, administered by Russia, claimed by Japan; maritime dispute with Norway over portion of the Barents Sea; Russia may dispute current de facto maritime border of midpoint of Caspian Sea from shore; potential dispute with Ukraine over Crimea; has made no territorial claim in Antarctica (but has reserved the right to do so) and does not recognize the claims of any other nation
Climate: ranges from steppes in the south through humid continental in much of European Russia; subarctic in Siberia to tundra climate in the polar north; winters vary from cool along Black Sea coast to frigid in Siberia; summers vary from warm in the steppes to cool along Arctic coast
Terrain: broad plain with low hills west of Urals; vast coniferous forest and tundra in Siberia; uplands and mountains along southern border regions
Natural resources: wide natural resource base including major deposits of oil, natural gas, coal, and many strategic minerals, timber
note: formidable obstacles of climate, terrain, and distance hinder exploitation of natural resources
Land use:
arable land: 8%
permanent crops: NA%
meadows and pastures: NA%
forest and woodland: NA%
other: NA%
note: agricultural land accounts for 13% of the total land area
Irrigated land: 56,000 sq km (1992)
Environment:
current issues: air pollution from heavy industry, emissions of coal-fired electric plants, and transportation in major cities; industrial and agricultural pollution of inland

waterways and sea coasts; deforestation; soil erosion; soil contamination from improper application of agricultural chemicals; scattered areas of sometimes intense radioactive contamination
natural hazards: permafrost over much of Siberia is a major impediment to development
international agreements: party to—Air Pollution, Air Pollution-Nitrogen Oxides, Air Pollution-Sulphur, Antarctic Treaty, Environmental Modification, Marine Dumping, Ozone Layer Protection, Ship Pollution, Tropical Timber, Wetlands; signed, but not ratified—Antarctic-Environmental Protocol, Biodiversity, Climate Change, Hazardous Wastes, Law of the Sea
Note: largest country in the world in terms of area but unfavorably located in relation to major sea lanes of the world; despite its size, much of the country lacks proper soils and climates (either too cold or too dry) for agriculture

People

Population: 149,608,953 (July 1994 est.)
Population growth rate: 0.2% (1994 est.)
Birth rate: 12.67 births/1,000 population (1994 est.)
Death rate: 11.34 deaths/1,000 population (1994 est.)
Net migration rate: 0.7 migrant(s)/1,000 population (1994 est.)
Infant mortality rate: 27 deaths/1,000 live births (1994 est.)
Life expectancy at birth:
total population: 68.89 years
male: 63.85 years
female: 74.2 years (1994 est.)
Total fertility rate: 1.83 children born/woman (1994 est.)
Nationality:
noun: Russian(s)
adjective: Russian
Ethnic divisions: Russian 81.5%, Tatar 3.8%, Ukrainian 3%, Chuvash 1.2%, Bashkir 0.9%, Byelorussian 0.8%, Moldavian 0.7%, other 8.1%
Religions: Russian Orthodox, Muslim, other
Languages: Russian, other
Literacy: age 9-49 can read and write (1970)
total population: 100%
male: 100%
female: 100%
Labor force: 75 million (1993 est.)
by occupation: production and economic services 83.9%, government 16.1%

Government

Names:
conventional long form: Russian Federation
conventional short form: Russia
local long form: Rossiyskaya Federatsiya
local short form: Rossiya
former: Russian Soviet Federative Socialist Republic
Digraph: RS
Type: federation
Capital: Moscow
Administrative divisions: 21 autonomous republics (avtomnykh respublik, singular—avtomnaya respublika); Adygea (Maykop), Bashkortostan (Ufa), Buryatia (Ulan-Ude), Chechenia (Groznyy), Chuvashia (Cheboksary), Dagestan (Makhachkala), Gorno-Altay (Gorno-Altaysk), Ingushetia (Nazran'), Kabardino-Balkaria (Nal'chik), Kalmykia (Elista), Karachay-Cherkessia (Cherkessk), Karelia (Petrozavodsk), Khakassia (Abakan), Komi (Syktyvkar), Mari El (Yoshkar-Ola), Mordovia (Saransk), North Ossetia (Vladikavkaz), Tatarstan (Kazan'), Tuva (Kyzyl), Udmurtia (Izhevsk), Yakutia (Yakutsk); 49 oblasts (oblastey, singular—oblast'); Amur (Blagoveshchensk), Arkhangel'sk, Astrakhan', Belgorod, Bryansk, Chelyabinsk, Chita, Irkutsk, Ivanovo, Kaliningrad, Kaluga, Kamchatka (Petropavlovsk-Kamchatskiy), Kemerovo, Kirov, Kostroma, Kurgan, Kursk, Leningrad (St. Petersburg), Lipetsk, Magadan, Moscow, Murmansk, Nizhniy Novgorod, Novgorod, Novosibirsk, Omsk, Orel, Orenburg, Penza, Perm', Pskov, Rostov, Ryazan', Sakhalin (Yuzhno-Sakhalinsk), Samara, Saratov, Smolensk, Sverdlovsk (Yekaterinburg), Tambov, Tomsk, Tula, Tver', Tyumen', Ul'yanovsk, Vladimir, Volgograd, Vologda,

Voronezh, Yaroslavl'; 6 krays (krayev, singular—kray); Altay (Barnaul), Khabarovsk, Krasnodar, Krasnoyarsk, Primorskiy (Vladivostok), Stavropol'
note: the autonomous republics of Chechenia and Ingushetia were formerly the automous republic of Checheno-Ingushetia (the boundary between Chechenia and Ingushetia has yet to be determined); the cities of Moscow and St. Petersburg are federal cities; an administrative division has the same name as its administrative center (exceptions have the administrative center name following in parentheses)
Independence: 24 August 1991 (from Soviet Union)
National holiday: Independence Day, June 12 (1990)
Constitution: adopted 12 December 1993
Legal system: based on civil law system; judicial review of legislative acts
Suffrage: 18 years of age; universal
Executive branch:
chief of state: President Boris Nikolayevich YEL'TSIN (since 12 June 1991) election last held 12 June 1991 (next to be held 1996); results—percent of vote by party NA%; note—no vice president; if the president dies in office, cannot exercise his powers because of ill health, is impeached, or resigns, the premier succeeds him; the premier serves as acting president until a new presidential election, which must be held within three months
head of government: Premier and Chairman of the Council of Ministers Viktor Stepanovich CHERNOMYRDIN (since 14 December 1992); First Deputy Chairman of the Council of Ministers Oleg SOSKOVETS (since 30 April 1993)
Security Council: (originally established as a presidential advisory body in June 1991, but restructured in March 1992 with responsibility for managing individual and state security)
Presidential Administration: (drafts presidential edicts and provides staff and policy support to the entire executive branch)
cabinet: Council of Ministers; appointed by the president
Group of Assistants: (schedules president's appointments, processes presidential edicts and other official documents, and houses the president's press service and primary speechwriters)
Council of Heads of Republics: (includes the leaders of the 21 ethnic-based Republics)
Council of Heads of Administrations: (includes the leaders of the 68 autonomous territories and regions, and the mayors of Moscow and St. Petersburg)
Presidential Council: (prepares policy papers for the president)
Legislative branch: bicameral Federal Assembly
Federation Council: elections last held 12 December 1993 (next to be held NA); note—two members elected from each of Russia's 89 territorial units for a total of 176 deputies; 2 seats unfilled as of 15 May 1994 (Chechenia did not participate in the election); Speaker Vladimir SHUMEYKO (Russia's Choice)
State Duma: elections last held 12 December 1993 (next to be held NA December 1995); results—percent of vote by party NA; seats—(450 total) Russia's Choice 78, New Regional Policy 66, Liberal Democrats 63, Agrarian Party 55, Communist Party of the Russian Federation 45, Unity and Accord 30, Yavlinskiy Bloc 27, Women of Russia 23, Democratic Party of Russia 15, Russia's Path 12, other parties 23, affiliation unknown 12, unfilled (as of 13 March 1994; Chechnya did not participate in the election) 1; Speaker Ivan RYBKIN (Agrarian Party)
Judicial branch: Constitutional Court, Supreme Court (highest court for criminal, civil, and administrative cases), Superior Court of Arbitration (highest court that resolves economic disputes)
Political parties and leaders:
pro-market democrats: Party of Russian Unity and Accord, Sergey SHAKHRAY; Russia's Choice electoral association, Yegor GAYDAR; Russian Movement for Democratic Reforms electoral association, Anatoliy SOBCHAK; Yavlinskiy-Boldyrev-Lukin Bloc electoral association, Grigoriy YAVLINSKIY
centrists/special interest parties: Civic Union for Stability, Justice, and Progress, Arkadiy VOL'SKIY; Constructive-Ecological Movement of Russia, Anatoliy PANFILOV;

Democratic Party of Russia, Nikolay TRAVKIN; Dignity and Charity Federal Political Movement, Konstantin FROLOV; Russia's Future-New Names electoral association, Vyacheslav LASHCHEVSKIY; Women of Russia Party, Alevtina FEDULOVA
anti-market and/or ultranationalist parties: Agrarian Party, Mikhail LAPSHIN; Communist Party of the Russian Federation, Gennadiy ZYUGANOV; Liberal Democratic Party of Russia, Vladimir ZHIRINOVSKIY
note: more than 20 political parties and associations tried to gather enough signatures to run slates of candidates in the 12 December 1993 legislative elections, but only 13 succeeded
Other political or pressure groups: NA
Member of: BSEC, CBSS, CCC, CE (guest), CERN (observer), CIS, CSCE, EBRD, ECE, ESCAP, IAEA, IBRD, ICAO, IDA, IFC, ILO, IMF, IMO, INMARSAT, INTELSAT, INTERPOL, IOC, IOM (observer), ISO, ITU, LORCS, MINURSO, NACC, NSG, OAS (observer), PCA, UN, UNCTAD, UNESCO, UNIDO, UNIKOM, UNOMOZ, UNPROFOR UN Security Council, UNTAC, UN Trusteeship Council, UNTSO, UPU, WHO, WIPO, WMO, WTO, ZC
Diplomatic representation in US:
chief of mission: Ambassador Vladimir Petrovich LUKIN
chancery: 1125 16th Street NW, Washington, DC 20036
telephone: (202) 628-7551 and 8548
consulate(s) general: New York, San Francisco, and Seattle
consulate(s): Washington
US diplomatic representation:
chief of mission: Ambassador Thomas R. PICKERING
embassy: Novinskiy Bul'var 19/23, Moscow
mailing address: APO AE 09721
telephone: [7] (095) 252-2451 through 2459
FAX: [7] (095)-4261/4270
consulate(s): St. Petersburg, Vladivostok
Flag: three equal horizontal bands of white (top), blue, and red

---

U.S. Government Contacts:

U.S. Trade Desk: (202) 482-0988

Legal Services:

Studio Uckmar
UL Medvedeva 13/1
103006 Moscow, Russia
Tel: 007-095-9730547
007-095-9730549
Fax: 007-095-9730551
Taxation, Corporate, General International Business Law, Administrative Law, Litigation.

Travel:

International Hotels in Country:
Moscow:
Metropole, Tel: 7-095-927-6000
Savoy, Tel: 7-095-929-8500
Slavianskaya, Tel: 7-095-941-8020.

SERBIA AND MOTENEGRO

Note: Serbia and Montenegro have asserted the formation of a joint independent state, but this entity has not been formally recognized as a state by the US; the US view is that the Socialist Federal Republic of Yugoslavia (SFRY) has dissolved and that none of the successor republics represents its continuation

Economy

Overview: The swift collapse of the Yugoslav federation has been followed by bloody ethnic warfare, the destabilization of republic boundaries, and the breakup of important interrepublic trade flows. Serbia and Montenegro faces major economic problems; output has dropped sharply, particularly in 1993. First, like the other former Yugoslav republics, it depended on its sister republics for large amounts of foodstuffs, energy supplies, and manufactures. Wide varieties in climate, mineral resources, and levels of technology among the republics accentuate this interdependence, as did the communist practice of concentrating much industrial output in a small number of giant plants. The breakup of many of the trade links, the sharp drop in output as industrial plants lost suppliers and markets, and the destruction of physical assets in the fighting all have contributed to the economic difficulties of the republics. One singular factor in the economic situation of Serbia and Montenegro is the continuation in office of a communist government that is primarily interested in political and military mastery, not economic reform. A further complication is the imposition of economic sanctions by the UN.

National product: GDP—exchange rate conversion—$10 billion (1993 est.)

National product real growth rate: NA%

National product per capita: $1,000 (1993 est.)

Inflation rate (consumer prices): hyperinflation (1993)

Unemployment rate: more than 60% (1993 est.)

Budget:

revenues: $NA

expenditures: $NA, including capital expenditures of $NA

Exports: $4.4 billion (f.o.b., 1990)

commodities: machinery and transport equipment 29%, manufactured goods 28.5%, miscellaneous manufactured articles 13.5%, chemicals 11%, food and live animals 9%, raw materials 6%, fuels and lubricants 2%, beverages and tobacco 1%

partners: prior to the imposition of sanctions by the UN Security Council trade partners were principally the other former Yugoslav republics; Italy, Germany, other EC, the FSU countries, East European countries, US

Imports: $6.4 billion (c.i.f., 1990)

commodities: machinery and transport equipment 26%, fuels and lubricants 18%, manufactured goods 16%, chemicals 12.5%, food and live animals 11%, miscellaneous manufactured items 8%, raw materials, including coking coal for the steel industry 7%, beverages, tobacco, and edible oils 1.5%

partners: prior to the imposition of sanctions by the UN Security Council the trade partners were principally the other former Yugoslav republics; the FSU countries, EC countries (mainly Italy and Germany), East European countries, US
External debt: $4.2 billion (1993 est.)
Industrial production: growth rate -42% (1993 est.)
Electricity:
capacity: 8,850,000 kW
production: 42 billion kWh
consumption per capita: 3,950 kWh (1992)
Industries: machine building (aircraft, trucks, and automobiles; armored vehicles and weapons; electrical equipment; agricultural machinery), metallurgy (steel, aluminum, copper, lead, zinc, chromium, antimony, bismuth, cadmium), mining (coal, bauxite, nonferrous ore, iron ore, limestone), consumer goods (textiles, footwear, foodstuffs, appliances), electronics, petroleum products, chemicals, and pharmaceuticals
Agriculture: the fertile plains of Vojvodina produce 80% of the cereal production of the former Yugoslavia and most of the cotton, oilseeds, and chicory; Vojvodina also produces fodder crops to support intensive beef and dairy production; Serbia proper, although hilly, has a well-distributed rainfall and a long growing season; produces fruit, grapes, and cereals; in this area, livestock production (sheep and cattle) and dairy farming prosper; Kosovo produces fruits, vegetables, tobacco, and a small amount of cereals; the mountainous pastures of Kosovo and Montenegro support sheep and goat husbandry; Montenegro has only a small agriculture sector, mostly near the coast where a Mediterranean climate permits the culture of olives, citrus, grapes, and rice
Illicit drugs: NA
Economic aid: $NA
Currency: 1 Yugoslav New Dinar (YD) = 100 paras
Exchange rates: Yugoslav New Dinars (YD) per US $1—1,100,000 (15 June 1993), 28.230 (December 1991), 15.162 (1990), 15.528 (1989), 0.701 (1988), 0.176 (1987)
Fiscal year: calendar year

Communications

Railroads: NA
Highways:
total: 46,019 km
paved: 26,949 km
unpaved: gravel 10,373 km; earth 8,697 km (1990)
Inland waterways: NA km
Pipelines: crude oil 415 km, petroleum products 130 km, natural gas 2,110 km
Ports: coastal—Bar; inland—Belgrade
Merchant marine:
Montenegro: 42 ships (1,000 GRT or over) totaling 804,156 GRT/1,368,813 DWT (controlled by Montenegrin beneficial owners) cargo 16, container 5, bulk 19, passenger ship 1, combination ore/oil 1
note: most under Maltese flag
Serbia: total 3 (1,000 GRT or over) totaling 246,631 GRT/451,843 DWT (controlled by Serbian beneficial owners)
bulk 2, conbination tanker/ore carrier 1
note: all under the flag of Saint Vincent and the Grenadines; no ships remain under Yugoslav flag
Airports:
total: 55
usable: 51
with permanent-surface runways: 18
with runways over 3,659 m: 0
with runways 2,440-3,659 m: 7
with runways 1,220-2,439 m: 11
Telecommunications: 700,000 telephones; broadcast stations—26 AM, 9 FM, 18 TV; 2,015,000 radios; 1,000,000 TVs; satellite ground stations—1 Atlantic Ocean INTELSAT

Defense Forces

Branches: People's Army—Ground Forces (internal and border troops), Naval Forces, Air and Air Defense Forces, Frontier Guard, Territorial Defense Force, Civil Defense
Manpower availability:
Montenegro: males age 15-49 179,868; fit for military service 146,158; reach military age (19) annually 5,399 (1994 est.)

Serbia: males age 15-49 2,546,717; fit for military service 2,048,921; reach military age (19) annually 80,937 (1994 est.)
Defense expenditures: 245 billion dinars, 4%-6% of GDP (1992 est.); note—conversion of defense expenditures into US dollars using the prevailing exchange rate could produce misleading results

Geography

Location: Balkan State, Southeastern Europe, bordering the Adriatic Sea, between Bosnia and Herzegovina and Bulgaria
Map references: Ethnic Groups in Eastern Europe, Europe, Standard Time Zones of the World
Area:
total area: 102,350 sq km
land area: 102,136 sq km
comparative area: slightly larger than Kentucky
note: Serbia has a total area and a land area of 88,412 sq km making it slightly larger than Maine; Montenegro has a total area of 13,938 sq km and a land area of 13,724 sq km making it slightly larger than Connecticut
Land boundaries: total 2,246 km, Albania 287 km (114 km with Serbia; 173 km with Motenegro), Bosnia and Herzegovina 527 km (312 km with Serbia; 215 km with Montenegro), Bulgaria 318 km, Croatia (north) 241 km, Croatia (south) 25 km, Hungary 151 km, The Former Yugoslav Republic of Macedonia 221 km, Romania 476 km
note: the internal boundary between Montenegro and Serbia is 211 km
Coastline: 199 km (Montenegro 199 km, Serbia 0 km)
Maritime claims:
territorial sea: 12 nm
International disputes: Sandzak region bordering northern Montenegro and southeastern Serbia—Muslims seeking autonomy; disputes with Bosnia and Herzegovina and Croatia over Serbian populated areas; Albanian majority in Kosovo seeks independence from Serbian Republic
Climate: in the north, continental climate (cold winter and hot, humid summers with well distributed rainfall); central portion, continental and Mediterranean climate; to the south, Adriatic climate along the coast, hot, dry summers and autumns and relatively cold winters with heavy snowfall inland
Terrain: extremely varied; to the north, rich fertile plains; to the east, limestone ranges and basins; to the southeast, ancient mountain and hills; to the southwest, extremely high shoreline with no islands off the coast; home of largest lake in former Yugoslavia, Lake Scutari
Natural resources: oil, gas, coal, antimony, copper, lead, zinc, nickel, gold, pyrite, chrome
Land use:
arable land: 30%
permanent crops: 5%
meadows and pastures: 20%
forest and woodland: 25%
other: 20%
Irrigated land: NA sq km
Environment:
current issues: coastal water pollution from sewage outlets, especially in tourist-related areas such as Kotor; air pollution around Belgrade and other industrial cities; water pollution from industrial wastes dumped into the Sava which flows into the Danube
natural hazards: subject to destructive earthquakes
international agreements: NA
Note: controls one of the major land routes from Western Europe to Turkey and the Near East; strategic location along the Adriatic coast

People

Population:
total: 10,759,897 (July 1994 est.)
Montenegro: 666,583 (July 1994 est.)
Serbia: 10,093,314 (July 1994 est.)
Population growth rate:
Montenegro: 0.79% (1994 est.)
Serbia: 0.54% (1994 est.)
Birth rate:
Montenegro: 13.72 births/1,000 population (1994 est.)
Serbia: 14.35 births/1,000 population (1994 est.)
Death rate:

Montenegro: 5.84 deaths/1,000 population (1994 est.)
Serbia: 8.94 deaths/1,000 population (1994 est.)
Net migration rate:
Montenegro: 0 migrant(s)/1,000 population (1994 est.)
Serbia: 0 migrant(s)/1,000 population (1994 est.)
Infant mortality rate:
Montenegro: 10.8 deaths/1,000 live births (1994 est.)
Serbia: 21.4 deaths/1,000 live births (1994 est.)

Life expectancy at birth:
Montenegro:
total population: 79.44 years
male: 76.57 years
female: 82.5 years (1994 est.)
Serbia:
total population: 73.39 years
male: 70.9 years
female: 76.07 years (1994 est.)
Total fertility rate:
Montenegro: 1.74 children born/woman (1994 est.)
Serbia: 2.06 children born/woman (1994 est.)
Nationality:
noun: Serb(s) and Montenegrin(s)
adjective: Serbian and Montenegrin
Ethnic divisions: Serbs 63%, Albanians 14%, Montenegrins 6%, Hungarians 4%, other 13%
Religions: Orthodox 65%, Muslim 19%, Roman Catholic 4%, Protestant 1%, other 11%
Languages: Serbo-Croatian 95%, Albanian 5%
Literacy:
total population: NA%
male: NA%
female: NA%
Labor force: 2,640,909
by occupation: industry, mining 40%, agriculture 5% (1990)

Government

Names:
conventional long form: none
conventional short form: Serbia and Montenegro
local long form: none
local short form: Srbija-Crna Gora
Digraph:
Serbia: SR
Montenegro: MW
Type: republic
Capital: Belgrade
Administrative divisions: 2 republics (pokajine, singular—pokajina); and 2 autonomous provinces*; Kosovo*, Montenegro, Serbia, Vojvodina*
Independence: 11 April 1992 (Federal Republic of Yugoslavia formed as self-proclaimed successor to the Socialist Federal Republic of Yugoslavia—SFRY)
National holiday: NA
Constitution: 27 April 1992
Legal system: based on civil law system
Suffrage: 16 years of age, if employed; 18 years of age, universal
Executive branch:
chief of state: Zoran LILIC (since 25 June 1993); note—Slobodan MILOSEVIC is president of Serbia (since 9 December 1990); Momir BULATOVIC is president of Montenegro (since 23 December 1990); Federal Assembly elected Zoran LILIC on 25 June 1993
head of government: Prime Minister Radoje KONTIC (since 29 December 1992); Deputy Prime Ministers Jovan ZEBIC (since NA March 1993), Asim TELACEVIC (since NA March 1993), Zeljko SIMIC (since NA 1993)
cabinet: Federal Executive Council
Legislative branch: bicameral Federal Assembly
Chamber of Republics: elections last held 31 May 1992 (next to be held NA 1996); results—percent of vote by party NA; seats—(40 total; 20 Serbian, 20 Montenegrin)
Chamber of Citizens: elections last held 31 May 1992 (next to be held NA 1996); results—percent of votes by party NA; seats—(138 total; 108 Serbian, 30 Montenegrin) SPS 73, SRS 33, DPSCG 23, SK-PJ 2, DZVM 2, independents 2, vacant 3
Judicial branch: Savezni Sud (Federal Court), Constitutional Court

Political parties and leaders: Serbian Socialist Party (SPS; former Communist Party), Slobodan MILOSEVIC; Serbian Radical Party (SRS), Vojislav SESELJ; Serbian Renewal Movement (SPO), Vuk DRASKOVIC, president; Democratic Party (DS), Zoran DJINDJIC; Democratic Party of Serbia, Vojlslav KOSTUNICA; Democratic Party of Socialists (DPSCG), Momir BULATOVIC, president; People's Party of Montenegro (NS), Novak KILIBARDA; Liberal Alliance of Montenegro, Slavko PEROVIC; Democratic Community of Vojvodina Hungarians (DZVM), Agoston ANDRAS; League of Communists-Movement for Yugoslavia (SK-PJ), Dragan ATANASOVSKI; Democratic Alliance of Kosovo (LDK), Dr. Ibrahim RUGOVA, president
Other political or pressure groups: Serbian Democratic Movement (DEPOS; coalition of opposition parties)
Diplomatic representation in US: US and Serbia and Montenegro do not maintain full diplomatic relations; the Embassy of the former Socialist Federal Republic of Yugoslavia continues to function in the US
US diplomatic representation:
chief of mission: (vacant); Charge d'Affaires Rudolf V. PERINA
embassy: address NA, Belgrade
mailing address: American Embassy Box 5070, Unit 25402, APO AE 09213-5070
telephone: [38] (11) 645-655
FAX: [38] (1) 645-221
Flag: three equal horizontal bands of blue (top), white, and red

SLOVAKIA

Economy

Overview: The dissolution of Czechoslovakia into two independent states—the Czech Republic and Slovakia—on 1 January 1993 has complicated the task of moving toward a more open and decentralized economy. The old Czechoslovakia, even though highly industrialized by East European standards, suffered from an aging capital plant, lagging technology, and a deficiency in energy and many raw materials. In January 1991, approximately one year after the end of communist control of Eastern Europe, the Czech and Slovak Federal Republic launched a sweeping program to convert its almost entirely state-owned and controlled economy to a market system. In 1991-92 these measures resulted in privatization of some medium- and small-scale economic activity and the setting of more than 90% of prices by the market—but at a cost in inflation, unemployment, and lower output. For Czechoslovakia as a whole inflation in 1991 was roughly 50% and output fell 15%. In 1992 in Slovakia, inflation slowed to an estimated 8.7% and the estimated fall in GDP was a more moderate 7%. In 1993 GDP fell roughly 5%, with the disruptions from the separation from the Czech lands probably accounting for half the decline; exports to the Czech Republic fell about 35%. Bratislava adopted an austerity program in June and devalued its currency 10% in July. In 1993, inflation rose an estimated 23%, unemployment topped 14%, and the budget deficit exceeded the IMF target of $485 million by over $200 million. By yearend 1993 Bratislava estimated that 29% of GDP was being produced in the private sector. The forecast for 1994 is gloomy; Bratislava optimistically projects no growth in GDP, 17% unemployment, a $425 million budget deficit, and 12% inflation. At best, if Slovakia stays on track with the IMF, GDP could fall by only 2-3% in 1994 and unemployment could be held under 18%, but a currency devaluation will likely drive inflation above 15%.

National product: GDP—purchasing power equivalent—$31 billion (1993 est.)

National product real growth rate: -5% (1993 est.)

National product per capita: $5,800 (1993 est.)

Inflation rate (consumer prices): 23% (1993 est.)

Unemployment rate: 14.4% (1993 est.)

Budget:
revenues: $4.5 billion
expenditures: $5.2 billion, including capital expenditures of $NA (1993 est.)

Exports: $5.13 billion (f.o.b., 1993 est.)
commodities: machinery and transport equipment; chemicals; fuels, minerals, and metals; agricultural products
partners: Czech Republic, CIS republics, Germany, Poland, Austria, Hungary, Italy, France, US, UK

Imports: $5.95 billion (f.o.b., 1993 est.)
commodities: machinery and transport equipment; fuels and lubricants; manufactured goods; raw materials; chemicals; agricultural products

partners: Czech Republic, CIS republics, Germany, Austria, Poland, Switzerland, Hungary, UK, Italy
External debt: $3.2 billion hard currency indebtedness (31 December 1993)
Industrial production: growth rate -13.5% (December 1993 over December 1992)
Electricity:
capacity: 6,800,000 kW
production: 24 billion kWh
consumption per capita: 4,550 kWh (1992)
Industries: brown coal mining, chemicals, metal-working, consumer appliances, fertilizer, plastics, armaments
Agriculture: largely self-sufficient in food production; diversified crop and livestock production, including grains, potatoes, sugar beets, hops, fruit, hogs, cattle, and poultry; exporter of forest products
Illicit drugs: transshipment point for Southwest Asian heroin bound for Western Europe
Economic aid:
donor: the former Czechoslovakia was a donor—$4.2 billion in bilateral aid to non-Communist less developed countries (1954-89)
Currency: 1 koruna (Sk) = 100 halierov
Exchange rates: koruny (Sk) per US$1—32.9 (December 1993), 28.59 (December 1992), 28.26 (1992), 29.53 (1991), 17.95 (1990), 15.05 (1989); note—values before 1993 reflect Czechoslovak exchange rate
Fiscal year: calendar year

Communications

Railroads: 3,669 km total (1990)
Highways:
total: 17,650 km (1990)
paved: NA
unpaved: NA
Inland waterways: NA km
Pipelines: natural gas 2,700 km; petroleum products NA km
Ports: maritime outlets are in Poland (Gdynia, Gdansk, Szczecin), Croatia (Rijeka), Slovenia (Koper), Germany (Hamburg, Rostock); principal river ports are Komarno on the Danube and Bratislava on the Danube
Merchant marine: 19 ships (1,000 GRT or over) totaling 309,502 GRT/521,997 DWT, bulk 13, cargo 6; note—most under the flag of Saint Vincent and the Grenadines
Airports:
total: 46
usable: 32
with permanent-surface runways: 7
with runways over 3,659 m: 0
with runways 2,440-3,659 m: 6
with runways 1,060-2,439 m: 18
note: a C-130 can land on a 1,060-m airstrip
Telecommunications: NA

Defense Forces

Branches: Army, Air and Air Defense Forces, Civil Defense, Railroad Units
Manpower availability: males age 15-49 1,426,290; fit for military service 1,095,604; reach military age (18) annually 48,695 (1994 est.)
Defense expenditures: 8.2 billion koruny, NA% of GDP (1993 est.); note—conversion of defense expenditures into US dollars using the current exchange rate could produce misleading results

Geography

Location: Central Europe, between Hungary and Poland
Map references: Ethnic Groups in Eastern Europe, Europe, Standard Time Zones of the World
Area:
total area: 48,845 sq km
land area: 48,800 sq km
comparative area: about twice the size of New Hampshire
Land boundaries: total 1,355 km, Austria 91 km, Czech Republic 215 km, Hungary 515 km, Poland 444 km, Ukraine 90 km
Coastline: 0 km (landlocked)
Maritime claims: none; landlocked
International disputes: Gabcikovo Dam dispute with Hungary; unresolved property

issues with Czech Republic over redistribution of former Czechoslovak federal property
Climate: temperate; cool summers; cold, cloudy, humid winters
Terrain: rugged mountains in the central and northern part and lowlands in the south
Natural resources: brown coal and lignite; small amounts of iron ore, copper and manganese ore; salt
Land use:
arable land: NA%
permanent crops: NA%
meadows and pastures: NA%
forest and woodland: NA%
other: NA%
Irrigated land: NA sq km
Environment:
current issues: acid rain damaging forests
natural hazards: NA
international agreements: party to—Air Pollution, Air Pollution-Nitrogen Oxides, Air Pollution-Sulphur, Antarctic Treaty, Environmental Modification, Hazardous Wastes, Law of the Sea, Nuclear Test Ban, Ozone Layer Protection; signed, but not ratified—Antarctic-Environmental Protocol, Biodiversity, Climate Change
Note: landlocked

People

Population: 5,403,505 (July 1994 est.)
Population growth rate: 0.53% (1994 est.)
Birth rate: 14.55 births/1,000 population (1994 est.)
Death rate: 9.28 deaths/1,000 population (1994 est.)
Net migration rate: 0 migrant(s)/1,000 population (1994 est.)
Infant mortality rate: 10.4 deaths/1,000 live births (1994 est.)
Life expectancy at birth:
total population: 72.81 years
male: 68.66 years
female: 77.2 years (1994 est.)
Total fertility rate: 1.96 children born/woman (1994 est.)
Nationality:
noun: Slovak(s)
adjective: Slovak
Ethnic divisions: Slovak 85.6%, Hungarian 10.8%, Gypsy 1.5% (the 1992 census figures underreport the Gypsy/Romany community, which could reach 500,000 or more), Czech 1.1%, Ruthenian 15,000, Ukrainian 13,000, Moravian 6,000, German 5,000, Polish 3,000
Religions: Roman Catholic 60.3%, atheist 9.7%, Protestant 8.4%, Orthodox 4.1%, other 17.5%
Languages: Slovak (official), Hungarian
Literacy:
total population: NA%
male: NA%
female: NA%
Labor force: 2.484 million
by occupation: industry 33.2%, agriculture 12.2%, construction 10.3%, communication and other 44.3% (1990)

Government

Names:
conventional long form: Slovak Republic
conventional short form: Slovakia
local long form: Slovenska Republika
local short form: Slovensko
Digraph: LO
Type: parliamentary democracy
Capital: Bratislava
Administrative divisions: 4 departments (kraje, singular—Kraj) Bratislava, Zapadoslovensky, Stredoslovensky, Vychodoslovensky
Independence: 1 January 1993 (from Czechoslovakia)
National holiday: Anniversary of Slovak National Uprising, August 29 (1944)
Constitution: ratified 1 September 1992; fully effective 1 January 1993
Legal system: civil law system based on Austro-Hungarian codes; has not accepted compulsory ICJ jurisdiction; legal code modified to comply with the obligations of Conference on Security and Cooperation in Europe (CSCE) and to expunge Marxist-Leninist legal theory
Suffrage: 18 years of age; universal
Executive branch:
chief of state: President Michal KOVAC (since 8 February 1993); election last held 8

February 1993 (next to be held NA 1998); results—Michal KOVAC elected by the National Council
head of government: Prime Minister Jozef MORAVCIK (since 16 March 1994)
cabinet: Cabinet; appointed by the president on recommendation of the prime minister
Legislative branch: unicameral
National Council (Narodni Rada): elections last held 5-6 June 1992 (next to be held 31 September-1 October 1994); results—percent of vote by party NA; seats—(150 total) Movement for a Democratic Slovakia 55, Party of the Democratic Left 28, Christian Democratic Movement 18, Slovak National Party 9, National Democratic Party 5, Hungarian Christian Democratic Movement/ Coexistence 14, Democratic Union of Slovakia 16, independents 5
Judicial branch: Supreme Court
Political parties and leaders: Movement for a Democratic Slovakia, Vladimir MECIAR, chairman; Party of the Democratic Left, Peter WEISS, chairman; Christian Democratic Movement, Jan CARNOGURSKY; Slovak National Party, Jan SLOTA, chairman; Hungarian Christian Democratic Movement, Vojtech BUGAR; National Democratic Party-New Alternative, Ludovit CERNAK, chairman; Democratic Union of Slovakia, Jozef MORAVCIK, chairman; Coexistence Movement, Miklos DURAY, chairman
Other political or pressure groups: Green Party; Social Democratic Party in Slovakia; Freedom Party; Slovak Christian Union; Hungarian Civic Party
Member of: BIS, CCC, CE (guest), CEI, CERN, COCOM (cooperating), CSCE, EBRD, ECE, FAO, GATT, IAEA, IBRD, ICAO, ICFTU, IDA, IFC, ILO, IMF, IMO, INMARSAT, INTELSAT (nonsignatory user), INTERPOL, IOC, IOM (observer), ISO, ITU, LORCS, NACC, NSG, PCA, UN (as of 8 January 1993), UNAVEM II, UNCTAD, UNESCO, UNIDO, UNOMUR, UNPROFOR, UPU, WFTU, WHO, WIPO, WMO, WTO, ZC
Diplomatic representation in US:
chief of mission: Ambassador-designate Bravislav LICHARDUS
chancery: (temporary) Suite 330, 2201 Wisconsin Avenue NW, Washington, DC 20007
telephone: (202) 965-5161
FAX: (202) 965-5166
US diplomatic representation:
chief of mission: Ambassdor Theodore RUSSELL
embassy: Hviezdoslavovo Namesite 4, 81102 Bratislava
mailing address: use embassy street address
telephone: [42] (7) 330-861
FAX: [42] (7) 335-439
Flag: three equal horizontal bands of white (top), blue, and red superimposed with the Slovak cross in a shield centered on the hoist side; the cross is white centered on a background of red and blue

---

U.S. Government Contacts:

U.S. Trade Desk: (202) 482-4915

Chambers of Commerce & Organizations:

American Chamber of Commerce in the Slovak Republic
Mileticova 23, Suite 307
821 08 Bratislova, Slovak Republic
Phone/Fax: (427) 214-730

Travel:

International Hotels in Country:
Bratislava:
Danube, Tel: 427/340833, Fax: 427/314311
Forum Bratislava, Tel: 427/348111, Fax: 427/314645.

SLOVENIA

Economy

Overview: Slovenia was by far the most prosperous of the former Yugoslav republics, with a per capita income more than twice the Yugoslav average, indeed not far below the levels in neighboring Austria and Italy. Because of its strong ties to Western Europe and the small scale of damage during its brief fight for independence from Yugoslavia, Slovenia has the brightest prospects among the former Yugoslav republics for economic recovery over the next few years. The dissolution of Yugoslavia, however, has led to severe short-term dislocations in production, employment, and trade ties. For example, overall industrial production has fallen 26% since 1990; particularly hard hit have been the iron and steel, machine-building, chemical, and textile industries. Meanwhile, the continued fighting in other former Yugoslav republics has led to further destruction of long-established trade channels and to an influx of tens of thousands of Croatian and Bosnian refugees. The key program for breaking up and privatizing major industrial firms was established in late 1992. Despite slow progress in privatization Slovenia has reasonable prospects for an upturn in 1994. Bright spots for encouraging Western investors are Slovenia's comparatively well-educated work force, its developed infrastructure, and its Western business attitudes, but instability in Croatia is a deterrent. Slovenia in absolute terms is a small economy, and a little Western investment would go a long way.

National product: GDP—purchasing power equivalent—$15 billion (1993 est.)

National product real growth rate: 0% (1993 est.)

National product per capita: $7,600 (1993 est.)

Inflation rate (consumer prices): 22.9% (1993)

Unemployment rate: 15.5% (1993)

Budget:
revenues: $NA
expenditures: $NA, including capital expenditures of $NA

Exports: $5.1 billion (f.o.b., 1993)
commodities: machinery and transport equipment 38%, other manufactured goods 44%, chemicals 9%, food and live animals 4.6%, raw materials 3%, beverages and tobacco less than 1% (1992)
partners: Germany 27%, Croatia 14%, Italy 13%, France 9% (1992)

Imports: $5.3 billion (c.i.f., 1993)
commodities: machinery and transport equipment 35%, other manufactured goods 26.7%, chemicals 14.5%, raw materials 9.4%, fuels and lubricants 7%, food and live animals 6% (1992)
partners: Germany 23%, Croatia 14%, Italy 14%, France 8%, Austria 8% (1992)

External debt: $1.9 billion

Industrial production: growth rate -2.8% (1993); accounts for 30% of GDP

Electricity:
capacity: 2,900,000 kW
production: 10 billion kWh
consumption per capita: 5,090 kWh (1992)

Industries: ferrous metallurgy and rolling mill products, aluminum reduction and rolled products, lead and zinc smelting, electronics (including military electronics), trucks, electric power equipment, wood products, textiles, chemicals, machine tools
Agriculture: accounts for 5% of GDP; dominated by stock breeding (sheep and cattle) and dairy farming; main crops—potatoes, hops, hemp, flax; an export surplus in these commodities; Slovenia must import many other agricultural products and has a negative overall trade balance in this sector
Illicit drugs: NA
Economic aid: $NA
Currency: 1 tolar (SIT) = 100 stotins
Exchange rates: tolars (SIT) per US$1—112 (June 1993), 28 (January 1992)
Fiscal year: calendar year

Communications

Railroads: 1,200 km, 1.435 m gauge (1991)
Highways:
total: 14,553 km
paved: 10,525 km
unpaved: gravel 4,028 km
Inland waterways: NA
Pipelines: crude oil 290 km, natural gas 305 km
Ports: coastal—Koper
Merchant marine: 19 ships (1,000 GRT or over) totaling 309,502 GRT/521,997 DWT controlled by Slovenian owners, bulk 13, cargo 6
note: most under the flag of Saint Vincent and the Grenadines; no ships remain under the Slovenian flag
Airports:
total: 14
usable: 13
with permanent-surface runways: 6
with runways over 3,659 m: 0
with runways 2,440-3,659 m: 2
with runways 1,220-2,439 m: 2
Telecommunications: 130,000 telephones; broadcast stations—6 AM, 5 FM, 7 TV; 370,000 radios; 330,000 TVs

Defense Forces

Branches: Slovene Defense Forces
Manpower availability: males age 15-49 513,885; fit for military service 411,619; reach military age (19) annually 15,157 (1994 est.)
Defense expenditures: 13.5 billion tolars, 4.5% of GDP (1993); note—conversion of the military budget into US dollars using the current exchange rate could produce misleading results

Geography

Location: Balkan State, Southeastern Europe, bordering the Adriatic Sea, between Austria and Croatia
Map references: Ethnic Groups in Eastern Europe, Europe, Standard Time Zones of the World
Area:
total area: 20,296 sq km
land area: 20,296 sq km
comparative area: slightly larger than New Jersey
Land boundaries: total 1,045 km, Austria 262 km, Croatia 501 km, Italy 199 km, Hungary 83 km
Coastline: 32 km
Maritime claims:
continental shelf: 200-m depth or to depth of exploitation
territorial sea: 12 nm
International disputes: dispute with Croatia over fishing rights in the Adriatic and over some border areas; the border issue is currently under negotiation
Climate: Mediterranean climate on the coast, continental climate with mild to hot summers and cold winters in the plateaus and valleys to the east
Terrain: a short coastal strip on the Adriatic, an alpine mountain region adjacent to Italy, mixed mountain and valleys with numerous rivers to the east
Natural resources: lignite coal, lead, zinc, mercury, uranium, silver
Land use:
arable land: 10%

permanent crops: 2%
meadows and pastures: 20%
forest and woodland: 45%
other: 23%
Irrigated land: NA sq km
Environment:
current issues: Sava River polluted with domestic and industrial waste; heavy metals and toxic chemicals along coastal waters; forest damage near Koper from air pollution originating at metallurgical and chemical plants
natural hazards: subject to flooding and earthquakes
international agreements: party to—Air Pollution, Hazardous Wastes, Marine Dumping, Nuclear Test Ban, Ozone Layer Protection, Ship Pollution; signed, but not ratified—Biodiversity, Climate Change

People

Population: 1,972,227 (July 1994 est.)
Population growth rate: 0.23% (1994 est.)
Birth rate: 11.81 births/1,000 population (1994 est.)
Death rate: 9.5 deaths/1,000 population (1994 est.)
Net migration rate: 0 migrant(s)/1,000 population (1994 est.)
Infant mortality rate: 8.1 deaths/1,000 live births (1994 est.)
Life expectancy at birth:
total population: 74.36 years
male: 70.49 years
female: 78.44 years (1994 est.)
Total fertility rate: 1.67 children born/woman (1994 est.)
Nationality:
noun: Slovene(s)
adjective: Slovenian
Ethnic divisions: Slovene 91%, Croat 3%, Serb 2%, Muslim 1%, other 3%
Religions: Roman Catholic 96% (including 2% Uniate), Muslim 1%, other 3%
Languages: Slovenian 91%, Serbo-Croatian 7%, other 2%
Literacy:
total population: NA%
male: NA%
female: NA%
Labor force: 786,036
by occupation: agriculture 2%, manufacturing and mining 46%

Government

Names:
conventional long form: Republic of Slovenia
conventional short form: Slovenia
local long form: Republika Slovenije
local short form: Slovenija
Digraph: SI
Type: emerging democracy
Capital: Ljubljana
Administrative divisions: 60 provinces (pokajine, singular—pokajina) Ajdovscina, Brezice, Celje, Cerknica, Crnomelj, Dravograd, Gornja Radgona, Grosuplje, Hrastnik Lasko, Idrija, Ilirska Bistrica, Izola, Jesenice, Kamnik, Kocevje, Koper, Kranj, Krsko, Lenart, Lendava, Litija, Ljubljana-Bezigrad, Ljubljana-Center, Ljubljana-Moste-Polje, Ljubljana-Siska, Ljubljana-Vic-Rudnik, Ljutomer, Logatec, Maribor, Metlika, Mozirje, Murska Sobota, Nova Gorica, Novo Mesto, Ormoz, Pesnica, Piran, Postojna, Ptuj, Radlje Ob Dravi, Radovljica, Ravne Na Koroskem, Ribnica, Ruse, Sentjur Pri Celju, Sevnica, Sezana, Skofja Loka, Slovenj Gradec, Slovenska Bistrica, Slovenske Konjice, Smarje Pri Jelsah, Tolmin, Trbovlje, Trebnje, Trzic, Velenje, Vrhnika, Zagorje Ob Savi, Zalec
Independence: 25 June 1991 (from Yugoslavia)
National holiday: Statehood Day, 25 June (1991)
Constitution: adopted 23 December 1991, effective 23 December 1991
Legal system: based on civil law system
Suffrage: 16 years of age, if employed; 18 years of age, universal
Executive branch:
chief of state: President Milan KUCAN (since 22 April 1990); election last held 6 December 1992 (next to be held NA 1996); results—Milan KUCAN reelected by direct popular vote
head of government: Prime Minister Janez DRNOVSEK (since 14 May 1992); Deputy

Prime Minister Lojze PETERLE (since NA)
cabinet: Council of Ministers
Legislative branch: bicameral National Assembly
State Assembly: elections last held 6 December 1992 (next to be held NA 1996); results—percent of vote by party NA; seats—(total 90) LDS 22, SKD 15, United List (former Communists and allies) 14, Slovene National Party 12, SLS 10, Democratic Party 6, ZS 5, SDSS 4, Hungarian minority 1, Italian minority 1
State Council: will become operational after next election in 1996; in the election of 6 December 1992 40 members were elected to represent local and socioeconomic interests
Judicial branch: Supreme Court, Constitutional Court
Political parties and leaders: Slovene Christian Democrats (SKD), Lozje PETERLE, chairman; Liberal Democratic (LDS), Janez DRNOVSEK, chairman; Social-Democratic Party of Slovenia (SDSS), Joze PUCNIK, chairman; Socialist Party of Slovenia (SSS), Viktor ZAKELJ, chairman; Greens of Slovenia (ZS), Dusan PLUT, chairman; National Democratic, Rajko PIRNAT, chairman; Democratic Peoples Party, Marjan PODOBNIK, chairman; Reformed Socialists (former Communist Party), Ciril RIBICIC, chairman; United List (former Communists and allies); Slovene National Party, leader NA; Democratic Party, Igor BAVCAR; Slovene People's Party (SLS), Ivan OMAN
note: parties have changed as of the December 1992 elections
Other political or pressure groups: none
Member of: CCC, CE, CEI, CSCE, EBRD, ECE, IAEA, IBRD, ICAO, IDA, IFC, ILO, IMF, IMO, INTELSAT (nonsignatory user), INTERPOL, IOC, IOM (observer), ITU, NAM (guest), UN, UNCTAD, UNESCO, UNIDO, UPU, WHO, WIPO, WMO
Diplomatic representation in US:
chief of mission: Ambassador Ernest PETRIC
chancery: 1525 New Hampshir Avenue NW, Washington, DC, 20036
telephone: (202) 667-5363
consulate(s) general: New York
US diplomatic representation:
chief of mission: Ambassador E. Allan WENDT
embassy: P.O. Box 254, Prazakova 4, 61000 Ljubljana
mailing address: use embassy street address
telephone: [386] (61) 301-427/472/485
FAX: [386] (61) 301-401
Flag: three equal horizontal bands of white (top), blue, and red with the Slovenian seal (a shield with the image of Triglav in white against a blue background at the center, beneath it are two wavy blue lines depicting seas and rivers, and around it, there are three six-sided stars arranged in an inverted triangle); the seal is located in the upper hoist side of the flag centered in the white and blue bands

TAJIKISTAN

Economy

Overview: Tajikistan had the lowest per capita GDP in the former USSR, the highest rate of population growth, and the lowest standard of living. Its economy at the start of 1994 is producing at roughly the 1989 level and faces urgent reconstruction tasks from the 1992 civil war. Tajikistan's economy was severely disrupted by the breakup of the Soviet economy, which provided guaranteed trade relations and heavy subsidies and in which specialized tasks were assigned to each republic. Its economy is highly agricultural (43% of the work force); it has specialized in growing cotton for export and must import a large share of its food. Its industry (14% of the work force) produces aluminum, hydropower, machinery, and household appliances. Nearly all petroleum products must be imported. Constant political turmoil and continued dominance of former Communist officials have slowed the process of economic reform and brought near economic collapse while limiting foreign assistance. Tajikistan is in the midst of a prolonged monetary crisis in which it is attempting to continue to use the Russian ruble as its currency while its neighbors have switched to new independent currencies; Russia is unwilling to advance sufficient rubles without attaching stringent reform conditions.

National product: GDP—purchasing power equivalent—$6.9 billion (1993 estimate from the UN International Comparison Program, as extended to 1991 and published in the World Bank's World Development Report 1993; and as extrapolated to 1993 using official Tajik statistics, which are very uncertain because of major economic changes since 1990)

National product real growth rate: -21% (1993 est.)

National product per capita: $1,180 (1993 est.)

Inflation rate (consumer prices): 38% per month (1993 average)

Unemployment rate: 1.1% includes only officially registered unemployed; also large numbers of underemployed workers and unregistered unemployed people

Budget:
revenues: $NA
expenditures: $NA, including capital expenditures of $NA

Exports: $263 million to outside the FSU countries (1993)
commodities: cotton, aluminum, fruits, vegetable oil, textiles
partners: Russia, Kazakhstan, Ukraine, Uzbekistan, Turkmenistan

Imports: $371 million from outside the FSU countries (1993)
commodities: fuel, chemicals, machinery and transport equipment, textiles, foodstuffs
partners: Russia, Uzbekistan, Kazakhstan

External debt: $NA

Industrial production: growth rate -20% (1993 est.)

Electricity:
capacity: 4,585,000 kW
production: 16.8 billion kWh
consumption per capita: 2,879 kWh (1992)

Industries: aluminum, zinc, lead, chemicals and fertilizers, cement, vegetable oil, metal-cutting machine tools, refrigerators and freezers

Agriculture: cotton, grain, fruits, grapes, vegetables; cattle, sheep and goats
Illicit drugs: illicit cultivation of cannabis and opium poppy; mostly for CIS consumption; limited government eradication programs; used as transshipment points for illicit drugs from Southwest Asia to Western Europe and North America
Economic aid:
recipient: Russia reportedly provided substantial general assistance throughout 1993 and continues to provide assistance in 1994; Western aid and credits promised through the end of 1993 were $700 million but disbursements were only $104 million; large scale development loans await IMF approval of a reform and stabilization plan
Currency: 1 ruble (R) = 100 kopeks; acquiring new Russian rubles as currency under December 1993 agreement
Exchange rates: NA
Fiscal year: calendar year

Communications

Railroads: 480 km; does not include industrial lines (1990)
Highways:
total: 29,900 km
paved: 21,400 km
unpaved: earth 8,500 km (1990)
Pipelines: natural gas 400 km (1992)
Ports: none; landlocked
Airports:
total: 58
usable: 30
with permanent-surface runways: 12
with runways over 3,659 m: 0
with runways 2,440-3,659 m: 4
with runways 1,060-2,439 m: 13
note: a C-130 can land on a 1,060-m airstrip
Telecommunications: poorly developed and not well maintained; many towns are not reached by the national network; 303,000 telephone circuits (December 1991); telephone density about 55 per 1000 persons(1951); linked by cable and microwave to other CIS republics, and by leased connections to the Moscow international gateway switch; Dushanbe linked by INTELSAT to international gateway switch in Ankara; satellite earth stations—1 Orbita and 2 INTELSAT (one INTELSAT earth station provides TV receive-only service from Turkey)

Defense Forces

Branches: Army (being formed), National Guard, Security Forces (internal and border troops)
Manpower availability: males age 15-49 1,361,143; fit for military service 1,116,246; reach military age (18) annually 57,681 (1994 est.)
Defense expenditures: $NA, NA% of GDP

Geography

Location: Central Asia, between Uzbekistan and China
Map references: Asia, Commonwealth of Independent States—Central Asian States, Standard Time Zones of the World
Area:
total area: 143,100 sq km
land area: 142,700 sq km
comparative area: slightly smaller than Wisconsin
Land boundaries: total 3,651 km, Afghanistan 1,206 km, China 414 km, Kyrgyzstan 870 km, Uzbekistan 1,161 km
Coastline: 0 km (landlocked)
Maritime claims: none; landlocked
International disputes: boundary with China in dispute; territorial dispute with Kyrgyzstan on northern boundary in Isfara Valley area; Afghanistan's and other foreign support to Tajik rebels based in northern Afghanistan
Climate: midlatitude continental, hot summers, mild winters; semiarid to polar in Pamir Mountains
Terrain: Pamir and Alay Mountains dominate landscape; western Fergana Valley in north, Kofarnihon and Vakhsh Valleys in southwest
Natural resources: significant hydropower potential, some petroleum, uranium, mercury, brown coal, lead, zinc, antimony, tungsten

Land use:
arable land: 6%
permanent crops: 0%
meadows and pastures: 23%
forest and woodland: 0%
other: 71%
Irrigated land: 6,940 sq km (1990)
Environment:
current issues: inadequate sanitation facilities; increasing levels of soil salinity; industrial pollution; excessive pesticides; Tajikistan is part of the basin of the shrinking Aral Sea which suffers from severe overutilization of available water for irrigation and associated pollution
natural hazards: NA
international agreements: NA
Note: landlocked

People

Population: 5,995,469 (July 1994 est.)
Population growth rate: 2.67% (1994 est.)
Birth rate: 34.79 births/1,000 population (1994 est.)
Death rate: 6.71 deaths/1,000 population (1994 est.)
Net migration rate: -1.43 migrant(s)/1,000 population (1994 est.)
Infant mortality rate: 62 deaths/1,000 live births (1994 est.)
Life expectancy at birth:
total population: 68.76 years
male: 65.88 years
female: 71.79 years (1994 est.)
Total fertility rate: 4.62 children born/woman (1994 est.)
Nationality:
noun: Tajik(s)
adjective: Tajik
Ethnic divisions: Tajik 64.9%, Uzbek 25%, Russian 3.5% (declining because of emigration), other 6.6%
Religions: Sunni Muslim 80%, Shi'a Muslim 5%
Languages: Tajik (official), Russian widely used in government and business
Literacy: age 9-49 can read and write (1970)
total population: 100%
male: 100%
female: 99%
Labor force: 1.95 million (1992)
by occupation: agriculture and forestry 43%, government and services 24%, industry 14%, trade and communications 11%, construction 8% (1990)

Government

Names:
conventional long form: Republic of Tajikistan
conventional short form: Tajikistan
local long form: Respublika i Tojikiston
local short form: none
former: Tajik Soviet Socialist Republic
Digraph: TI
Type: republic
Capital: Dushanbe
Administrative divisions: 2 oblasts (viloyotho, singular—viloyat) and one autonomous oblast* (viloyati avtonomii); Viloyati Avtonomii Badakhshoni Kuni* (Khorugh—formerly Khorog), Viloyati Khatlon (Qurghonteppa—formerly Kurgan-Tyube), Viloyati Leninobad (Khujand—formerly Leninabad)
note: the administrative center names are in parentheses
Independence: 9 September 1991 (from Soviet Union)
National holiday: National Day, 9 September (1991)
Constitution: a referendum on new constitution planned for June 1994
Legal system: based on civil law system; no judicial review of legislative acts
Suffrage: 18 years of age; universal
Executive branch:
chief of state: Head of State and Assembly Chairman Emomili RAKHMONOV (since NA November 1992); election last held 27 October 1991 (next to be held NA September 1994); results—Rakhman NABIYEV, Communist Party 60%; Davlat KHUDONAZAROV, Democratic Party, Islamic Rebirth Party and Rastokhoz Party 30%
head of government: Prime Minister Abdujalil

SAMADOV (since 27 December 993)
cabinet: Council of Ministers
note: the presidency was abolished in November 1992, when RAKHMANOV became head of state; a referendum on presidential or parliamentary system is planned for June 1994
Legislative branch: unicameral
Supreme Soviet: elections last held 25 February 1990 (next to be held NA September 1994); results—Communist Party 99%, other 1%; seats—(230 total) Communist Party 227, other 3
Judicial branch: Prosecutor General
Political parties and leaders: Communist Party (Tajik Socialist Party—TSP), Shodi SHABDOLOV, chairman; Tajik Democratic Party (TDP), Shodmon YUSUF; Islamic Revival Party (IRP), Mohammed Sharif HIMOTZODA, Davat OUSMAN; Rastokhez Movement, Tohir ABDUJABBAR; Lali Badakhshan Society, Atobek AMIRBEK
note: all the above-listed parties but the Communist Party were banned in June 1993
Other political or pressure groups: Tajikistan Opposition Movement based in northern Afghanistan
Member of: CIS, CSCE, EBRD, ECO, ESCAP, IBRD, IDA, IDB, IMF, INTELSAT (nonsignatory user), IOC, NACC, OIC, UN, UNCTAD, UNESCO, UNIDO, WHO, WMO
Diplomatic representation in US:
chief of mission: NA
chancery: NA
telephone: NA
US diplomatic representation:
chief of mission: Ambassador Stanley T. ESCUDERO
embassy: Hotel October, 105A Rudaki Prospect, Dushanbe
mailing address: use embassy street address
telephone: [7] (3772) 21-03-56 and 21-03-60
Flag: three horizontal stripes of red (top), a wider stripe of white, and green; a crown surmounted by seven five-pointed stars is located in the center of the white stripe

---

U.S. Government Contacts:

U.S. Trade Desk: (202) 482-0360

TURKEY

Economy

Overview: In early 1994, after an impressive economic performance through most of the 1980s, Turkey faces its most damaging economic crisis in the last 15 years. Sparked by the downgrading in mid-January of Turkey's international credit rating by two US credit rating agencies, the crisis stems from two years of loose fiscal and monetary policies that have exacerbated inflation and allowed the public debt, money supply, and current account deficit to explode. Under Prime Minister CILLER, Ankara has followed seriously flawed policies that have destroyed public confidence in the government's ability to manage the economy. Inflation is now running at an annual rate of 107% and the public sector deficit is equivalent to 16% of GDP. Turkish firms have been hurt by high interest rates and a dramatic drop in consumer demand. Three Turkish banks have folded and the stock market has fallen 48% since the beginning of the year. Economic growth may drop to between 0% and 2% in 1994, compared to 7.3% in 1993. Moreover, the government is facing a severe cash crunch. In March 1994, the treasury came close to defaulting on a loan, and official foreign currency reserves are equal to less than two months' worth of imports. The unprecedented effort by the Kurdistan Workers' Party (PKK) to raise the economic costs of its insurgency against the Turkish state is adding to Turkey's economic problems. Attacks against the tourism industry have cut tourist revenues, which account for about 3% of GDP, while economic activity in southeastern Turkey, where most of the violence occurs, has dropped considerably. To cope with the economic crisis and instill domestic and international investor confidence in the fragile coalition government, CILLER has asked the IMF to endorse a stabilization package she introduced in early April 1994. Negotiations are underway for a standby agreement, which would give Turkey access to $450 million this year and enable her cash-starved government to return to the foreign capital markets.
National product: GDP—purchasing power equivalent—$312.4 billion (1993)
National product real growth rate: 7.3% (1993)
National product per capita: $5,100 (1993)
Inflation rate (consumer prices): 65% (1993)
Unemployment rate: 12.2% (1993)
Budget:
revenues: $36.5 billion
expenditures: $47.6 billion, including capital expenditures of $5 billion (1994)
Exports: $14.9 billion (f.o.b., 1992)
commodities: manufactured products 72%, foodstuffs 23%, mining products 4%
partners: EC countries 53%, US 6%, Russia 4%, Saudi Arabia 3%
Imports: $22.9 billion (c.i.f., 1992)
commodities: manufactured products 68%, fuels 17%, foodstuffs 4%
partners: EC countries 44%, US 11%, Saudi Arabia 7%, Russia 5%
External debt: $59.4 billion (1993)
Industrial production: growth rate 4.3% (1992); accounts for 28% of GDP

Electricity:
capacity: 14,400,000 kW
production: 44 billion kWh
consumption per capita: 750 kWh (1991)
Industries: textiles, food processing, mining (coal, chromite, copper, boron minerals), steel, petroleum, construction, lumber, paper
Agriculture: accounts for 16% of GDP and employs about half of working force; products—tobacco, cotton, grain, olives, sugar beets, pulses, citrus fruit, variety of animal products; self-sufficient in food most years
Illicit drugs: major transit route for Southwest Asian heroin and hashish to Western Europe and the US via air, land, and sea routes; major Turkish, Iranian, and other international trafficking organizations operate out of Istanbul; laboratories to convert imported morphine base into heroin are in remote regions of Turkey as well as near Istanbul; government maintains strict controls over areas of legal opium poppy cultivation and output of poppy straw concentrate
Economic aid:
recipient: US commitments, including Ex-Im (FY70-89), $2.3 billion; Western (non-US) countries, ODA and OOF bilateral commitments (1970-89), $10.1 billion; OPEC bilateral aid (1979-89), $665 million; Communist countries (1970-89), $4.5 billion
note: aid for Persian Gulf war efforts from coalition allies (1991), $4.1 billion; aid pledged for Turkish Defense Fund, $2.5 billion
Currency: 1 Turkish lira (TL) = 100 kurus
Exchange rates: Turkish liras (TL) per US$1—15,196.1 (January 1994), 10,983.3 (1993), 6,872.4 (1992), 4,171.8 (1991), 2,608.6 (1990), 2,121.7 (1989)
Fiscal year: calendar year

Communications

Railroads: 8,429 km 1.435-meter gauge (including 795 km electrified)
Highways:
total: 320,611 km
paved: 27,000 km (including 138 km of expressways)
unpaved: gravel 18,500 km; earth 275,111 km (1988)
Inland waterways: about 1,200 km
Pipelines: crude oil 1,738 km, petroleum products 2,321 km, natural gas 708 km
Ports: Iskenderun, Istanbul, Mersin, Izmir
Merchant marine: 390 ships (1,000 GRT or over) totaling 4,664,205 GRT/8,163,379 DWT, short-sea passenger 7, passenger-cargo 1, cargo 195, container 2, roll-on/roll-off cargo 5, refrigerated cargo 2, livestock carrier 1, oil tanker 41, chemical tanker 10, liquefied gas 4, combination ore/oil 12, specialized tanker 2, bulk 103, combination bulk 5
Airports:
total: 113
usable: 105
with permanent-surface runways: 69
with runways over 3,659 m: 3
with runways 2,440-3,659 m: 32
with runways 1,220-2,439 m: 27
Telecommunications: fair domestic and international systems; trunk radio relay microwave network; limited open wire network; 3,400,000 telephones; broadcast stations—15 AM; 94 FM; 357 TV; 1 satellite ground station operating in the INTELSAT (2 Atlantic Ocean antennas) and EUTELSAT systems; 1 submarine cable

Defense Forces

Branches: Land Forces, Navy (including Naval Air and Naval Infantry), Air Force, Coast Guard, Gendarmerie
Manpower availability: males age 15-49 16,112,783; fit for military service 9,828,853; reach military age (20) annually 614,252 (1994 est.)
Defense expenditures: exchange rate conversion—$14 billion, 5.6% of GDP (1994)

Geography

Location: Southwestern Asia (that part west of the Bosporus is sometimes included with Europe), bordering the Mediterranean Sea and Black Sea, between Bulgaria and Iran
Map references: Africa, Europe, Middle East, Standard Time Zones of the World
Area:
total area: 780,580 sq km

land area: 770,760 sq km
comparative area: slightly larger than Texas
Land boundaries: total 2,627 km, Armenia 268 km, Azerbaijan 9 km, Bulgaria 240 km, Georgia 252 km, Greece 206 km, Iran 499 km, Iraq 331 km, Syria 822 km
Coastline: 7,200 km
Maritime claims:
exclusive economic zone: in Black Sea only—to the maritime boundary agreed upon with the former USSR
territorial sea: 6 nm in the Aegean Sea, 12 nm in the Black Sea and in the Mediterranean Sea
International disputes: complex maritime and air (but not territorial) disputes with Greece in Aegean Sea; Cyprus question; Hatay question with Syria; ongoing dispute with downstream riparians (Syria and Iraq) over water development plans for the Tigris and Euphrates Rivers
Climate: temperate; hot, dry summers with mild, wet winters; harsher in interior
Terrain: mostly mountains; narrow coastal plain; high central plateau (Anatolia)
Natural resources: antimony, coal, chromium, mercury, copper, borate, sulphur, iron ore
Land use:
arable land: 30%
permanent crops: 4%
meadows and pastures: 12%
forest and woodland: 26%
other: 28%
Irrigated land: 22,200 sq km (1989 est.)
Environment:
current issues: water pollution from dumping of chemicals and detergents; air pollution; deforestation
natural hazards: subject to very severe earthquakes, especially in northern Turkey, along an arc extending from the Sea of Marmara to Lake Van
international agreements: party to—Air Pollution, Nuclear Test Ban, Ozone Layer Protection, Ship Pollution; signed, but not ratified—Biodiversity, Environmental Modification, Hazardous Wastes,
Note: strategic location controlling the Turkish Straits (Bosporus, Sea of Marmara, Dardanelles) that link Black and Aegean Seas

People

Population: 62,153,898 (July 1994 est.)
Population growth rate: 2.02% (1994 est.)
Birth rate: 25.98 births/1,000 population (1994 est.)
Death rate: 5.8 deaths/1,000 population (1994 est.)
Net migration rate: 0 migrant(s)/1,000 population (1994 est.)
Infant mortality rate: 48.8 deaths/1,000 live births (1994 est.)
Life expectancy at birth:
total population: 70.94 years
male: 68.61 years
female: 73.38 years (1994 est.)
Total fertility rate: 3.21 children born/woman (1994 est.)
Nationality:
noun: Turk(s)
adjective: Turkish
Ethnic divisions: Turkish 80%, Kurdish 20%
Religions: Muslim 99.8% (mostly Sunni), other 0.2% (Christian and Jews)
Languages: Turkish (official), Kurdish, Arabic
Literacy: age 15 and over can read and write (1990 est.)
total population: 81%
male: 90%
female: 71%
Labor force: 20.8 million
by occupation: agriculture 48%, services 32%, industry 20%
note: about 1,800,000 Turks work abroad (1993)

Government

Names:
conventional long form: Republic of Turkey
conventional short form: Turkey
local long form: Turkiye Cumhuriyeti
local short form: Turkiye
Digraph: TU
Type: republican parliamentary democracy
Capital: Ankara
Administrative divisions: 73 provinces (iller, singular—il); Adana, Adiyaman, Afyon, Agri, Aksaray, Amasya, Ankara, Antalya,

Artvin, Aydin, Balikesir, Batman, Bayburt, Bilecik, Bingol, Bitlis, Bolu, Burdur, Bursa, Canakkale, Cankiri, Corum, Denizli, Diyarbakir, Edirne, Elazig, Erzincan, Erzurum, Eskisehir, Gazi Antep, Giresun, Gumushane, Hakkari, Hatay, Icel, Isparta, Istanbul, Izmir, Kahraman Maras, Karaman, Kars, Kastamonu, Kayseri, Kirikkale, Kirklareli, Kirsehir, Kocaeli, Konya, Kutahya, Malatya, Manisa, Mardin, Mugla, Mus, Nevsehir, Nigde, Ordu, Rize, Sakarya, Samsun, Sanli Urfa, Siirt, Sinop, Sirnak, Sivas, Tekirdag, Tokat, Trabzon, Tunceli, Usak, Van, Yozgat, Zonguldak
Independence: 29 October 1923 (successor state to the Ottoman Empire)
National holiday: Anniversary of the Declaration of the Republic, 29 October (1923)
Constitution: 7 November 1982
Legal system: derived from various continental legal systems; accepts compulsory ICJ jurisdiction, with reservations
Suffrage: 21 years of age; universal
Executive branch:
chief of state: President Suleyman DEMIREL (since 16 May 1993)
head of government: Prime Minister Tansu CILLER (since 5 July 1993)
National Security Council: advisory body to the President and the Cabinet
cabinet: Council of Ministers; appointed by the president on nomination of the prime minister
Legislative branch: unicameral
Turkish Grand National Assembly: (Turkiye Buyuk Millet Meclisi) elections last held 20 October 1991 (next to be held NA October 1996); results—DYP 27.03%, ANAP 24.01%, SHP 20.75%, RP 16.88%, DSP 10.75%, SBP 0.44%, independent 0.14%; seats—(450 total) DYP 178, ANAP 115, SHP 86, RP 40, MCP 19, DSP 7, other 5
note: seats held by various parties are subject to change due to defections, creation of new parties, and ouster or death of sitting deputies; present seats by party are as follows: DYP 178, ANAP 101, SHP 55, RP 39, CHP 18, MHP 13, DEP 13, BBP 7, DSP 3, YP 3, MP 2, independents 10, vacant 8
Judicial branch: Court of Cassation
Political parties and leaders: Correct Way Party (DYP), Tansu CILLER; Motherland Party (ANAP), Mesut YILMAZ; Social Democratic Populist Party (SHP), Murat KARAYALCIN; Welfare Party (RP), Necmettin ERBAKAN; Democratic Left Party (DSP), Bulent ECEVIT; Nationalist Action Party (MHP), Alparslan TURKES; Democracy Party (DEP), Hatip DICLE; Socialist Unity Party (SBP), Sadun AREN; New Party (YP), Yusuf Bozkurt OZAL; Republican People's Party (CHP), Deniz BAYKAL; Labor Party (IP), Dogu PERINCEK; National Party (MP), Aykut EDIBALI; Democrat Party (DP), Aydin MENDERES; Grand Unity Party (BBP), Muhsin YAZICIOGLU; Rebirth Party (YDP), Hasan Celal GUZEL; People's Democracy Party (HADEP), Murat BOZLAK; Main Path Party (ANAYOL), Gurcan BASER
Other political or pressure groups: Turkish Confederation of Labor (TURK-IS), Bayram MERAL
Member of: AsDB, BIS, BSEC, CCC, CE, CERN (observer), COCOM, CSCE, EBRD, ECE, ECO, FAO, GATT, IAEA, IBRD, ICAO, ICC, ICFTU, IDA, IDB, IEA, IFAD, IFC, ILO, IMF, IMO, INMARSAT, INTELSAT, INTERPOL, IOC, IOM (observer), ISO, ITU, LORCS, NACC, NATO, NEA, OECD, OIC, PCA, UN, UNCTAD, UNESCO, UNHCR, UNIDO, UNIKOM, UNOSOM, UNRWA, UPU, WEU (associate), WFTU, WHO, WIPO, WMO, WTO
Diplomatic representation in US:
chief of mission: Ambassador Nuzhet KANDEMIR
chancery: 1714 Massachusetts Avenue NW, Washington, DC 20036
telephone: (202) 659-8200
consulate(s) general: Chicago, Houston, Los Angeles, and New York
US diplomatic representation:
chief of mission: Ambassador Richard C. BARKLEY
embassy: 110 Ataturk Boulevard, Ankara
mailing address: PSC 93, Box 5000, Ankara, or APO AE 09823
telephone: [90] (312) 468-6110 through 6128
FAX: [90] (312) 467-0019
consulate(s) general: Istanbul
consulate(s): Adana

Flag: red with a vertical white crescent (the closed portion is toward the hoist side) and white five-pointed star centered just outside the crescent opening

U.S. Government Contacts:

U.S. Trade Desk: (202) 482-3945

American Embassy Commercial Section
110 Ataturk Boulevard
Ankara, Turkey
APO AE 09822
Tel: 90-4-167-0949
Fax: 90-4-167-1366

American Consulate General - Istanbul Commercial Section
104-108 Mesrutiyet Caddesi
Tepebasl
Istanbul, Turkey
APO AE 09827
Tel: 90-1-151-1651
Fax: 90-1-152-2417

Turkey Government Contacts:

Embassy of Turkey Commercial Section
2523 Massachusetts Avenue, N.W.
Washington, DC 20008
Tel: (202) 483-5366

Turkish International Cooperation Agency (TICA)
P.O. Box 86 Ahmetler
06428 Ankara/Turkey
Tel: 90 312 417 27 90
Fax: 90 312 417 27 99

Turkish Ministry of Finance
(T.C. Maliye Bakanligi)
Ankara
Tel: 90 312 310 38 80 - 419 12 00
Fax: 90 312 310 51 59 - 324 14 26
310 52 23 - 311 83 78 - 425 00 58

Turkish Ministry of Industry and Commerce
(T.C. Sanayi ve Ticaret Bakanligi)
Ankara
Tel: 90 312 231 72 80
Fax: 90 312 230 87 04 - 230 81 47
230 87 85 - 230 42 51

Chambers of Commerce & Organizations:

Turkish-American Businessmen's Association
Fahri Gizdem Sokak 22/5
80280 Gayrettepe, Istanbul, Turkey
Tel: (901) 274-2824/288-6212
Fax: (901) 275-9316

Legal Services:

White and Case
1747 Penn. Ave
Suite 500
Washington, DC
Tel: (202) 872-0013
Fax: (202) 872-0210

Arnold and Porter
1200 New Hampshire Ave, N.E.
Washington, DC 20036
Tel: (202) 872-6784
Fax: (202) 872-6720

Consultants:

PROFIN - Project Development and Financing Consultant Co.
Cinnah Cad. 100/2 06550
Cankaya Ankara
Turkey
Tel: 90-312-440-23-17
Fax: 90-312-440-23-15

Travel:

International Hotels in Country:
Istanbul:
Ciragan Palace, Tel: 90 212/258-3377, Fax: 90 212/259-6687
Pera Palace, Tel: 90 212/251-4560, Fax: 90 212/251-4089
Hilton, 90 212/231-4646, Fax: 90 212/240-4165.

TURKMENISTAN

Economy

Overview: Turkmenistan is a largely desert country with nomadic cattle raising, intensive agriculture in irrigated oases, and huge gas and oil resources. Half of its irrigated land is planted in cotton; it is the world's tenth largest producer. It also is the world's fourth largest producer of natural gas and has the fifth largest reserves. Furthermore, Turkmenistan has substantial oil resources; its two oil refineries make it an exporter of refined products. Profiting from the move toward market prices for its oil and gas resources, Turkmenistan has suffered the least economic decline of the 15 states of the former USSR. With an authoritarian ex-Communist regime in power and a tribally based social structure, Turkmenistan has taken a cautious approach to questions of economic reform, using the profits from its gas and cotton exports to sustain a generally inefficient economy. Economic restructuring and privatization have just begun, and price liberalization and price increases have been accompanied by generous wage hikes and subsidies. At the same time, Turkmenistan faces serious constraints on its gas and oil earnings because of the inability of its traditional regional customers to pay for the current level of purchases and the lack of pipeline access to hard currency markets. Faced with financial shortfalls, rampant inflation, and the desire to ensure a stable currency, the regime has become more receptive to market reforms yet still seeks to offer widespread social benefits to its population and to retain state domination over the economy.

National product: GDP—purchasing power equivalent—$13 billion (1993 estimate from the UN International Comparison Program, as extended to 1991 and published in the World Bank's World Development Report 1993; and as extrapolated to 1993 using official Turkmen statistics, which are very uncertain because of major economic changes since 1990)

National product real growth rate: 7.8% (1993 est.)

National product per capita: $3,330 (1993 est.)

Inflation rate (consumer prices): 45% per month (1993 est.)

Unemployment rate: 2.9% (1992 est.); includes only officially registered unemployed; also large number of underemployed

Budget:
revenues: $NA
expenditures: $NA, including capital expenditures of $NA

Exports: $1.2 billion to states outside the FSU (1993)
commodities: natural gas, cotton, petroleum products, textiles, carpets
partners: Ukraine, Russia, Kazakhstan, Uzbekistan, Georgia, Eastern Europe, Turkey, Argentina

Imports: $490 million from states outside the FSU (1993)
commodities: machinery and parts, grain and food, plastics and rubber, consumer durables, textiles
partners: Russia, Azerbaijan, Uzbekistan, Kazakhstan, Turkey

External debt: NEGL
Industrial production: growth rate 5.3% (1993)
Electricity:
capacity: 2,920,000 kW
production: 13.1 billion kWh
consumption per capita: 3,079 kWh (1992)
Industries: natural gas, oil, petroleum products, textiles, food processing
Agriculture: cotton, grain, animal husbandry
Illicit drugs: illicit producer of cannabis and opium; mostly for CIS consumption; limited government eradication program; used as transshipment points for illicit drugs from Southwest Asia to Western Europe
Economic aid:
recipient: Turkmenistan has received about $200 million in bilateral aid credits
Currency: Turkmenistan introduced its national currency, the manat, on 1 November 1993
Exchange rates: NA
Fiscal year: calendar year

Communications

Railroads: 2,120 km; does not include industrial lines (1990)
Highways:
total: 23,000 km
paved and gravel: 18,300 km
unpaved: earth 4,700 km (1990)
Pipelines: crude oil 250 km, natural gas 4,400 km
Ports: inland—Krasnowodsk (Caspian Sea)
Airports:
total: 7
usable: 7
with permanent-surface runways: 4
with runways over 3,659 m: 0
with runways 2,440-3,659 m: 0
with runways 1,220-2,439 m: 4
Telecommunications: poorly developed; only 7.5 telephone circuits per 100 persons (1991); linked by cable and microwave to other CIS republics and to other countries by leased connections to the Moscow international gateway switch; a new telephone link from Ashgabat to Iran has been established; a new exchange in Ashgabat switches international traffic through Turkey via INTELSAT; satellite earth stations—1 Orbita and 1 INTELSAT

Defense Forces

Branches: National Guard, Republic Security Forces (internal and border troops), Joint Command Turkmenistan/Russia (Ground, Navy or Caspian Sea Flotilla, Air, and Air Defense)
Manpower availability: males age 15-49 962,987; fit for military service 787,991; reach military age (18) annually 40,079 (1994 est.)
Defense expenditures: exchange rate conversion—$NA, NA% of GDP

Geography

Location: Central Asia, bordering the Caspian Sea, between Iran and Uzbekistan
Map references: Asia, Commonwealth of Independent States—Central Asian States, Standard Time Zones of the World
Area:
total area: 488,100 sq km
land area: 488,100 sq km
comparative area: slightly larger than California
Land boundaries: total 3,736 km, Afghanistan 744 km, Iran 992 km, Kazakhstan 379 km, Uzbekistan 1,621 km
Coastline: 0 km
note: Turkmenistan borders the Caspian Sea (1,768 km)
Maritime claims: landlocked, but boundaries in the Caspian Sea with Azerbaijan, Kazakhstan, and Iran are under negotiations
International disputes: Russia may dispute current de facto maritime border to midpoint of Caspian Sea from shore
Climate: subtropical desert
Terrain: flat-to-rolling sandy desert with dunes rising to mountains in the south; low mountains along border with Iran; borders Caspian Sea in west
Natural resources: petroleum, natural gas, coal, sulphur, salt

Land use:
arable land: 3%
permanent crops: 0%
meadows and pastures: 69%
forest and woodland: 0%
other: 28%
Irrigated land: 12,450 sq km (1990)
Environment:
current issues: contamination of soil and groundwater with agricultural chemicals, pesticides; salinization, water-logging of soil due to poor irrigation methods; Caspian Sea pollution; diversion of a large share of the flow of the Amu Darya river into irrigation contributes to that river's inability to replenish the Aral Sea; desertification
natural hazards: NA
international agreements: party to—Ozone Layer Protection
Note: landlocked

People

Population: 3,995,122 (July 1994 est.)
Population growth rate: 2.01% (1994 est.)
Birth rate: 30.42 births/1,000 population (1994 est.)
Death rate: 7.44 deaths/1,000 population (1994 est.)
Net migration rate: -2.89 migrant(s)/1,000 population (1994 est.)
Infant mortality rate: 69.9 deaths/1,000 live births (1994 est.)
Life expectancy at birth:
total population: 65.14 years
male: 61.63 years
female: 68.82 years (1994 est.)
Total fertility rate: 3.77 children born/woman (1994 est.)
Nationality:
noun: Turkmen(s)
adjective: Turkmen
Ethnic divisions: Turkmen 73.3%, Russian 9.8%, Uzbek 9%, Kazakh 2%, other 5.9%
Religions: Muslim 87%, Eastern Orthodox 11%, unknown 2%
Languages: Turkmen 72%, Russian 12%, Uzbek 9%, other 7%
Literacy: age 9-49 can read and write (1970)
total population: 100%
male: 100%
female: 100%
Labor force: 1.573 million
by occupation: agriculture and forestry 44%, industry and construction 20%, other 36% (1992)

Government

Names:
conventional long form: none
conventional short form: Turkmenistan
local long form: Tiurkmenostan Respublikasy
local short form: Turkmenistan
former: Turkmen Soviet Socialist Republic
Digraph: TX
Type: republic
Capital: Ashgabat
Administrative divisions: 5 welayatlar (singular—welayat): Ahal Welayaty (Ashgabat), Balkan Welayaty (Nebitdag), Dashhowuz Welayaty (formerly Tashauz), Lebap Welayaty (Charjew), Mary Welayaty
note: names in parentheses are administrative centers when name differs from welayat name
Independence: 27 October 1991 (from the Soviet Union)
National holiday: Independence Day, 27 October (1991)
Constitution: adopted 18 May 1992
Legal system: based on civil law system
Suffrage: 18 years of age; universal
Executive branch:
chief of state: President Saparmurad NIYAZOV (since NA October 1990); election last held 21 June 1992 (next to be held NA 2002); results—Saparmurad NIYAZOV 99.5% (ran unopposed); note—a 15 January 1994 referendum extended NIYAZOV's term an additional five years until 2002 (99.99% approval)
head of government: Prime Minister (vacant); Deputy Prime Ministers Batyr SARDJAEV, Valery G. OCHERTSOV, Orazgeldi AIDOGDIEV, Djourakuli BABAKULIYEV, Rejep SAPAROV, Boris SHIKHMURADOV, Abad RIZAEVA, Yagmur OVEZOV (since NA)
cabinet: Council of Ministers

Legislative branch: under 1992 constitution there are two parliamentary bodies, a unicameral People's Council (Halk Maslahaty—having more than 100 members and meeting infrequently) and a 50-member unicameral Assembly (Majlis)
Assembly (Majlis): elections last held 7 January 1990 (next to be held late 1994 or early 1995); results—percent of vote by party NA; seats—(175 total) elections not officially by party, but Communist Party members won nearly 90% of seats; note—seats to be reduced to 50 at next election
Judicial branch: Supreme Court
Political parties and leaders:
ruling party: Democratic Party (formerly Communist), chairman vacant
opposition: Party for Democratic Development, Durdymurat HOJA-MUKHAMMED, chairman; Agzybirlik, Nurberdy NURMAMEDOV, cochairman, Hubayberdi HALLIYEV, cochairman
note: formal opposition parties are outlawed; unofficial, small opposition movements exist
Member of: CIS, CSCE, EBRD, ECE, ECO, ESCAP, IBRD, ICAO, IDB, ILO, IMF, IMO, INTELSAT (nonsignatory user), IOC, ITU, NACC, OIC, UN, UNCTAD, UNESCO, UPU, WHO, WMO
Diplomatic representation in US:
chief of mission: Ambassador Khalil UGUR
chancery: 1511 K Street NW, Suite 412, Washington, DC, 20005
telephone: NA
US diplomatic representation:
chief of mission: Ambassador Joseph S. HULINGS III
embassy: Yubilenaya Hotel, Ashgabat
mailing address: use embassy street address
telephone: [7] 36320 24-49-25 or 24-49-26
Flag: green field, including a vertical stripe on the hoist side, with a claret vertical stripe in between containing five white, black, and orange carpet guls (an assymetrical design used in producing rugs) associated with five different tribes; a white crescent and five white stars in the upper left corner to the right of the carpet guls

U.S. Government Contacts:

U.S. Trade Desk: (202) 482-0360

UKRAINE

Economy

Overview: After Russia, the Ukrainian republic was far and away the most important economic component of the former Soviet Union producing more than three times the output of the next-ranking republic. Its fertile black soil generated more than one-fourth of Soviet agricultural output, and its farms provided substantial quantities of meat, milk, grain and vegetables to other republics. Likewise, its diversified heavy industry supplied equipment and raw materials to industrial and mining sites in other regions of the former USSR. In 1992 the Ukrainian Government liberalized most prices and erected a legal framework for privatizing state enterprises while retaining many central economic controls and continuing subsidies to state production enterprises. In November 1992 the new Prime Minister KUCHMA launched a new economic reform program promising more freedom to the agricultural sector, faster privatization of small and medium enterprises, and stricter control over state subsidies. In 1993, however, severe internal political disputes over the scope and pace of economic reform and payment arrears on energy imports have led to further declines in output, and inflation of 50% or more per month by the last quarter. In first quarter 1994, national income and industrial output were less than two-thirds the first quarter 1993 figures, according to official statistics. At the same time an increasing number of people are developing small private businesses and exploiting opportunities in non-official markets. Even so, the magnitude of the problems and the slow pace in building new market-oriented institutions preclude a near-term recovery of output to the 1990 level. A vital economic concern in 1994 will continue to be Russia's decisions on the prices and quantities of oil and gas to be shipped to the Ukraine.

National product: GDP—purchasing power equivalent—$205.4 billion (1993 estimate from the UN International Comparison Program, as extended to 1991 and published in the World Bank's World Development Report 1993; and as extrapolated to 1993 using official Ukrainian statistics, which are very uncertain because of major economic changes since 1990)

National product real growth rate: -16% (1993 est.)

National product per capita: $3,960 (1993 est.)

Inflation rate (consumer prices): 45% per month (1993)

Unemployment rate: 0.4% officially registered; large number of unregistered or underemployed workers

Budget:

revenues: $NA

expenditures: $NA, including capital expenditures of $NA

Exports: $3 billion to countries outside of the FSU (1993)

commodities: coal, electric power, ferrous and nonferrous metals, chemicals, machinery and transport equipment, grain, meat

partners: FSU countries, Germany, China, Austria

Imports: $2.2 billion from outside of the FSU countries (1993)
commodities: machinery and parts, transportation equipment, chemicals, textiles
partners: FSU countries, Germany, China, Austria
External debt: $NA
Industrial production: growth rate -14% (1993); accounts for 50% of GDP
Electricity:
capacity: 55,882,000 kW
production: 281 billion kWh
consumption per capita: 5,410 kWh (1992)
Industries: coal, electric power, ferrous and nonferrous metals, machinery and transport equipment, chemicals, food-processing (especially sugar)
Agriculture: accounts for about 25% of GDP; grain, vegetables, meat, milk, sugar beets
Illicit drugs: illicit cultivator of cannabis and opium poppy; mostly for CIS consumption; limited government eradication program; used as transshipment points for illicit drugs to Western Europe
Economic aid: $350 million economic aid and $350 million to help disassemble the atomic weapons from the US in 1994
Currency: Ukraine withdrew the Russian ruble from circulation on 12 November 1992 and declared the karbovanets (plural karbovantsi) sole legal tender in Ukrainian markets; Ukrainian officials claim this is an interim move toward introducing a new currency—the hryvnya—possibly in mid-1994
Exchange rates: NA
Fiscal year: calendar year

Communications

Railroads: 23,350 km (1,524-mm gauge); 8,600 km electrified
Highways:
total: 273,700 km
paved and gravel: 236,400 km
unpaved: earth 37,300 km
Inland waterways: 1,672 km perennially navigable (Pryp''yat' and Dnipro Rivers)
Pipelines: crude oil 2,010 km, petroleum products 1,920 km, natural gas 7,800 km (1992)
Ports: coastal—Berdyans'k, Illichivs'k, Kerch, Kherson, Mariupol', Mykolayiv, Odesa, Sevastopol', Pivdenne; inland—Kiev (Kyyiv)
Merchant marine: 390 ships (1,000 GRT or over) totaling 3,932,009 GRT/5,236,134 DWT, cargo 231, container 18, barge carriers 7, bulk cargo 55, oil tanker 10, chemical tanker 2, liquefied gas 1, passenger 12, passenger cargo 5, short-sea passenger 8, roll-on/roll-off cargo 33, railcar carrier 2, multi-function-large-load-carrier 1, refrigerated cargo 5
Airports:
total: 694
usable: 199
with permanent-surface runways: 111
with runways over 3,659 m: 3
with runways 2,440-3,659 m: 81
with runways 1,060-2,439 m: 78
note: a C-130 can land on a 1,060-m airstrip
Telecommunications: the telephone system is inadequate both for business and for personal use; about 7,886,000 telephone circuits serve 52,056,000 people (1991); telephone density is 151.4 telephone circuits per 1,000 persons (1991); 3.56 million applications for telephones had not been satisfied as of January 1991; calls to other CIS countries are carried by land line or microwave; other international calls to 167 countries are carried by satellite or by the 150 leased lines through the Moscow gateway switch; an NMT-450 analog cellular telephone network operates in Kiev (Kyyiv) and allows direct dialing of international calls through Kiev's EWSD digital exchange; electronic mail services have been established in Kiev, Odessa, and Lugansk by Sprint; satellite earth stations employ INTELSAT, INMARSAT, and Intersputnik

Defense Forces

Branches: Army, Navy, Air and Air Defense Forces, Republic Security Forces (internal and border troops), National Guard
Manpower availability: males age 15-49 12,191,984; fit for military service 9,591,276; reach military age (18) annually 364,676 (1994 est.)

Defense expenditures: 544,256 million karbovantsi, NA% of GDP (forecast for 1993); note—conversion of the military budget into US dollars using the current exchange rate could produce misleading results

Geography

Location: Eastern Europe, bordering the Black Sea, between Poland and Russia
Map references: Asia, Commonwealth of Independent States—European States, Europe, Standard Time Zones of the World
Area:
total area: 603,700 sq km
land area: 603,700 sq km
comparative area: slightly smaller than Texas
Land boundaries: total 4,558 km, Belarus 891 km, Hungary 103 km, Moldova 939 km, Poland 428 km, Romania (southwest) 169 km, Romania (west) 362 km, Russia 1,576 km, Slovakia 90 km
Coastline: 2,782 km
Maritime claims: NA
International disputes: potential future border disputes with Moldova and Romania in Northern Bukovina and southern Odes'ka Oblast'; potential dispute with Moldova over former southern Bessarabian area; potential dispute with Russia over Crimea; has made no territorial claim in Antarctica (but has reserved the right to do so) and does not recognize the claims of any other nation
Climate: temperate continental; subtropical only on the southern Crimean coast; precipitation disproportionately distributed, highest in west and north, lesser in east and southeast; winters vary from cool along the Black Sea to cold farther inland; summers are warm across the greater part of the country, hot in the south
Terrain: most of Ukraine consists of fertile plains (steppes) and plateaux, mountains being found only in the west (the Carpathians), and in the Crimean Peninsula in the extreme south
Natural resources: iron ore, coal, manganese, natural gas, oil, salt, sulphur, graphite, titanium, magnesium, kaolin, nickel, mercury, timber
Land use:
arable land: 56%
permanent crops: 2%
meadows and pastures: 12%
forest and woodland: 0%
other: 30%
Irrigated land: 26,000 sq km (1990)
Environment:
current issues: unsafe drinking water; air and water pollution; deforestation; radiation contamination in the northeast from 1986 accident at Chornobyl' Nuclear Power Plant
natural hazards: NA
international agreements: party to—Air Pollution, Air Pollution-Nitrogen Oxides, Air Pollution-Sulphur, Antarctic Treaty, Environmental Modification, Marine Dumping, Ozone Layer Protection, Ship Pollution; signed, but not ratified—Air Pollution-Volatile Organic Compounds, Biodiversity, Climate Change, Law of the Sea
Note: strategic position at the crossroads between Europe and Asia; second largest country in Europe

People

Population: 51,846,958 (July 1994 est.)
Population growth rate: 0.05% (1994 est.)
Birth rate: 12.34 births/1,000 population (1994 est.)
Death rate: 12.6 deaths/1,000 population (1994 est.)
Net migration rate: 0.71 migrant(s)/1,000 population (1994 est.)
Infant mortality rate: 20.7 deaths/1,000 live births (1994 est.)
Life expectancy at birth:
total population: 69.99 years
male: 65.45 years
female: 74.76 years (1994 est.)
Total fertility rate: 1.82 children born/woman (1994 est.)
Nationality:
noun: Ukrainian(s)
adjective: Ukrainian
Ethnic divisions: Ukrainian 73%, Russian 22%, Jewish 1%, other 4%
Religions: Ukrainian Orthodox—Moscow

Patriarchate, Ukrainian Orthodox—Kiev Patriarchate, Ukrainian Autocephalous Orthodox, Ukrainian Catholic (Uniate), Protestant, Jewish
Languages: Ukrainian, Russian, Romanian, Polish, Hungarian
Literacy: age 9-49 can read and write (1979)
total population: 100%
male: 100%
female: 100%
Labor force: 23.985 million
by occupation: industry and construction 33%, agriculture and forestry 21%, health, education, and culture 16%, trade and distribution 7%, transport and communication 7%, other 16% (1992)

Government

Names:
conventional long form: none
conventional short form: Ukraine
local long form: none
local short form: Ukrayina
former: Ukrainian Soviet Socialist Republic
Digraph: UP
Type: republic
Capital: Kiev (Kyyiv)
Administrative divisions: 24 oblasti (singular—oblast'), 1 autonomous republic* (avtomnaya respublika), and 2 municipalites (mista, singular—misto) with oblast status**; Cherkas'ka (Cherkasy), Chernihivs'ka (Chernihiv), Chernivets'ka (Chernitsi), Dnipropetrovs'ka (Dnipropetrovs'k), Donets'ka (Donets'k), Ivano-Frankivs'ka (Ivano-Frankivs'k), Kharkivs'ka (Kharkiv), Khersons'ka (Kherson), Khmel'nyts'ka (Khmel'nyts'kyy), Kirovohrads'ka (Kirovohrad), Kyyiv**, Kyyivs'ka (Kiev), Luhans'ka (Luhans'k), L'vivs'ka (L'viv), Mykolayivs'ka (Mykolayiv), Odes'ka (Odesa), Poltavs'ka (Poltava), Respublika Krym* (Simferopol'), Rivnens'ka (Rivne), Sevastopol'**,Sums'ka (Sevastopol'), Ternopil's'ka (Ternopil'), Vinnyts'ka (Vinnytsya), Volyns'ka (Luts'k), Zakarpats'ka (Uzhhorod), Zaporiz'ka (Zaporizhzhya), Zhytomyrs'ka (Zhytomyr)
note: names in parentheses are administrative centers when name differs from oblast' name
Independence: 1 December 1991 (from Soviet Union)
National holiday: Independence Day, 24 August (1991)
Constitution: using 1978 pre-independence constitution; new constitution currently being drafted
Legal system: based on civil law system; no judicial review of legislative acts
Suffrage: 18 years of age; universal
Executive branch:
chief of state: President Leonid Makarovych KRAVCHUK (since 5 December 1991); election last held 1 December 1991 (next to be held 26 June 1994); results—Leonid KRAVCHUK 61.59%, Vyacheslav CHORNOVIL 23.27%, Levko LUKYANENKO 4.49%, Volodymyr HRYNYOV 4.17%, Iher YUKHNOVSKY 1.74%, Leopold TABURYANSKYY 0.57%, other 4.17%
head of government: Prime Minister (vacant); Acting First Deputy Prime Minister (and Acting Prime Minister since September 1993) Yukhym Leonidovych ZVYAHIL'SKYY (since 11 June 1993) and five deputy prime ministers
cabinet: Council of Ministers; appointed by the president and approved by the Supreme Council
Legislative branch: unicameral
Supreme Council: elections last held 27 March 1994 (next to be held NA); results—percent of vote by party NA; seats—(450 total) number of seats by party NA; note—338 deputies were elected; the remaining 112 seats to be filled on 24 July 1994
Judicial branch: being organized
Political parties and leaders: Green Party of Ukraine, Vitaliy KONONOV, leader; Liberal Party of Ukraine, Ihor MERKULOV, chairman; Liberal Democratic Party of Ukraine, Volodymyr KLYMCHUK, chairman; Democratic Party of Ukraine, Volodymyr Oleksandrovych YAVORIVSKIY, chairman; People's Party of Ukraine, Leopol'd TABURYANSKYY, chairman; Peasants' Party of Ukraine, Serhiy

DOVGRAN', chairman; Party of Democratic Rebirth of Ukraine, Volodymyr FILENKO, chairman; Social Democratic Party of Ukraine, Yuriy ZBITNEV, chairman; Socialist Party of Ukraine, Oleksandr MOROZ, chairman; Ukrainian Christian Democratic Party, Vitaliy ZHURAVSKYY, chairman; Ukrainian Conservative Republican Party, Stepan KHMARA, chairman; Ukrainian Labor Party, Valentyn LANDYK, chairman; Ukrainian Party of Justice, Mykhaylo HRECHKO, chairman; Ukrainian Peasants' Democratic Party, Serhiy PLACHINDA, chairman; Ukrainian Republican Party, Mykhaylo HORYN', chairman; Ukrainian National Conservative Party, Viktor RADIONOV, chairman; Ukrainian People's Movement for Restructuring (Rukh), Vyacheslav CHORNOUL, chairman; Ukrainian Communist Party, Petr SYMONENKO
Other political or pressure groups: New Ukraine (Nova Ukrayina); Congress of National Democratic Forces
Member of: BSEC, CBSS (observer), CCC, CE (guest), CEI (participating), CIS, CSCE, EBRD, ECE, IAEA, IBRD, ICAO, ILO, IMF, INMARSAT, INTELSAT (nonsignatory user), INTERPOL, IOC, ITU, NACC, PCA, UN, UNCTAD, UNESCO, UNIDO, UNPROFOR, UPU, WHO, WIPO, WMO
Diplomatic representation in US:
chief of mission: Ambassador Oleh Hryhorovych BILORUS
chancery: 3350 M Street NW, Suite 200, Washington, DC 20007
telephone: (202) 333-0606
FAX: (202) 333-0817
consulate(s) general: Chicago and New York
US diplomatic representation:
chief of mission: Ambassador William MILLER
embassy: 10 Yuria Kotsyubinskovo, 252053 Kiev 53
mailing address: use embassy street address
telephone: [7] (044) 244-7349 or 244-7344
FAX: [7] (044) 244-7350
Flag: two equal horizontal bands of azure (top) and golden yellow represent grainfields under a blue sky

U.S. Government Contacts:

U.S. Trade Desk: (202) 482-1104

Chambers of Commerce & Organizations:

American Chamber of Commerce in Ukraine
7 Kudriavsky Uzviv, 2nd Floor
Kiev 252053, Ukraine
Tel: (7044) 417-1015
Fax: (7044) 416-9841

UZBEKISTAN

Economy

Overview: Uzbekistan is a dry, landlocked country of which 20% is intensely cultivated, irrigated river valleys. It is one of the poorest states of the former USSR with 60% of its population living in overpopulated rural communities. Nevertheless, Uzbekistan is the world's third largest cotton exporter, a major producer of gold and natural gas, and a regionally significant producer of chemicals and machinery. Since independence, the government has sought to prop up the Soviet-style command economy with subsidies and tight controls on prices and production. Such policies have buffered the economy from the sharp declines in output and high inflation experienced by many other former Soviet republics. By late 1993, however, they had become increasingly unsustainable as inflation soared and Russia forced the Uzbek Government to introduce its own currency. Faced with mounting economic problems, the government has increased its cooperation with international financial institutions, announced an acceleration of privatization, and stepped up efforts to attract foreign investors. Nevertheless, the regime is likely to resist full-fledged market reforms.

National product: GDP—purchasing power equivalent—$53.7 billion (1993 estimate from the UN International Comparison Program, as extended to 1991 and published in the World Bank's World Development Report 1993; and as extrapolated to 1993 using official Uzbek statistics, which are very uncertain because of major economic changes since 1990)
National product real growth rate: -3.5% (1993 est.)
National product per capita: $2,430 (1993 est.)
Inflation rate (consumer prices): 18% per month (1993)
Unemployment rate: 0.2% includes only officially registered unemployed; large numbers of underemployed workers
Budget:
revenues: $NA
expenditures: $NA, including capital expenditures of $NA
Exports: $706.5 million to outside the FSU countries (1993)
commodities: cotton, gold, natural gas, mineral fertilizers, ferrous metals, textiles, food products
partners: Russia, Ukraine, Eastern Europe, US
Imports: $947.3 million from outside the FSU countries (1993)
commodities: grain, machinery and parts, consumer durables, other foods
partners: principally other FSU countries, Czech Republic
External debt: $NA
Industrial production: growth rate -7% (1993)
Electricity:
capacity: 11,950,000 kW
production: 50.9 billion kWh
consumption per capita: 2,300 kWh (1992)
Industries: textiles, food processing, machine building, metallurgy, natural gas
Agriculture: livestock, cotton, vegetables, fruits, grain
Illicit drugs: illicit cultivator of cannabis and

opium poppy; mostly for CIS consumption; limited government eradication programs; used as transshipment points for illicit drugs to Western Europe
Economic aid:
recipient: $125 million by yearend 1993; future commitments for about $500 million
Currency: introduced provisional som-coupons 10 November 1993 which circulated parallel to the Russian rubles; became the sole legal currency 31 January 1994; will be replaced in July 1994 by the som currency
Exchange rates: NA
Fiscal year: calendar year

Communications

Railroads: 3,460 km; does not include industrial lines (1990)
Highways:
total: 78,400 km
paved and gravel: 67,000 km
unpaved: earth 11,400 km (1990)
Pipelines: crude oil 250 km, petroleum products 40 km, natural gas 810 km (1992)
Ports: none; landlocked
Airports:
total: 265
usable: 74
with permanent-surface runways: 30
with runways over 3,659 m: 2
with runways 2,440-3,659 m: 20
with runways 1,060-2,439 m: 19
note: a C-130 can land on a 1,060-m airstrip
Telecommunications: poorly developed; 1,458,000 telephone circuits with 68.75 circuits per 1000 persons (1991); linked by landline or microwave with CIS member states and by leased connection via the Moscow international gateway switch to other countries; new INTELSAT links to Tokyo and Ankara give Uzbekistan international access independent of Russian facilities; satellite earth stations—Orbita and INTELSAT; NMT-450 analog cellular network established in Tashkent

Defense Forces

Branches: Army, National Guard, Republic Security Forces (internal and border troops)
Manpower availability: males age 15-49 5,388,456; fit for military service 4,403,497; reach military age (18) annually 222,405 (1994 est.)
Defense expenditures: exchange rate conversion—$NA, NA% of GDP

Geography

Location: Central Asia, bordering the Aral Sea, between Kazakhstan and Turkmenistan
Map references: Asia, Commonwealth of Independent States—Central Asian States, Standard Time Zones of the World
Area:
total area: 447,400 sq km
land area: 425,400 sq km
comparative area: slightly larger than California
Land boundaries: total 6,221 km, Afghanistan 137 km, Kazakhstan 2,203 km, Kyrgyzstan 1,099 km, Tajikistan 1,161 km, Turkmenistan 1,621 km
Coastline: 0 km
note: Uzbekistan borders the Aral Sea (420 km)
Maritime claims: none; landlocked
International disputes: Russia may dispute current de facto maritime border to midpoint of Caspian Sea from shore
Climate: mostly midlatitude desert, long, hot summers, mild winters; semiarid grassland in east
Terrain: mostly flat-to-rolling sandy desert with dunes; broad, flat intensely irrigated river valleys along course of Amu Darya and Sirdaryo Rivers; Fergana Valley in east surrounded by mountainous Tajikistan and Kyrgyzstan; shrinking Aral Sea in west
Natural resources: natural gas, petroleum, coal, gold, uranium, silver, copper, lead and zinc, tungsten, molybdenum
Land use:
arable land: 10%
permanent crops: 1%
meadows and pastures: 47%
forest and woodland: 0%
other: 42%

Irrigated land: 41,550 sq km (1990)
Environment:
current issues: drying up of the Aral Sea is resulting in growing concentrations of chemical pesticides and natural salts; these substances are then blown from the increasingly exposed lake bed and contribute to desertification; water pollution from industrial wastes is the cause of many human health disorders; increasing soil salinization; soil contamination from agricultural chemicals, including DDT
natural hazards: NA
international agreements: party to—Climate Change, Environmental Modification, Ozone Layer Protection
Note: landlocked

People

Population: 22,608,866 (July 1994 est.)
Population growth rate: 2.13% (1994 est.)
Birth rate: 30.01 births/1,000 population (1994 est.)
Death rate: 6.51 deaths/1,000 population (1994 est.)
Net migration rate: -2.22 migrant(s)/1,000 population (1994 est.)
Infant mortality rate: 53.2 deaths/1,000 live births (1994 est.)
Life expectancy at birth:
total population: 68.58 years
male: 65.28 years
female: 72.04 years (1994 est.)
Total fertility rate: 3.73 children born/woman (1994 est.)
Nationality:
noun: Uzbek(s)
adjective: Uzbek
Ethnic divisions: Uzbek 71.4%, Russian 8.3%, Tajik 4.7%, Kazakh 4.1%, Tatar 2.4%, Karakalpak 2.1%, other 7%
Religions: Muslim 88% (mostly Sunnis), Eastern Orthodox 9%, other 3%
Languages: Uzbek 74.3%, Russian 14.2%, Tajik 4.4%, other 7.1%
Literacy: age 9-49 can read and write (1970)
total population: 100%
male: 100%
female: 100%
Labor force: 8.234 million
by occupation: agriculture and forestry 43%, industry and construction 22%, other 35% (1992)

Government

Names:
conventional long form: Republic of Uzbekistan
conventional short form: Uzbekistan
local long form: Uzbekiston Respublikasi
local short form: none
former: Uzbek Soviet Socialist Republic
Digraph: UZ
Type: republic
Capital: Tashkent (Toshkent)
Administrative divisions: 12 wiloyatlar (singular—wiloyat), 1 autonomous republic* (respublikasi, singular—respublika), and 1 city** (shahri); Andijon Wiloyati, Bukhoro Wiloyati, Jizzakh Wiloyati, Farghona Wiloyati, Karakalpakstan* (Nukus), Qashqadaryo Wiloyati (Qarshi), Khorazm Wiloyati (Urganch), Namangan Wiloyati, Nawoiy Wiloyati, Samarqand Wiloyati, Sirdaryo Wiloyati (Guliston), Surkhondaryo Wiloyati (Termiz), Toshkent Shahri**, Toshkent Wiloyati
note: an administrative division has the same name as its administrative center (exceptions have the administrative center name following in parentheses)
Independence: 31 August 1991 (from Soviet Union)
National holiday: Independence Day, 1 September (1991)
Constitution: new constitution adopted 8 December 1992
Legal system: evolution of Soviet civil law; still lacks independent judicial system
Suffrage: 18 years of age; universal
Executive branch:
chief of state: President Islam KARIMOV (since NA March 1990); election last held 29 December 1991 (next to be held NA December 1996); results—Islam KARIMOV 86%, Mukhammad SOLIKH 12%, other 2%
head of government: Prime Minister Abdulkhashim MUTALOV (since 13 January

1992), First Deputy Prime Minister Ismail Hakimovitch DJURABEKOV (since NA)
cabinet: Cabinet of Ministers; appointed by the president with approval of the Supreme Assembly
Legislative branch: unicameral
Supreme Soviet: elections last held 18 February 1990 (next to be held winter 1994); results—percent of vote by party NA; seats—(500 total) Communist 450, ERK 10, other 40; note—total number of seats will be reduced to 250 in next election
Judicial branch: Supreme Court
Political parties and leaders: People's Democratic Party (PDP; formerly Communist Party), Islam A. KARIMOV, chairman; Erk (Freedom) Democratic Party (EDP), Muhammad SOLIKH, chairman (in exile); note—ERK was banned 9 December 1992
Other political or pressure groups: Birlik (Unity) People's Movement (BPM), Abdul Rakhim PULATOV, chairman (in exile); Islamic Rebirth Party (IRP), Abdullah UTAYEV, chairman
note: PULATOV (BPM) and SOLIKH (EDP) are both in exile in the West; UTAYEV (IRP) is either in prison or in exile
Member of: CCC, CIS, CSCE, EBRD, ECE, ECO, ESCAP, IBRD, ICAO, IDA, IFC, ILO, IMF, IOC, ITU, NACC, NAM, UN, UNCTAD, WHO, WMO
Diplomatic representation in US:
chief of mission: Ambassador Fatikh TESHABAYEV
chancery: Suites 619 and 623, 1511 K Street NW, Washington DC, 20005
telephone: (202) 638-4266/4267
FAX: (202) 638-4268
consulate(s) general: New York
US diplomatic representation:
chief of mission: Ambassador Henry L. CLARKE
embassy: 82 Chelanzanskaya, Tashkent
mailing address: use embassy street address
telephone: [7] (3712) 77-14-07, 77-11-32
FAX: [7] (3712) 77-69-53
Flag: three equal horizontal bands of blue (top), white, and green separated by red fimbriations with a crescent moon and 12 stars in the upper hoist-side quadrant

U.S. Government Contacts:

U.S. Trade Desk: (202) 482-0360

ADDENDA

Abbreviations & Definitions

avdp.	avoirdupois
c.i.f.	cost, insurance, and freight
CY	calendar year
DWT	deadweight ton
est.	estimate
Ex-Im	Export-Import Bank of the United States
f.o.b.	free on board
FRG	Federal Republic of Germany (West Germany); used for information dated before 3 October 1990 or CY91
FSU	former Soviet Union
FY	fiscal year
FYROM	The Former Yugoslav Republic of Macedonia
GDP	gross domestic product
GDR	German Democratic Republic (East Germany); used for information dated before 3 October 1990 or CY91
GNP	gross national product
GRT	gross register ton
GWP	gross world product
km	kilometer
kW	kilowatt
kWh	kilowatt hour
m	meter
NA	not available
NEGL	negligible
nm	nautical mile
NZ	New Zealand
ODA	official development assistance
OOF	other official flows
PDRY	People's Democratic Republic of Yemen [Yemen (Aden) or South Yemen]; used for information dated before 22 May 1990 or CY91
sq km	square kilometer
sq mi	square mile
UAE	United Arab Emirates
UK	United Kingdom
US	United States
USSR	Union of Soviet Socialist Republics (Soviet Union); used for information dated before 25 December 1991
YAR	Yemen Arab Republic [Yemen (Sanaa) or North Yemen]; used for information dated before 22 May 1990 or CY91

Administrative divisions: The numbers, designatory terms, and first-order administrative divisions are generally those approved by the US Board on Geographic Names (BGN). Changes that have been reported but not yet acted on by BGN are noted.

Area: Total area is the sum of all land and water areas delimited by international boundaries and/or coastlines. Land area is the aggregate of all surfaces delimited by international boundaries and/or coastlines, excluding inland water bodies (lakes, reservoirs, rivers). Comparative areas are based on total area equivalents. Most entities are compared with the entire US or one of the 50 states. The smaller entities are compared with Washington, DC (178 sq km, 69 sq mi) or The Mall in Washington, DC (0.59 sq km, 0.23 sq mi, 146 acres).

Birth rate: The average annual number of births during a year per 1,000 population at midyear; also known as crude birth rate.

Dates of information: In general, information available as of 1 January 1994 was used in the preparation of this edition. Population figures are estimates for 1 July 1994, with population growth rates estimated for calendar year 1994. Major political events have been updated through May 1994.

Death rate: The average annual number of deaths during a year per 1,000 population at midyear; also known as crude death rate.

Digraphs: The digraph is a two-letter "country code" that precisely identifies every entity without overlap, duplication, or omission. AF, for example, is the digraph for Afghanistan. It is a standardized geopolitical data element promulgated in the *Federal Information Processing Standards Publication* (FIPS) 10-3 by the National Institute of Standards and Technology (US Department of Commerce) and maintained by the Office of the Geographer (US Department of State). The digraph is used to eliminate confusion and incompatibility in the collection, processing, and dissemination of area-specific data and is particularly useful for interchanging data between databases.

Diplomatic representation: The US Government has diplomatic relations with 183 nations, including 177 of the 184 UN members (excluded UN members are Bhutan, Cuba, Iran, Iraq, North Korea, Vietnam, and former Yugoslavia). In addition, the US has diplomatic relations with 6 nations that are not in the UN—Holy See, Kiribati, Nauru, Switzerland, Tonga, and Tuvalu.

Economic aid: This entry refers to bilateral commitments of official development assistance (ODA) and other official flows (OOF). ODA is defined as financial assistance which is concessional in character, has the main objective to promote economic development and welfare of LDCs. and contains a grant element of at least 25%. OOF transactions are also official government assistance, but with a main objective other than development and with a grant element less than 25%. OOF transactions include official export credits (such as Ex-Im Bank credits), official equity and portfolio investment, and debt reorganization by the official sector that does not meet concessional terms. Aid is considered to have been committed when agreements are initialed by the parties involved and constitute a formal declaration of intent.

Entities: Some of the nations, dependent areas, areas of special sovereignty, and governments included in this publication are not independent, and others are not officially recognized by the US Government. "Nation" refers to a people politically organized into a sovereign state with a definite territory. "Dependent area" refers to a broad category of political entities that are associated in some way with a nation. Names used for page headings are usually the short-form names as approved by the US Board on Geographic Names. There are 266 entities in *The World Factbook* that may be categorized as follows:

NATIONS

183 UN members (excluding both the Socialist Federal Republic of Yugoslavia and the Federal Republic of Yugoslavia; membership status in the UN is still to be determined)

7 nations that are not members of the UN—Holy See, Kiribati, Nauru, Serbia and Montenegro, Switzerland, Tonga, Tuvalu

OTHER

1 Taiwan

DEPENDENT AREAS

6 Australia—Ashmore and Cartier Islands, Christmas Island, Cocos (Keeling) Islands, Coral Sea Islands, Heard Island and McDonald Islands, Norfolk Island

2 Denmark—Faroe Islands, Greenland

16 France—Bassas da India, Clipperton Island, Europa Island, French Guiana, French Polynesia, French Southern and Antarctic Lands, Glorioso Islands, Guadeloupe, Juan de Nova Island, Martinique, Mayotte, New Caledonia, Reunion, Saint Pierre and Miquelon, Tromelin Island, Wallis and Futuna

2 Netherlands—Aruba, Netherlands Antilles

3 New Zealand—Cook Islands, Niue, Tokelau

3 Norway—Bouvet Island, Jan Mayen, Svalbard

1 Portugal—Macau

16 United Kingdom—Anguilla, Bermuda, British Indian Ocean Territory, British Virgin Islands, Cayman Islands, Falkland Islands, Gibraltar, Guernsey, Hong Kong, Jersey, Isle of Man, Montserrat, Pitcairn Islands, Saint Helena, South Georgia and the South Sandwich Islands, Turks and Caicos Islands

15 United States—American Samoa, Baker Island, Guam, Howland Island, Jarvis Island, Johnston Atoll, Kingman Reef, Midway

Islands, Navassa Island, Northern Mariana Islands, Trust Territory of the Pacific Islands (Palau), Palmyra Atoll, Puerto Rico, Virgin Islands, Wake Island

MISCELLANEOUS

6 Antarctica, Gaza Strip, Paracel Islands, Spratly Islands, West Bank, Western Sahara

OTHER ENTITIES

4 oceans—Arctic Ocean, Atlantic Ocean, Indian Ocean, Pacific Ocean

1 World

266 total

Exchange rate: The value of a nation's monetary unit at a given date or over a given period of time, as expressed in units of local currency per US dollar and as determined by international market forces or official fiat.

Gross domestic product (GDP): The value of all final goods and services produced within a nation in a given year.

Gross national product (GNP): The value of all final goods and services produced within a nation in a given year, plus income earned abroad, minus income earned by foreigners from domestic production.

Gross world product (GWP): The aggregate value of all goods and services produced worldwide in a given year.

GNP/GDP methodology: In the "Economy" section, GNP/GDP dollar estimates for the great majority of countries are derived from *purchasing power parity* (PPP) calculations rather than from conversions at official currency exchange rates. The PPP method normally involves the use of international dollar price weights, which are applied to the quantities of goods and services produced in a given economy. In addition to the lack of reliable data from the majority of countries, the statistician faces a major difficulty in specifying, identifying, and allowing for the quality of goods and services. The division of a GNP/GDP estimate in local currency by the corresponding PPP estimate in dollars gives *the PPP conversion rate*. On average, one thousand dollars will buy the same market basket of goods in the US as one thousand dollars—converted to the local currency at the PPP conversion rate—will buy in the other country. Whereas PPP estimates for OECD countries are quite reliable, PPP estimates for developing countries are often rough approximations. The latter estimates are based on extrapolation of numbers published by the UN International Comparison Program and by Professors Robert Summers and Alan Heston of the University of Pennsylvania and their colleagues. Because currency exchange rates depend on a variety of international and domestic financial forces that often have little relation to domestic output, use of these rates is less satisfactory for calculating GNP/GDP than the PPP method. In developing countries with weak currencies the exchange rate estimate of GNP/GDP in dollars is typically one-fourth to one-half the

PPP estimate. Furthermore, exchange rates may suddenly go up or down by 10% or more because of market forces or official fiat whereas real output has remained unchanged. On 12 January 1994, for example, the 14 countries of the African Financial Community (whose currencies are tied to the French franc) devalued their currencies by 50%. This move, of course, did not cut the real output of these countries by half. One additional caution: the proportion of, say, defense expenditures as a percent of GNP/GDP in local currency accounts may differ substantially from the proportion when GNP/GDP accounts are expressed in PPP terms, as, for example, when an observer estimates the dollar level of Russian or Japanese military expenditures.

Growth rate (population): The annual percent change in the population, resulting from a surplus (or deficit) of births over deaths and the balance of migrants entering and leaving a country. The rate may be positive or negative.

Illicit drugs: There are five categories of illicit drugs—narcotics, stimulants, depressants (sedatives), hallucinogens, and cannabis. These categories include many drugs legally produced and prescribed by doctors as well as those illegally produced and sold outside medical channels.

Cannabis (Cannabis sativa) is the common hemp plant, which provides hallucinogens with some sedative properties, and includes marijuana (pot, Acapulco gold, grass, reefer), tetrahydrocannabinol (THC, Marinol), hashish (hash), and hashish oil (hash oil).

Coca (Erythroxylon coca) is a bush, and the leaves contain the stimulant cocaine. Coca is not to be confused with cocoa, which comes from cacao seeds and is used in making chocolate, cocoa, and cocoa butter.

Cocaine is a stimulant derived from the leaves of the coca bush.

Depressants (sedatives) are drugs that reduce tension and anxiety and include chloral hydrate, barbiturates (Amytal, Nembutal, Seconal, phenobarbital), benzodiazepines (Librium, Valium), methaqualone (Quaalude), glutethimide (Doriden), and others (Equanil, Placidyl, Valmid).

Drugs are any chemical substances that effect a physical, mental, emotional, or behavioral change in an individual.

Drug abuse is the use of any licit or illicit chemical substance that results in physical, mental, emotional, or behavioral impairment in an individual.

Hallucinogens are drugs that affect sensation, thinking, self-awareness, and emotion. Hallucinogens include LSD (acid, microdot), mescaline and peyote (mexc, buttons, cactus), amphetamine variants (PMA, STP, DOB), phencyclidine (PCP, angel dust, hog), phencyclidine analogues (PCE, PCPy, TCP), and others (psilocybin, psilocyn).

Hashish is the resinous exudate of the cannabis or hemp plant (Cannabis sativa).

Heroin is a semisynthetic derivative of morphine.

Mandrax is a synthetic chemical depressant, the same as, or similar to, Quaalude.

Marijuana is the dried leaves of the cannabis or hemp plant (Cannabis sativa).

Narcotics are drugs that relieve pain, often induce sleep, and refer to opium, opium derivatives, and synthetic substitutes. Natural narcotics include opium (paregoric, parepectolin), morphine (MS-Contin, Roxanol), codeine (Tylenol with codeine, Empirin with codeine, Robitussan AC), and thebaine. Semisynthetic narcotics include heroin (horse, smack), and hydromorphone (Dilaudid). Synthetic narcotics include meperidine or Pethidine (Demerol, Mepergan), methadone (Dolophine, Methadose), and others (Darvon, Lomotil).

Opium is the milky exudate of the incised, unripe seedpod of the opium poppy.

Opium poppy (Papaver somniferum) is the source for many natural and semisynthetic narcotics.

Poppy straw concentrate is the alkaloid derived from the mature dried opium poppy.

Qat (kat, khat) is a stimulant from the buds or leaves of catha edulis that is chewed or drunk as tea.

Stimulants are drugs that relieve mild depression, increase energy and activity, and include cocaine (coke, snow, crack), amphetamines (Desoxyn, Dexedrine), phenmetrazine (Preludin), methylphenidate (Ritalin), and others (Cylert, Sanorex, Tenuate).

Infant mortality rate: The number of deaths to infants under one year old in a given year per 1,000 live births occurring in the same year.

International disputes: This category includes a wide variety of situations that range from traditional bilateral boundary disputes to unilateral claims of one sort or another. Information regarding disputes over international boundaries and maritime boundaries has been reviewed by the Department of State. References to other situations involving borders or frontiers may also be included, such as resource disputes, geopolitical questions, or irredentist issues. However, inclusion does not necessarily constitute official acceptance or recognition by the US Government.

Irrigated land: The figure refers to the land area that is artificially supplied with water.

Land use: Human use of the land surface is categorized as *arable land*—land cultivated for crops that are replanted after each harvest (wheat, maize, rice); *permanent crops*—land cultivated for crops that are not replanted after each harvest (citrus, coffee, rubber); *meadows and pastures*—land permanently used for herbaceous forage crops; *forest and woodland*—under dense or open stands of trees; and *other*—any land type not specifically mentioned above (urban areas, roads, desert).

Leaders: The chief of state is the titular leader of the country who represents the state at official and ceremonial functions but is not involved with the day-to-day activities of the government. The head of government is the administrative leader who manages the day-to-day activities of the government. In the UK, the monarch is the chief of state, and the Prime Minister is the head of government. In the US, the President is both the chief of state and the head of government.

Life expectancy at birth: The average number of years to be lived by a group of people all born in the same year, if mortality at each age remains constant in the future.

Literacy: There are no universal definitions and standards of literacy. Unless otherwise noted, all rates are based on the most common definition—the ability to read and write at a specified age. Detailing the standards that individual countries use to assess the ability to read and write is beyond the scope of this publication.

Maritime claims: The proximity of neighboring states may prevent some national claims from being extended the full distance.

Merchant marine: All ships engaged in the carriage of goods. All commercial vessels (as opposed to all nonmilitary ships), which excludes tugs, fishing vessels, offshore oil rigs, etc.; also, a grouping of merchant ships by nationality or register.

Captive register—A register of ships maintained by a territory, possession, or colony primarily or exclusively for the use of ships owned in the parent country; also referred to as an offshore register, the offshore equivalent of an internal register. Ships on a captive register will fly the same flag as the parent country, or a local variant of it, but will be subject to the maritime laws and taxation rules of the offshore territory. Although the nature of a captive register makes it especially desirable for ships owned in the parent country, just as in the internal register, the ships may also be owned abroad. The captive register then acts as a flag of convenience register, except that it is not the register of an independent state.

Flag of convenience register—A national register offering registration to a merchant ship not owned in the flag state. The major flags of convenience (FOC) attract ships to their register by virtue of low fees, low or nonexistent taxation of profits, and liberal manning requirements. True FOC registers are characterized by having relatively few of the ships registered actually owned in the flag state. Thus, while virtually any flag can be used for ships under a given set of circumstances, an FOC register is one where the majority of the merchant fleet is owned abroad. It is also referred to as an open register.

Flag state—The nation in which a ship is registered and which holds legal jurisdiction over operation of the ship, whether at home or abroad. Differences in flag state maritime legislation determine how a ship is manned and taxed and whether a foreign-owned ship may be placed on the register.

Internal register—A register of ships maintained as a subset of a national register. Ships on the internal register fly the national flag and have that nationality but are subject to a separate set of maritime rules from those on the main national register. These differences usually include lower taxation of profits, manning by foreign nationals, and, usually, ownership outside the flag state (when it functions as an FOC register). The Norwegian International Ship Register and Danish International Ship

Register are the most notable examples of an internal register. Both have been instrumental in stemming flight from the national flag to flags of convenience and in attracting foreign owned ships to the Norwegian and Danish flags.

Merchant ship—A vessel that carries goods against payment of freight; commonly used to denote any nonmilitary ship but accurately restricted to commercial vessels only.

Register—The record of a ship's ownership and nationality as listed with the maritime authorities of a country; also, the compendium of such individual ships' registrations. Registration of a ship provides it with a nationality and makes it subject to the laws of the country in which registered (the flag state) regardless of the nationality of the ship's ultimate owner.

Money figures: All money figures are expressed in contemporaneous US dollars unless otherwise indicated.

National product: The total output of goods and services in a country in a given year. See Gross domestic product (GDP), Gross national product (GNP), and GNP/GDP methodology.

Net migration rate: The balance between the number of persons entering and leaving a country during the year per 1,000 persons (based on midyear population). An excess of persons entering the country is referred to as net immigration (3.56 migrants/1,000 population); an excess of persons leaving the country as net emigration (-9.26 migrants/1,000 population).

Population: Figures are estimates from the Bureau of the Census based on statistics from population censuses, vital statistics registration systems, or sample surveys pertaining to the recent past, and on assumptions about future trends. Starting with the 1993 Factbook, demographic estimates for some countries (mostly African) have taken into account the effects of the growing incidence of AIDS infections; in 1993 these countries were Burkina, Burundi, Central African Republic, Congo, Cote d'Ivoire, Haiti, Kenya, Malawi, Rwanda, Tanzania, Uganda, Zaire, Zambia, Zimbabwe, Thailand, and Brazil.

Total fertility rate: The average number of children that would be born per woman if all women lived to the end of their childbearing years and bore children according to a given fertility rate at each age.

Years: All year references are for the calendar year (CY) unless indicated as fiscal year (FY).

International Organizations Abbreviations

ABEDA	Arab Bank for Economic Development in Africa
ACC	Arab Cooperation Council
ACCT	Agence de Cooperation Culturelle et Technique; see Agency for Cultural and Technical Cooperation
ACP	African, Caribbean, and Pacific Countries
AfDB	African Development Bank
AFESD	Arab Fund for Economic and Social Development
AG	Andean Group
AL	Arab League
ALADI	Asociacion Latinoamericana de Integracion; see Latin American Integration Association (LAIA)
AMF	Arab Monetary Fund
AMU	Arab Maghreb Union
ANZUS	Australia-New Zealand-United States Security Treaty
APEC	Asia Pacific Economic Cooperation
AsDB	Asian Development Bank
ASEAN	Association of Southeast Asian Nations
BAD	Banque Africaine de Developpement; see African Development Bank (AfDB)
BADEA	Banque Arabe de Developpement Economique en Afrique; see Arab Bank for Economic Development in Africa (ABEDA)
BCIE	Banco Centroamericano de Integracion Economico; see Central American Bank for Economic Integration (BCIE)
BDEAC	Banque de Developpment des Etats de l'Afrique Centrale; see Central African States Development Bank (BDEAC)
Benelux	Benelux Economic Union
BID	Banco Interamericano de Desarrollo; see Inter-American Development Bank (IADB)
BIS	Bank for International Settlements
BOAD	Banque Ouest-Africaine de Developpement; see West African Development Bank (WADB)
BSEC	Black Sea Economic Cooperation Zone
C	Commonwealth
CACM	Central American Common Market
CAEU	Council of Arab Economic Unity

CARICOM	Caribbean Community and Common Market
CBSS	Council of the Baltic Sea States
CCC	Customs Cooperation Council
CDB	Caribbean Development Bank
CE	Council of Europe
CEAO	Communaute Economique de l'Afrique de l'Ouest; see West African Economic Community (CEAO)
CEEAC	Communaute Economique des Etats de l'Afrique Centrale; see Economic Community of Central African States (CEEAC)
CEI	Central European Initiative
CEMA	Council for Mutual Economic Assistance; also known as CMEA or Comecon; abolished 1 January 1991
CEPGL	Communaute Economique des Pays des Grands Lacs; see Economic Community of the Great Lakes Countries (CEPGL)
CERN	Conseil Europeen pour la Recherche Nucleaire; see European Organization for Nuclear Research (CERN)
CG	Contadora Group
CIS	Commonwealth of Independent States
CMEA	Council for Mutual Economic Assistance (CEMA); also known as Comecon; abolished 1 January 1991
COCOM	Coordinating Committee on Export Controls
Comecon	Council for Mutual Economic Assistance (CEMA); also known as CMEA; abolished 1 January 1991
CP	Colombo Plan
CSCE	Conference on Security and Cooperation in Europe
DC	developed country
EADB	East African Development Bank
EBRD	European Bank for Reconstruction and Development
EC	European Community; see European Union (EU)
ECA	Economic Commission for Africa
ECAFE	Economic Commission for Asia and the Far East; see Economic and Social Commission for Asia and the Pacific (ESCAP)
ECE	Economic Commission for Europe
ECLA	Economic Commission for Latin America; see Economic Commission for Latin America and the Caribbean (ECLAC)
ECLAC	Economic Commission for Latin America and the Caribbean
ECO	Economic Cooperation Organization
ECOSOC	Economic and Social Council
ECOWAS	Economic Community of West African States

ECSC	European Coal and Steel Community
ECWA	Economic Commission for Western Asia: see Economic and Social Commission for Western Asia (ESCWA)
EEC	European Economic Community
EFTA	European Free Trade Association
EIB	European Investment Bank
Entente	Council of the Entente
ESA	European Space Agency
ESCAP	Economic and Social Commission for Asia and the Pacific
ESCWA	Economic and Social Commission for Western Asia
EU	European Union
Euratom	European Atomic Energy Community
FAO	Food and Agriculture Organization
FLS	Front Line States
FZ	Franc Zone
G-2	Group of 2
G-3	Group of 3
G-5	Group of 5
G-6	Group of 6 (not to be confused with the Big Six)
G-7	Group of 7
G-8	Group of 8
G-9	Group of 9
G-10	Group of 10
G-11	Group of 11
G-15	Group of 15
G-19	Group of 19
G-24	Group of 24
G-30	Group of 30
G-33	Group of 33
G-77	Group of 77
GATT	General Agreement on Tariffs and Trade
GCC	Gulf Cooperation Council
Habitat	Commission on Human Settlements
IADB	Inter-American Development Bank
IAEA	International Atomic Energy Agency
IBEC	International Bank for Economic Cooperation

IBRD	International Bank for Reconstruction and Development
ICAO	International Civil Aviation Organization
ICC	International Chamber of Commerce
ICEM	Intergovernmental Committee for European Migration: see International Organization for Migration (IOM)
ICFTU	International Confederation of Free Trade Unions
ICJ	International Court of Justice
ICM	Intergovernmental Committee for Migration: see International Organization for Migration (IOM)
ICRC	International Committee of the Red Cross
IDA	International Development Association
IDB	Islamic Development Bank
IEA	International Energy Agency
IFAD	International Fund for Agricultural Development
IFC	International Finance Corporation
IFCTU	International Federation of Christian Trade Unions
IGADD	Inter-Governmental Authority on Drought and Development
IIB	International Investment Bank
ILO	International Labor Organization
IMCO	Intergovernmental Maritime Consultative Organization: see International Maritime Organization (IMO)
IMF	International Monetary Fund
IMO	International Maritime Organization
INMARSAT	International Maritime Satellite Organization
INTELSAT	International Telecommunications Satellite Organization
INTERPOL	International Criminal Police Organization
IOC	International Olympic Committee
IOM	International Organization for Migration
ISO	International Organization for Standardization
ITU	International Telecommunication Union
LAES	Latin American Economic System
LAIA	Latin American Integration Association
LAS	League of Arab States: see Arab League (AL)
LDC	less developed country
LLDC	least developed country
LORCS	League of Red Cross and Red Crescent Societies

MERCOSUR	Mercado Comun del Cono Sur; see Southern Cone Common Market
MINURSO	United Nations Mission for the Referendum in Western Sahara
MTCR	Missile Technology Control Regime
NACC	North Atlantic Cooperation Council
NAM	Nonaligned Movement
NATO	North Atlantic Treaty Organization
NC	Nordic Council
NEA	Nuclear Energy Agency
NIB	Nordic Investment Bank
NIC	newly industrializing country; see newly industrializing economy (NIE)
NIE	newly industrializing economy
NSG	Nuclear Suppliers Group
OAPEC	Organization of Arab Petroleum Exporting Countries
OAS	Organization of American States
OAU	Organization of African Unity
OECD	Organization for Economic Cooperation and Development
OECS	Organization of Eastern Caribbean States
OIC	Organization of the Islamic Conference
ONUSAL	United Nations Observer Mission in El Salvador
OPANAL	Organismo para la Proscripcion de las Armas Nucleares en la America Latina y el Caribe; see Agency for the Prohibition of Nuclear Weapons in Latin America and the Caribbean
OPEC	Organization of Petroleum Exporting Countries
PCA	Permanent Court of Arbitration
RG	Rio Group
SAARC	South Asian Association for Regional Cooperation
SACU	Southern African Customs Union
SADC	Southern African Development Community
SADCC	Southern African Development Coordination Conference
SELA	Sistema Economico Latinoamericana; see Latin American Economic System (LAES)
SPARTECA	South Pacific Regional Trade and Economic Cooperation Agreement
SPC	South Pacific Commission
SPF	South Pacific Forum
UDEAC	Union Douaniere et Economique de l'Afrique Centrale; see Central African Customs and Economic Union (UDEAC)

UN	United Nations
UNAVEM II	United Nations Angola Verification Mission
UNCTAD	United Nations Conference on Trade and Development
UNDOF	United Nations Disengagement Observer Force
UNDP	United Nations Development Program
UNEP	United Nations Environment Program
UNESCO	United Nations Educational, Scientific, and Cultural Organization
UNFICYP	United Nations Force in Cyprus
UNFPA	United Nations Fund for Population Activities: see UN Population Fund (UNFPA)
UNHCR	United Nations Office of the High Commissioner for Refugees
UNICEF	United Nations Children's Fund
UNIDO	United Nations Industrial Development Organization
UNIFIL	United Nations Interim Force in Lebanon
UNIKOM	United Nations Iraq-Kuwait Observation Mission
UNMOGIP	United Nations Military Observer Group in India and Pakistan
UNOMIG	United Nations Observer Mission in Georgia
UNOMOZ	United Nations Operation in Mozambique
UNOMUR	United Nations Observer Mission Uganda-Rwanda
UNOSOM	United Nations Operation in Somalia
UNPROFOR	United Nations Protection Force
UNRWA	United Nations Relief and Works Agency for Palestine Refugees
UNTAC	United Nations Transitional Authority in Cambodia
UNTSO	United Nations Truce Supervision Organization
UPU	Universal Postal Union
WADB	West African Development Bank
WCL	World Confederation of Labor
WEU	Western European Union
WFC	World Food Council
WFP	World Food Program
WFTU	World Federation of Trade Unions
WHO	World Health Organization
WIPO	World Intellectual Property Organization
WMO	World Meteorological Organization
WP	Warsaw Pact (members met 1 July 1991 to dissolve the alliance)
WTO	World Tourism Organization
ZC	Zangger Committee

International Economic Statistics

Selected World Statistics [a]

	1990	1991	1992	1993
Gross domestic product *(billion 1993 US $)*[b]	28,028.0	28,044.0	28,528.0	29,132.0
Population *(million persons, midyear)*	5,295.0	5,381.0	5,469.0	5,556.0
Exports *(billion US $)*	3,424.6	3,533.2	3,759.6	3,730.7
Crude oil, excluding natural gas liquids *(million b/d)*	60.6	60.1	60.0	59.6
Natural gas *(trillion cubic meters)*	2.1	2.1	2.1	2.1
Hard coal *(million metric tons)*[c]	3,515.0	3,450.0	3,530.0	3,640.0
Brown coal and lignite *(million metric tons)*	1,210.0	1,180.0	970.0	945.0
Electricity *(billion kilowatt-hours)*	11,800.0	12,035.0	11,460.0	11,985.0
Iron ore *(million metric tons)*	893.0	956.0	930.0	940.0
Bauxite *(million metric tons)*	109.0	107.9	101.6	105.6
Pig iron *(million metric tons)*	555.0	526.0	517.0	528.0
Crude steel *(million metric tons)*	771.0	736.0	722.0	725.0
Refined copper *(thousand metric tons)*	10,696.0	10,637.0	10,917.0	NA
Primary aluminum *(million metric tons)*	19.3	19.6	19.5	19.8
Smelter lead *(thousand metric tons)*	3,098.0	3,008.0	3,042.0	NA
Refined zinc *(thousand metric tons)*	7,109.0	7,101.0	6,210.0	NA
Primary tin *(thousand metric tons)*	227.0	183.0	190.0	NA
Mineral fertilizer[d] *(million metric tons)*	152.6	147.9	144.2	138.3
Nitrogen fertilizer[d] *(million metric tons of N)*	84.6	81.9	80.6	79.9
Phosphate fertilizer[d] *(million metric tons of P_2O_5)*	39.7	39.0	38.6	34.8
Potassium fertilizer[d] *(million metric tons of K_2O)*	28.3	26.7	25.0	23.5
Synthetic fibers *(thousand metric tons)*	13,265.0	11,598.0	11,200.0	11,300.0
Automobiles *(thousand units)*	35,700.0	34,400.0	34,000.0	NA
Grain *(million metric tons)*	1,930.0	1,860.0	1,936.0	1,853.0
Wheat *(million metric tons)*	589.0	543.0	560.0	562.0
Coarse grain *(million metric tons)*	821.0	803.0	856.0	777.0
Rice *(million metric tons)*	518.0	515.0	520.0	514.0
Sugar *(million metric tons)*	113.6	115.9	111.3	112.7
Coffee *(thousand metric tons)*	6,028.0	6,259.0	5,575.0	5,650.0

[a] For more detailed descriptions and definitions, refer to the respective table.

[b] Data were converted to US dollars by the use of purchasing power parities used by international organizations and academia.

[c] Including brown coal at its hard coal equivalent.

[d] Fertilizer year ending 30 June of the stated year.

Percent

Share of Global Exports of High-Technology Products

Microelectronics		Computers	
1980	1990	1980	1990
United States (18.3)	United States (27.5)	United States (38.6)	United States (24.2)
Japan (13.2)	Japan (21.7)	Germany[a] (11.5)	Japan (17.3)
Singapore (10.1)	Malaysia (7.2)	United Kingdom (10.4)	United Kingdom (8.7)
Malaysia (8.9)	South Korea (6.7)	France (8.6)	Germany[a] (6.6)
Germany[a] (8.4)	Germany[a] (4.0)	Italy (6.6)	Taiwan (6.3)
France (4.9)	Taiwan (3.8)	Japan (4.3)	Singapore (6.1)
Hong Kong (4.8)	Singapore (3.6)	Canada (3.4)	Netherlands (4.2)
United Kingdom (4.5)	United Kingdom (3.5)	Sweden (2.9)	France (4.0)
South Korea (4.2)	France (2.7)	Hong Kong (1.9)	Italy (3.3)
Philippines (3.8)	Canada (2.3)	Netherlands (1.6)	South Korea (2.5)

Machine Tools and Robotics		Scientific/Precision Equipment	
1980	1990	1980	1990
Germany[a] (25.8)	Japan (21.8)	United States (28.3)	United States (27.4)
United States (14.1)	Germany[a] (20.2)	Germany[a] (18.1)	Germany[a] (16.9)
Japan (11.3)	United States (13.1)	United Kingdom (9.4)	Japan (12.9)
Switzerland (9.1)	Italy (9.7)	France (8.0)	United Kingdom (7.0)
Italy (8.7)	Switzerland (7.3)	Japan (7.1)	France (5.6)
United Kingdom (6.9)	United Kingdom (4.5)	Switzerland (5.5)	Switzerland (4.1)
France (6.3)	France (3.6)	Netherlands (4.2)	Netherlands (3.8)
Sweden (2.4)	Netherlands (2.5)	Italy (3.0)	Italy (2.9)
Canada (1.8)	Sweden (2.5)	Belgium (2.7)	Sweden (2.4)
Netherlands (1.8)	Taiwnan (2.1)	Sweden (2.7)	Belgium (2.3)

Telecommunications Equipment		Aerospace	
1980	1990	1980	1990
Germany[a] (16.7)	Japan (28.4)	United States (47.6)	United States (50.3)
Sweden (15.3)	United States (15.9)	United Kingdom (19.7)	France (17.5)
United States (10.9)	Sweden (6.9)	Germany[a] (9.1)	United Kingdom (7.7)
Japan (10.3)	Germany[a] (6.5)	France (6.0)	Germany[a] (4.1)
Netherlands (9.3)	Canada (4.7)	Canada (4.4)	Canada (4.0)
Belgium (7.4)	Taiwan (3.9)	Netherlands (2.5)	Netherlands (2.5)
France (6.5)	South Korea (3.4)	Italy (2.1)	Italy (0.9)
Canada (5.1)	Netherlands (3.3)	Belgium (1.2)	Japan (0.9)
United Kingdom (4.1)	France (3.1)	Switzerland (0.8)	Sweden (0.9)
Italy (2.7)	United Kingdom (3.1)	Japan (0.6)	Switzerland (0.5)

Medicine and Biologicals		Organic Chemicals	
1980	1990	1980	1990
Germany[a] (16.7)	Germany[a] (15.4)	Germany[a] (19.1)	Germany[a] (16.0)
Switzerland (12.5)	United States (13.5)	United States (13.9)	United States (14.9)
United Kingdom (12.0)	Switzerland (12.3)	Netherlands (10.9)	Netherlands (11.8)
France (11.9)	United Kingdom (12.2)	France (10.7)	France (9.2)
United States (11.4)	France (8.6)	United Kingdom (8.4)	United Kingdom (7.2)
Italy (5.4)	Italy (5.1)	Japan (6.3)	Japan (7.1)
Belgium (5.2)	Belgium (4.9)	Belgium (6.1)	Belgium, (6.7)
Netherlands (4.7)	Netherlands (4.7)	Italy (4.6)	Italy (4.8)
Sweden (2.5)	Sweden (4.6)	Switzerland (3.3)	Switzerland (3.3)
Japan (2.2)	Japan (2.8)	Canada (2.5)	Canada (2.1)

Thousand barrels per day of oil equivalent

Primary Energy Production[a]

	1990	1991	1992	1993
OECD				
United States	33,015	33,285	33,175	32,525
Canada	5,510	5,730	5,900	6,275
Japan	1,380	1,455	1,480	1,485
Norway	2,400	2,615	2,910	3,050
European Union				
Germany	3,700	3,325	3,220	3,010
France	2,085	2,185	2,230	2,215
Netherlands	1,195	1,335	1,335	1,360
United Kingdom	4,150	4,275	4,270	4,325
Selected East European				
Russia	25,260	23,890	22,270	20,900
Ukraine	NA	2,040	1,978	1,770
Bulgaria	195	179	176	173
Hungary	297	294	276	256
Poland	1,955	1,900	1,790	1,792
Romania	818	729	693	692
Other				
China	14,470	NA	NA	NA

[a]Data are for coal, crude oil, natural gas, natural gas liquids, and hydroelectric and nuclear electric power expressed in terms of oil equivalent.

Thousand barrels per day of oil equivalent

Primary Energy Production, by Type[a]

	1993			
	Coal	Crude Oil	Natural Gas	Hydro/ Nuclear
OECD				
United States	11,725	8,000	8,650	4,150
Canada	925	2,075	2,300	975
Japan	80	15	40	1,350
European Union				
Germany	1,825	60	275	850
France	200	65	50	1,900
Netherlands	5	60	1,275	20
United Kingdom	850	2,000	1,050	425
Selected East European				
Russia	2,560	7,040	9,965	1,335
Ukraine	980	85	310	395
Bulgaria	97	1	NEGL	75
Hungary	60	32	90	74
Poland	1,702	4	70	16
Romania	156	139	334	63
Other				
China	10,700[b]	2,770[b]	290[b]	710[b]

[a]Data are for coal, crude oil, natural gas, natural gas liquids, and hydroelectric and nuclear electric power expressed in terms of oil equivalent.
[b]Data are for 1990.

Thousand barrels per day

Crude Oil Production[a]

	1990	1991	1992	1993
OECD[b]				
United States	7,355	7,417	7,171	6,838
Canada	1,518	1,548	1,604	1,684
Norway	1,620	1,876	2,144	2,247
European Union				
United Kingdom	1,850	1,823	1,864	1,866
Selected East European				
Russia[c]	10,320	9,220	7,880	7,040
Kazakhstan[c]	510	530	514	460
Azerbaijan[c]	248	234	226	201
Hungary	40	39	33	32
Romania	160	140	136	139
OPEC				
Algeria	794	803	772	750
Indonesia	1,289	1,411	1,346	1,323
Iran	3,252	3,358	3,455	3,640
Iraq	2,080	283	425	436
Kuwait[d]	1,235	200	1,050	1,873
Libya	1,374	1,509	1,493	1,367
Nigeria	1,811	1,867	1,902	1,896
Saudi Arabia[d]	6,414	8,223	8,308	8,162
United Arab Emirates	2,117	2,416	2,322	2,225
Venezuela	2,085	2,350	2,314	2,332
Other				
China	2,769	2,785	2,835	2,900
Mexico	2,648	2,774	2,668	2,664

[a] Unless otherwise indicated, data are for crude oil and exclude natural gas liquids, shale oil, natural gasoline, and synthetic crude oil.
[b] Including shale oil.
[c] Including natural gas liquids.
[d] Including about one-half of Neutral Zone production.

World Crude Oil Prices

	1990	1991	1992	1993
OPEC official average sales price[a]				
US $ per barrel	21.76	18.58	18.33	16.08
1993 US $ per barrel[c]	23.86	19.60	18.80	16.08
World average price				
US $ per barrel	22.12	18.72	18.24	16.13
1993 US $ per barrel[c]	24.25	19.75	18.71	16.13

[a] F.o.b. prices set by the OPEC governments for direct sales

[b] Posted prices.

[c] Nominal price deflated by the US GDP deflator.

Proved Reserves of Crude Oil, and Natural Gas, Yearend 1993

	Crude Oil (*Billion barrels*)	Natural Gas (Trillion cubic feet)
OECD		
United States	24	165
Canada	5	95
Norway	9	70
European Union		
Germany	NEGL	12
Italy	1	11
Netherlands	NEGL	68
United Kingdom	5	22
Selected East European		
Russia	35	1,748
Poland	NEGL	5
Romania	2	8
Other		
OPEC		
Algeria	9	128
Indonesia	6	64
Iran	93	730
Iraq	100	110
Kuwait	94	52
Libya	23	46
Nigeria	18	120
Qatar	4	250
Saudi Arabia	259	185
United Arab Emirates	98	205
Venezuela	63	129
Other		
Brazil	4	5
Egypt	6	15
India	6	25
Malaysia	4	77
Mexico	51	71
Oman	5	20
Syria	2	7

Table 76 *Thousand troy ounces*

Selected Countries: Platinum-Group Metals Production

	1990	1991	1992	1993
South Africa[a]	4,563	4,593	4,916	4,800
Russia	4,019	3,906	3,346	2,400
Canada	376	376	329	444
United States[b]	249	250	267	268
Colombia	42	52	63	64
Japan	79	66	52	60
Australia	16	16	16	16
Finland	5	5	5	5
Serbia[c]	5	4	2	2
Zimbabwe	2	2	1	1

[a]Platinum-group metals from platinum ores and osmium and iridium from gold ores.
[b]Crude placer platinum and byproduct metals recovered largely from domestic copper refining.
[c]Including Montenegro.

Table 77 *Million troy ounces*

Selected Countries: Gold Production

	1990	1991	1992	1993
South Africa	19.45	19.33	19.74	19.92
United States	9.33	8.96	9.52	NA
Australia	7.85	7.53	7.83	7.72
China	3.22	3.86	4.50	5.14
Canada	5.45	5.68	5.17	4.92
Russia	NA	NA	4.69	4.18
Papua New Guinea	1.03	1.95	2.29	2.85
Uzbekistan	NA	NA	2.60	2.60
Brazil	3.28	2.87	2.86	1.89
Colombia	.94	1.12	1.03	1.06

Million persons, annual average

Industrial Employment [a]

	1990	1991	1992	1993
OECD				
United States	29.61	28.25	27.65	27.45
Canada	2.96	2.73	2.63	2.61
Japan	20.89	21.52	21.85	21.69
European Union				
France	6.42	6.33	6.12	5.87
Germany [b]	10.88	10.93	10.85	10.43
Italy	6.84	6.91	6.85	NA
United Kingdom	7.47	6.90	6.50	6.17
Selected East European				
Russia	25.09	25.28	25.55	25.66
Ukraine	6.87	6.91	NA	NA
Bulgaria [c]	1.77	1.55	1.35	1.14 [d]
Czech Republic	NA	NA	NA	2.04
Hungary [ce]	1.69	1.52	1.32	1.20 [d]
Poland [c]	5.76	5.18	4.81	4.45 [d]
Romania [ce]	4.58	4.15	3.30	NA
Slovakia	NA	NA	NA	.83
Other				
China [e]	121.58	124.71	NA	NA

[a] Includes employment in manufacturing, mining, and construction.
[b] Western area only.
[c] Official statistics. Beginning in 1990, figures are distorted because government statistical officials are not able to track all of private sector employment.
[d] Midyear data.
[e] Yearend data.

Million persons

Nonagricultural Labor Force[a]

	1990	1991	1992	1993
OECD				
United States	121.43	121.91	123.60	124.78
Canada	13.15	13.20	13.27	13.40
Japan	58.78	60.29	61.13	61.82
European Union				
France	23.05	23.28	23.39	23.52
Germany[b]	28.44	28.85	29.17	29.12
Italy	20.79	21.13	21.18	NA
United Kingdom	27.97	27.84	27.68	27.62
Selected East European				
Russia	71.88	71.93	73.26	73.58
Ukraine	22.81	22.95	23.40	23.44
Bulgaria[c]	3.40	3.16	3.05	NA
Czech Republic	NA	NA	NA	NA
Hungary[c]	4.79	4.81	4.74	4.67[d]
Poland[c]	12.54	12.90	13.19	13.44[d]
Romania[c]	7.69	7.91	7.94	NA
Slovakia	NA	NA	NA	2.14
Other				
China[e]	225.63	233.48	NA	NA

[a]Excludes the armed forces but includes the unemployed. Annual averages of monthly data, unless otherwise indicated.
[b]Western area only.
[c]Official statistics. Beginning in 1990, figures are distorted because government statistical officials are not able to track all of private sector employment.
[d]Midyear data.
[e]Yearend data, series revised in 1985.

Gross Domestic Product Per Capita, 1993[a]
(in 1993 US $)

More than $15,000

Aruba
Australia
Austria
Bahamas, The
Belgium
Bermuda
Canada
Cayman Islands
Denmark
Finland
France
Germany
Hong Kong
Iceland
Italy
Japan
Liechtenstein
Luxembourg
Monaco
Netherlands
New Zealand
Norway
Qatar
San Marino
Singapore
Sweden
Switzerland
United Arab Emirates
United Kingdom
United States

$10,001 to $15,000

Andorra
Bahrain
Brunei
Cyprus
Faroe Islands
Guam
Ireland
Israel
Korea, South
Kuwait
Northern Mariana Islands
Saudi Arabia
Spain
Taiwan
Virgin Islands, British
Virgin Islands, US

$3,001 to $10,000

Algeria
American Samoa
Anguilla
Antigua and Barbuda
Argentina
Barbados
Belarus
Bosnia and Herzegovina
Botswana
Brazil
Bulgaria
Chile
Colombia
Costa Rica
Croatia
Czech Republic
Ecuador
Estonia
Falkland Islands
Fiji
French Guiana
French Polynesia
Gabon
Gibraltar
Greece
Greenland
Grenada
Guadeloupe
Hungary
Iran
Jamaica
Kazakhstan
Latvia
Libya
Lithuania
Macau
Malaysia
Malta
Man, Isle of
Martinique
Mauritius
Mexico
Moldova
Montserrat
Nauru
Netherlands Antilles
New Caledonia
Oman
Pacific Islands, Trust Territory of the
Panama
Poland
Portugal
Puerto Rico
Reunion
Russia
St. Kitts and Nevis
St. Pierre and Miquelon
Seychelles
Slovakia
Slovenia
South Africa
Syria
Thailand
Trinidad and Tobago
Tunisia
Turkey
Turkmenistan
Turks and Caicos Islands
Ukraine
Uruguay
Venezuela

$1,000 to $3,000

Albania
Armenia
Azerbaijan
Bangladesh
Belize
Benin
Bolivia
Cameroon
Cape Verde
China
Congo
Cook Islands
Cote d'Ivoire
Cuba
Djibouti
Dominica
Dominican Republic
Egypt
El Salvador
Gaza Strip
Georgia
Ghana
Guatemala
Guyana
Honduras
India
Indonesia
Iraq
Jordan
Kenya
Korea, North
Kyrgyzstan
Lebanon
Lesotho
Marshall Islands
Mauritania
Micronesia, Federated States of
Mongolia
Morocco
Namibia
Nepal
Nicaragua
Nigeria
Niue
Pakistan
Papua New Guinea
Paraguay
Peru
Philippines
Romania
Saint Lucia
Saint Vincent and the Grenadines
Senegal
Serbia and Montenegro
Sierra Leone
Solomon Islands
Sri Lanka
Suriname
Swaziland
Tajikistan
The Former Yugoslav Republic of Macedonia
Tokelau
Tonga
Uganda
Uzbekistan
Vanuatu
Vietnam
Wallis and Futuna
West Bank
Western Samoa
Zimbabwe

[a] GDP per capita data are calculated using GDP converted at purchasing power exchange rates.

Geographic Name Reference Guide

Name	Geographic Area
Abidjan [US Embassy]	Cote d'Ivoire
Abu Dhabi [US Embassy]	United Arab Emirates
Abuja [US Embassy Branch Office]	Nigeria
Acapulco [US Consular Agency]	Mexico
Accra [US Embassy]	Ghana
Adamstown	Pitcairn Islands
Adana [US Consulate]	Turkey
Addis Ababa [US Embassy]	Ethiopia
Adelaide [US Consular Agency]	Australia
Adelie Land (Terre Adelie) [claimed by France]	Antarctica
Aden	Yemen
Aden, Gulf of	Indian Ocean
Admiralty Islands	Papua New Guinea
Adriatic Sea	Atlantic Ocean
Aegean Islands	Greece
Aegean Sea	Atlantic Ocean
Afars and Issas, French Territory of the (F.T.A.I.)	Djibouti
Agalega Islands	Mauritius
Agana	Guam
Aland Islands	Finland
Alaska	United States
Alaska, Gulf of	Pacific Ocean
Aldabra Islands	Seychelles
Alderney	Guernsey
Aleutian Islands	United States
Alexander Island	Antarctica
Alexandria [US Consulate General]	Egypt
Algiers [US Embassy]	Algeria
Alhucemas, Penon de	Spain
Alma-Ata (Almaty)	Kazakhstan
Almaty (Alma-Ata) [US Embassy]	Kazakhstan
Alofi	Niue
Alphonse Island	Seychelles
Amami Strait	Pacific Ocean
Amindivi Islands	India
Amirante Isles	Seychelles
Amman [US Embassy]	Jordan
Amsterdam [US Consulate General]	Netherlands
Amsterdam Island (Ile Amsterdam)	French Southern and Antarctic
Amundsen Sea	Pacific Ocean

Name	Geographic Area
Amur	China; Russia
Andaman Islands	India
Andaman Sea	Indian Ocean
Andorra la Vella	Andorra
Anegada Passage	Atlantic Ocean
Anglo-Egyptian Sudan	Sudan
Anjouan	Comoros
Ankara [US Embassy]	Turkey
Annobon	Equatorial Guinea
Antananarivo [US Embassy]	Madagascar
Antipodes Islands	New Zealand
Antwerp [US Consulate General]	Belgium
Aozou Strip	Chad
Apia [US Embassy]	Western Samoa
Aqaba, Gulf of	Indian Ocean
Arabian Sea	Indian Ocean
Arafura Sea	Pacific Ocean
Argun	China; Russia
Ascension Island	Saint Helena
Ashgabat (Ashkhabad)	Turkmenistan
Ashkhabad [US Embassy]	Turkmenistan
Asmara [US Embassy]	Eritrea
Asmera (see Asmara)	Eritrea
Assumption Island	Seychelles
Asuncion [US Embassy]	Paraguay
Asuncion Island	Northern Mariana Islands
Atacama	Chile
Athens [US Embassy]	Greece
Attu	United States
Auckland [US Consulate General]	New Zealand
Auckland Islands	New Zealand
Australes Iles (Iles Tubuai)	French Polynesia
Avarua	Cook Islands
Axel Heiberg Island	Canada
Azores	Portugal
Azov, Sea of	Atlantic Ocean
Bab el Mandeb	Indian Ocean
Babuyan Channel	Pacific Ocean
Babuyan Islands	Philippines
Baffin Bay	Arctic Ocean
Baffin Island	Canada
Baghdad [US Embassy temporarily suspended; US Interests Section located in Poland's embassy in Baghdad]	Iraq
Baku [US Embassy]	Azerbaijan

Name	Geographic Area
Baky (Baku)	Azerbaijan
Balabac Strait	Pacific Ocean
Balearic Islands	Spain
Balearic Sea (Iberian Sea)	Atlantic Ocean
Bali [US Consular Agency]	Indonesia
Bali Sea	Indian Ocean
Balintang Channel	Pacific Ocean
Balintang Islands	Philippines
Balleny Islands	Antarctica
Balochistan	Pakistan
Baltic Sea	Atlantic Ocean
Bamako [US Embassy]	Mali
Banaba (Ocean Island)	Kiribati
Bandar Seri Begawan [US Embassy]	Brunei
Banda Sea	Pacific Ocean
Bangkok [US Embassy]	Thailand
Bangui [US Embassy]	Central African Republic
Banjul [US Embassy]	Gambia, The
Banks Island	Canada
Banks Islands (Iles Banks)	Vanuatu
Barcelona [US Consulate General]	Spain
Barents Sea	Arctic Ocean
Barranquilla [US Consulate]	Colombia
Bashi Channel	Pacific Ocean
Basilan Strait	Pacific Ocean
Bass Strait	Indian Ocean
Basse-Terre	Gaudeloupe
Basseterre	Saint Kitts and Nevis
Batan Islands	Philippines
Basutoland	Lesotho
Bavaria (Bayern)	Germany
Beagle Channel	Atlantic Ocean
Bear Island (Bjornoya)	Svalbard
Beaufort Sea	Arctic Ocean
Bechuanaland	Botswana
Beijing [US Embassy]	China
Beirut [US Embassy]	Lebanon
Belau	Pacific Islands, Trust Territory
Belem [US Consular Agency]	Brazil
Belep Islands (Iles Belep)	New Caledonia
Belfast [US Consulate General]	United Kingdom
Belgian Congo	Zaire
Belgrade [US Embassy; US does not maintain full diplomatic relations with Serbia and Montenegro]	Serbia and Montenegro

Name	Geographic Area
Belize City [US Embassy]	Belize
Belle Isle, Strait of	Atlantic Ocean
Bellingshausen Sea	Pacific Ocean
Belmopan	Belize
Belorussia	Belarus
Bengal, Bay of	Indian Ocean
Bering Sea	Pacific Ocean
Bering Strait	Pacific Ocean
Berkner Island	Antarctica
Berlin [US Branch Office]	Germany
Berlin, East	Germany
Berlin, West	Germany
Bern [US Embassy]	Switzerland
Bessarabia	Romania; Moldova
Bijagos, Arquipelago dos	Guinea-Bissau
Bikini Atoll	Marshall Islands
Bilbao [US Consulate]	Spain
Bioko	Equatorial Guinea
Biscay, Bay of	Atlantic Ocean
Bishkek [Interim Chancery]	Kyrgyzstan
Bishop Rock	United Kingdom
Bismarck Archipelago	Papua New Guinea
Bismarck Sea	Pacific Ocean
Bissau [US Embassy]	Guinea-Bissau
Bjornoya (Bear Island)	Svalbard
Black Rock	Falkland Islands (Islas Malvinas)
Black Sea	Atlantic Ocean
Bloemfontein	South Africa
Boa Vista	Cape Verde
Bogota [US Embassy]	Colombia
Bombay [US Consulate General]	India
Bonaire	Netherlands Antilles
Bonifacio, Strait of	Atlantic Ocean
Bonin Islands	Japan
Bonn [US Embassy]	Germany
Bophuthatswana	South Africa
Bora-Bora	French Polynesia
Bordeaux [US Consulate General]	France
Borneo	Brunei; Indonesia; Malaysia
Bornholm	Denmark
Bosporus	Atlantic Ocean
Bothnia, Gulf of	Atlantic Ocean
Bougainville Island	Papua New Guinea

Name	Geographic Area
Bougainville Strait	Pacific Ocean
Bounty Islands	New Zealand
Brasilia [US Embassy]	Brazil
Bratislava [US Embassy]	Slovakia
Brazzaville [US Embassy]	Congo
Bridgetown [US Embassy]	Barbados
Brisbane [US Consulate]	Australia
British East Africa	Kenya
British Guiana	Guyana
British Honduras	Belize
British Solomon Islands	Solomon Islands
British Somaliland	Somalia
Brussels [US Embassy, US Mission to European Communities, US Mission to the North Atlantic Treaty Organization (USNATO)]	Belgium
Bucharest [US Embassy]	Romania
Budapest [US Embassy]	Hungary
Buenos Aires [US Embassy]	Argentina
Bujumbura [US Embassy]	Burundi
Burnt Pine	Norfolk Island
Byelorussia	Belarus
Cabinda	Angola
Cabot Strait	Atlantic Ocean
Caicos Islands	Turks and Caicos Islands
Cairo [US Embassy]	Egypt
Calcutta [US Consulate General]	India
Calgary [US Consulate General]	Canada
California, Gulf of	Pacific Ocean
Campbell Island	New Zealand
Canal Zone	Panama
Canary Islands	Spain
Canberra [US Embassy]	Australia
Cancun [US Consular Agency]	Mexico
Canton (Guangzhou)	China
Canton Island	Kiribati
Cape Town [US Consulate General]	South Africa
Caracas [US Embassy]	Venezuela
Cargados Carajos Shoals	Mauritius
Caroline Islands	Micronesia, Federated States of Territory of the
Caribbean Sea	Atlantic Ocean
Carpentaria, Gulf of	Pacific Ocean
Casablanca [US Consulate General]	Morocco
Castries	Saint Lucia

Name	Geographic Area
Cato Island	Australia
Cayenne	French Guiana
Cebu [US Consulate General]	Philippines
Celebes	Indonesia
Celebes Sea	Pacific Ocean
Celtic Sea	Atlantic Ocean
Central African Empire	Central African Republic
Ceuta	Spain
Ceylon	Sri Lanka
Chafarinas, Islas	Spain
Chagos Archipelago (Oil Islands)	British Indian Ocean Territory
Channel Islands	Guernsey; Jersey
Charlotte Amalie	Virgin Islands
Chatham Islands	New Zealand
Cheju-do	Korea, South
Cheju Strait	Pacific Ocean
Chengdu [US Consulate General]	China
Chesterfield Islands (Iles Chesterfield)	New Caledonia
Chiang Mai [US Consulate General]	Thailand
Chihli, Gulf of (Bo Hai)	Pacific Ocean
China, People's Republic of	China
China, Republic of	Taiwan
Chisinau [US Embassy]	Moldova
Choiseul	Solomon Islands
Christchurch [US Consular Agency]	New Zealand
Christmas Island [Indian Ocean]	Australia
Christmas Island [Pacific Ocean] (Kiritimati)	Kiribati
Chukchi Sea	Arctic Ocean
Ciskei	South Africa
Ciudad Juarez [US Consulate General]	Mexico
Cochabamba [US Consular Agency]	Bolivia
Coco, Isla del	Costa Rica
Cocos Islands	Cocos (Keeling) Islands
Colombo [US Embassy]	Sri Lanka
Colon [US Consular Agency]	Panama
Colon, Archipielago de (Galapagos Islands)	Ecuador
Commander Islands (Komandorskiye Ostrova)	Russia
Conakry [US Embassy]	Guinea
Congo (Brazzaville)	Congo
Congo (Kinshasa)	Zaire
Congo (Leopoldville)	Zaire
Con Son Islands	Vietnam
Cook Strait	Pacific Ocean
Copenhagen [US Embassy]	Denmark

Name	Geographic Area
Coral Sea	Pacific Ocean
Corn Islands (Islas del Maiz)	Nicaragua
Corsica	France
Cosmoledo Group	Seychelles
Cotonou [US Embassy]	Benin
Crete	Greece
Crooked Island Passage	Atlantic Ocean
Crozet Islands (Iles Crozet)	French Southern and Antarctic
Curacao [US Consulate General]	Netherlands Antilles
Cusco [US Consular Agency]	Peru
Czechoslovakia	Czech Republic; Slovakia
Dahomey	Benin
Daito Islands	Japan
Dakar [US Embassy]	Senegal
Daman (Damao)	India
Damascus [US Embassy]	Syria
Danger Atoll	Cook Islands
Danish Straits	Atlantic Ocean
Danzig (Gdansk)	Poland
Dao Bach Long Vi	Vietnam
Dardanelles	Atlantic Ocean
Dar es Salaam [US Embassy]	Tanzania
Davis Strait	Atlantic Ocean
Deception Island	Antarctica
Denmark Strait	Atlantic Ocean
D'Entrecasteaux Islands	Papua New Guinea
Devon Island	Canada
Dhahran [US Consulate General]	Saudi Arabia
Dhaka [US Embassy]	Bangladesh
Diego Garcia	British Indian Ocean Territory
Diego Ramirez	Chile
Diomede Islands	Russia [Big Diomede]
Diu	India
Djibouti [US Embassy]	Djibouti
Dodecanese	Greece
Dodoma	Tanzania
Doha [US Embassy]	Qatar
Douala [US Consulate]	Cameroon
Douglas	Man, Isle of
Dover, Strait of	Atlantic Ocean
Drake Passage	Atlantic Ocean
Dubai (Dubayy) [US Consulate General]	United Arab Emirates
Dublin [US Embassy]	Ireland
Durango [US Consular Agency]	Mexico

Name	Geographic Area
Durban [US Consulate General]	South Africa
Dushanbe [Interim Chancery]	Tajikistan
Dusseldorf [US Consulate General]	Germany
Dutch East Indies	Indonesia
Dutch Guiana	Suriname
East China Sea	Pacific Ocean
Easter Island (Isla de Pascua)	Chile
Eastern Channel (East Korea Strait or Tsushima Strait)	Pacific Ocean
East Germany (German Democratic Republic)	Germany
East Korea Strait (Eastern Channel or Tsushima Strait)	Pacific Ocean
East Pakistan	Bangladesh
East Siberian Sea	Arctic Ocean
East Timor (Portuguese Timor)	Indonesia
Edinburgh [US Consulate General]	United Kingdom
Elba	Italy
Ellef Ringnes Island	Canada
Ellesmere Island	Canada
Ellice Islands	Tuvalu
Elobey, Islas de	Equatorial Guinea
Enderbury Island	Kiribati
Enewetak Atoll (Eniwetok Atoll)	Marshall Islands
England	United Kingdom
English Channel	Atlantic Ocean
Eniwetok Atoll	Marshall Islands
Epirus, Northern	Albania; Greece
Essequibo [claimed by Venezuela]	Guyana
Etorofu	Russia [de facto]
Farquhar Group	Seychelles
Fernando de Noronha	Brazil
Fernando Po (Bioko)	Equatorial Guinea
Finland, Gulf of	Atlantic Ocean
Florence [US Consulate General]	Italy
Florida, Straits of	Atlantic Ocean
Formosa	Taiwan
Formosa Strait (Taiwan Strait)	Pacific Ocean
Fort-de-France [US Consulate General]	Martinique
Frankfurt am Main [US Consulate General]	Germany
Franz Josef Land	Russia
Freetown [US Embassy]	Sierra Leone
French Cameroon	Cameroon
French Indochina	Cambodia; Laos; Vietnam
French Guinea	Guinea
French Sudan	Mali

Name	Geographic Area
French Territory of the Afars and Issas (F.T.A.I.)	Djibouti
French Togo	Togo
Friendly Islands	Tonga
Frunze (Bishkek)	Kyrgyzstan
Fukuoka [US Consulate]	Japan
Funafuti	Tuvalu
Funchal [US Consular Agency]	Portugal
Fundy, Bay of	Atlantic Ocean
Futuna Islands (Hoorn Islands)	Wallis and Futuna
Gaborone [US Embassy]	Botswana
Galapagos Islands (Archipielago de Colon)	Ecuador
Galleons Passage	Atlantic Ocean
Gambier Islands (Iles Gambier)	French Polynesia
Gaspar Strait	Indian Ocean
Geneva [Branch Office of the US Embassy, US Mission to European Office of the UN and Other International Organizations]	Switzerland
Genoa [US Consulate General]	Italy
George Town [US Consular Agency]	Cayman Islands
Georgetown [US Embassy]	Guyana
German Democratic Republic (East Germany)	Germany
German Federal Republic of (West Germany)	Germany
Gibraltar	Gibraltar
Gibraltar, Strait of	Atlantic Ocean
Gilbert Islands	Kiribati
Goa	India
Gold Coast	Ghana
Golan Heights	Syria
Good Hope, Cape of	South Africa
Goteborg	Sweden
Gotland	Sweden
Gough Island	Saint Helena
Grand Banks	Atlantic Ocean
Grand Cayman	Cayman Islands
Grand Turk [US Consular Agency]	Turks and Caicos Islands
Great Australian Bight	Indian Ocean
Great Belt (Store Baelt)	Atlantic Ocean
Great Britain	United Kingdom
Great Channel	Indian Ocean
Greater Sunda Islands	Brunei; Indonesia; Malaysia
Green Islands	Papua New Guinea
Greenland Sea	Arctic Ocean
Grenadines, Northern	Saint Vincent and the Grenadines
Grenadines, Southern	Grenada

Name	Geographic Area
Guadalajara [US Consulate General]	Mexico
Guadalcanal	Solomon Islands
Guadalupe, Isla de	Mexico
Guangzhou [US Consulate General]	China
Guantanamo [US Naval Base]	Cuba
Guatemala [US Embassy]	Guatemala
Gubal, Strait of	Indian Ocean
Guinea, Gulf of	Atlantic Ocean
Guayaquil [US Consulate General]	Ecuador
Ha'apai Group	Tonga
Habomai Islands	Russia [de facto]
Hague, The [US Embassy]	Netherlands
Haifa [US Consular Agency]	Israel
Hainan Dao	China
Halifax [US Consulate General]	Canada
Halmahera	Indonesia
Hamburg [US Consulate General]	Germany
Hamilton [US Consulate General]	Bermuda
Hanoi	Vietnam
Harare [US Embassy]	Zimbabwe
Hatay	Turkey
Havana [US post not maintained; representation by US Interests Section (USINT) of the Swiss Embassy]	Cuba
Hawaii	United States
Heard Island	Heard Island
Helsinki [US Embassy]	Finland
Hermosillo [US Consulate]	Mexico
Hispaniola	Dominican Republic; Haiti
Hokkaido	Japan
Hong Kong [US Consulate General]	Hong Kong
Honiara [US Consulate]	Solomon Islands
Honshu	Japan
Hormuz, Strait of	Indian Ocean
Horn, Cape (Cabo de Hornos)	Chile
Horne, Iles de	Wallis and Futuna
Horn of Africa	Ethiopia; Somalia
Hudson Bay	Arctic Ocean
Hudson Strait	Arctic Ocean
Inaccessible Island	Saint Helena
Indochina	Cambodia; Laos; Vietnam
Inner Mongolia (Nei Mongol)	China
Ionian Islands	Greece
Ionian Sea	Atlantic Ocean
Irian Jaya	Indonesia

Name	Geographic Area
Irish Sea	Atlantic Ocean
Islamabad [US Embassy]	Pakistan
Islas Malvinas	Falkland Islands
Istanbul [US Consulate General]	Turkey
Italian Somaliland	Somalia
Ivory Coast	Cote d'Ivoire
Iwo Jima	Japan
Izmir [US Consulate General]	Turkey
Jakarta [US Embassy]	Indonesia
Jamestown	Saint Helena
Japan, Sea of	Pacific Ocean
Java	Indonesia
Java Sea	Indian Ocean
Jeddah [US Consulate General]	Saudi Arabia
Jerusalem [US Consulate General]	Israel; West Bank
Johannesburg [US Consulate General]	South Africa
Juan de Fuca, Strait of	Pacific Ocean
Juan Fernandez, Isla de	Chile
Juventud, Isla de la (Isle of Youth)	Cuba
Kabul [US Embassy now closed]	Afghanistan
Kaduna [US Consulate General]	Nigeria
Kalimantan	Indonesia
Kamchatka Peninsula (Poluostrov Kamchatka)	Russia
Kampala [US Embassy]	Uganda
Kampuchea	Cambodia
Karachi [US Consulate General]	Pakistan
Kara Sea	Arctic Ocean
Karimata Strait	Indian Ocean
Kathmandu [US Embassy]	Nepal
Kattegat	Atlantic Ocean
Kauai Channel	Pacific Ocean
Keeling Islands	Cocos (Keeling) Islands
Kerguelen, Iles	French Southern and Antarctic
Kermadec Islands	New Zealand
Khabarovsk	Russia
Khartoum [US Embassy]	Sudan
Khmer Republic	Cambodia
Khuriya Muriya Islands (Kuria Muria Islands)	Oman
Khyber Pass	Pakistan
Kiel Canal (Nord-Ostsee Kanal)	Atlantic Ocean
Kiev [US Embassy]	Ukraine
Kigali [US Embassy]	Rwanda
Kingston [US Embassy]	Jamaica

Name	Geographic Area
Kingston	Norfolk Island
Kingston	Saint Vincent and the Grenadines
Kinshasa [US Embassy]	Zaire
Kirghiziya	Kyrgyzstan
Kiritimati (Christmas Island)	Kiribati
Kishinev (Chisinau)	Moldova
Kithira Strait	Atlantic Ocean
Kodiak Island	United States
Kola Peninsula (Kol'skiy Poluostrov)	Russia
Kolonia [US Embassy]	Micronesia, Federated States
Korea Bay	Pacific Ocean
Korea, Democratic People's Republic of	Korea, North
Korea, Republic of	Korea, South
Korea Strait	Pacific Ocean
Koror [US Liaison Office]	Pacific Islands, Trust Territory
Kosovo	Serbia and Montenegro
Kowloon	Hong Kong
Krakow [US Consulate General]	Poland
Kuala Lumpur [US Embassy]	Malaysia
Kunashiri (Kunashir)	Russia [de facto]
Kuril Islands	Russia [de facto]
Kuwait [US Embassy]	Kuwait
Kwajalein Atoll	Marshall Islands
Kyushu	Japan
Kyyiv (Kiev)	Ukraine
Labrador	Canada
Laccadive Islands	India
Laccadive Sea	Indian Ocean
La Coruna [US Consular Agency]	Spain
Lagos [US Embassy]	Nigeria
Lahore [US Consulate General]	Pakistan
Lakshadweep	India
La Paz [US Embassy]	Bolivia
La Perouse Strait	Pacific Ocean
Laptev Sea	Arctic Ocean
Las Palmas [US Consular Agency]	Spain
Lau Group	Fiji
Leipzig [US Consulate General]	Germany
Leningrad (see Saint Petersburg)	Russia
Lesser Sunda Islands	Indonesia
Leyte	Philippines
Liancourt Rocks [claimed by Japan]	Korea, South
Libreville [US Embassy]	Gabon
Ligurian Sea	Atlantic Ocean

Name	Geographic Area
Lilongwe [US Embassy]	Malawi
Lima [US Embassy]	Peru
Lincoln Sea	Arctic Ocean
Line Islands	Kiribati; Palmyra Atoll
Lisbon [US Embassy]	Portugal
Ljubljana [US Embassy]	Slovenia
Lobamba	Swaziland
Lombok Strait	Indian Ocean
Lome [US Embassy]	Togo
London [US Embassy]	United Kingdom
Longyearbyen	Svalbard
Lord Howe Island	Australia
Louisiade Archipelago	Papua New Guinea
Loyalty Islands (Iles Loyaute)	New Caledonia
Luanda [US Liaison Office]	Angola
Lubumbashi [US Consulate General closed since October 1991]	Zaire
Lusaka [US Embassy]	Zambia
Luxembourg [US Embassy]	Luxembourg
Luzon	Philippines
Luzon Strait	Pacific Ocean
Lyon [US Consulate General]	France
Macao	Macau
Macedonia	The Former Yugoslav Republic
Macquarie Island	Australia
Madeira Islands	Portugal
Madras [US Consulate General]	India
Madrid [US Embassy]	Spain
Magellan, Strait of	Atlantic Ocean
Maghreb	Algeria, Libya, Mauritania
Mahe Island	Seychelles
Maiz, Islas del (Corn Islands)	Nicaragua
Majorca (Mallorca)	Spain
Majuro [US Embassy]	Marshall Islands
Makassar Strait	Pacific Ocean
Malabo [US Embassy]	Equatorial Guinea
Malacca, Strait of	Indian Ocean
Malaga [US Consular Agency]	Spain
Malagasy Republic	Madagascar
Male [US post not maintained; representation from Colombo, Sri Lanka]	Maldives
Mallorca (Majorca)	Spain
Malpelo, Isla de	Colombia
Malta Channel	Atlantic Ocean

Name	Geographic Area
Malvinas, Islas	Falkland Islands
Mamoutzou	Mayotte
Managua [US Embassy]	Nicaragua
Manama [US Embassy]	Bahrain
Manaus [US Consular Agency]	Brazil
Manchukuo	China
Manchuria	China
Manila [US Embassy]	Philippines
Manipa Strait	Pacific Ocean
Mannar, Gulf of	Indian Ocean
Manua Islands	American Samoa
Maputo [US Embassy]	Mozambique
Maracaibo [US Consulate]	Venezuela
Marcus Island (Minami-tori-shima)	Japan
Mariana Islands	Guam; Northern Mariana Islands
Marion Island	South Africa
Marmara, Sea of	Atlantic Ocean
Marquesas Islands (Iles Marquises)	French Polynesia
Marseille [US Consulate General]	France
Martin Vaz, Ilhas	Brazil
Mas a Tierra (Robinson Crusoe Island)	Chile
Mascarene Islands	Mauritius; Reunion
Maseru [US Embassy]	Lesotho
Matamoros [US Consulate]	Mexico
Mata Utu	Wallis and Futuna
Mazatlan [US Consulate]	Mexico
Mbabane [US Embassy]	Swaziland
McDonald Islands	Heard Island and McDonald
Medan [US Consulate]	Indonesia
Mediterranean Sea	Atlantic Ocean
Melbourne [US Consulate General]	Australia
Melilla	Spain
Mensk (Minsk)	Belarus
Merida [US Consulate]	Mexico
Messina, Strait of	Atlantic Ocean
Mexico [US Embassy]	Mexico
Mexico, Gulf of	Atlantic Ocean
Milan [US Consulate General]	Italy
Minami-tori-shima	Japan
Mindanao	Philippines
Mindoro Strait	Pacific Ocean
Minicoy Island	India
Minsk [US Embassy]	Belarus
Mogadishu [US Liaison Office]	Somalia

Name	Geographic Area
Moldovia	Moldova
Mombasa [US Consulate]	Kenya
Monaco	Monaco
Mona Passage	Atlantic Ocean
Monrovia [US Embassy]	Liberia
Montego Bay [US Consular Agency]	Jamaica
Montenegro	Serbia and Montenegro
Monterrey [US Consulate General]	Mexico
Montevideo [US Embassy]	Uruguay
Montreal [US Consulate General, US Mission to the International Civil Aviation Organization (ICAO)]	Canada
Moravian Gate	Czech Republic
Moroni [US Embassy]	Comoros
Mortlock Islands	Micronesia, Federated States of
Moscow [US Embassy]	Russia
Mozambique Channel	Indian Ocean
Mulege [US Consular Agency]	Mexico
Munich [US Consulate General]	Germany
Musandam Peninsula	Oman; United Arab Emirates
Muscat [US Embassy]	Oman
Muscat and Oman	Oman
Myanma, Myanmar	Burma
Naha [US Consulate General]	Japan
Nairobi [US Embassy]	Kenya
Nampo-shoto	Japan
Naples [US Consulate General]	Italy
Nassau [US Embassy]	Bahamas, The
Natuna Besar Islands	Indonesia
N'Djamena [US Embassy]	Chad
Netherlands East Indies	Indonesia
Netherlands Guiana	Suriname
Nevis	Saint Kitts and Nevis
New Delhi [US Embassy]	India
Newfoundland	Canada
New Guinea	Indonesia; Papua New Guinea
New Hebrides	Vanuatu
New Siberian Islands	Russia
New Territories	Hong Kong
New York, New York [US Mission to the United Nations (USUN)]	United States
Niamey [US Embassy]	Niger
Nice [US Consular Agency]	France
Nicobar Islands	India
Nicosia [US Embassy]	Cyprus
Nightingale Island	Saint Helena

Name	Geographic Area
North Atlantic Ocean	Atlantic Ocean
North Channel	Atlantic Ocean
Northeast Providence Channel	Atlantic Ocean
Northern Epirus	Albania; Greece
Northern Grenadines	Saint Vincent and the Grenadines
Northern Ireland	United Kingdom
Northern Rhodesia	Zambia
North Island	New Zealand
North Korea	Korea, North
North Pacific Ocean	Pacific Ocean
North Sea	Atlantic Ocean
North Vietnam	Vietnam
Northwest Passages	Arctic Ocean
North Yemen (Yemen Arab Republic)	Yemen
Norwegian Sea	Atlantic Ocean
Nouakchott [US Embassy]	Mauritania
Noumea	New Caledonia
Nuku'alofa	Tonga
Novaya Zemlya	Russia
Nuevo Laredo [US Consulate]	Mexico
Nuuk (Godthab)	Greenland
Nyasaland	Malawi
Oahu	United States
Oaxaca [US Consular Agency]	Mexico
Ocean Island (Banaba)	Kiribati
Ocean Island (Kure Island)	United States
Ogaden	Ethiopia; Somalia
Oil Islands (Chagos Archipelago)	British Indian Ocean Territory
Okhotsk, Sea of	Pacific Ocean
Okinawa	Japan
Oman, Gulf of	Indian Ocean
Ombai Strait	Pacific Ocean
Oporto [US Consulate]	Portugal
Oran [US Consulate]	Algeria
Oranjestad	Aruba
Oresund (The Sound)	Atlantic Ocean
Orkney Islands	United Kingdom
Osaka-Kobe [US Consulate General]	Japan
Oslo [US Embassy]	Norway
Otranto, Strait of	Atlantic Ocean
Ottawa [US Embassy]	Canada
Ouagadougou [US Embassy]	Burkina
Outer Mongolia	Mongolia

Name	Geographic Area
Pagan	Northern Mariana Islands
Pago Pago	American Samoa
Palau	Pacific Islands, Trust Territory
Palawan	Philippines
Palermo [US Consulate General]	Italy
Palk Strait	Indian Ocean
Palma de Mallorca [US Consular Agency]	Spain
Pamirs	China; Tajikistan
Panama [US Embassy]	Panama
Panama Canal	Panama
Panama, Gulf of	Pacific Ocean
Papeete	French Polynesia
Paramaribo [US Embassy]	Suriname
Parece Vela	Japan
Paris [US Embassy	France
Pascua, Isla de (Easter Island)	Chile
Passion, Ile de la	Clipperton Island
Pashtunistan	Afghanistan; Pakistan
Peking (Beijing)	China
Pemba Island	Tanzania
Pentland Firth	Atlantic Ocean
Perim	Yemen
Perouse Strait, La	Pacific Ocean
Persian Gulf	Indian Ocean
Perth [US Consulate General]	Australia
Pescadores	Taiwan
Peshawar [US Consulate]	Pakistan
Peter I Island	Antarctica
Philip Island	Norfolk Island
Philippine Sea	Pacific Ocean
Phnom Penh [US Embassy]	Cambodia
Phoenix Islands	Kiribati
Pines, Isle of (Isla de la Juventud)	Cuba
Piura [US Consular Agency]	Peru
Pleasant Island	Nauru
Plymouth	Montserrat
Ponape (Pohnpei)	Micronesia
Ponta Delgada [US Consulate]	Portugal
Port-au-Prince [US Embassy]	Haiti
Port Louis [US Embassy]	Mauritius
Port Moresby [US Embassy]	Papua New Guinea
Porto Alegre [US Consulate]	Brazil
Port-of-Spain [US Embassy]	Trinidad and Tobago
Porto-Novo	Benin

Name	Geographic Area
Port Said [US Consular Agency]	Egypt
Portuguese Guinea	Guinea-Bissau
Portuguese Timor (East Timor)	Indonesia
Port-Vila	Vanuatu
Poznan [US Consulate General]	Poland
Prague [US Embassy]	Czech Republic
Praia [US Embassy]	Cape Verde
Pretoria [US Embassy]	South Africa
Pribilof Islands	United States
Prince Edward Island	Canada
Prince Edward Islands	South Africa
Prince Patrick Island	Canada
Principe	Sao Tome and Principe
Puerto Plata [US Consular Agency]	Dominican Republic
Puerto Vallarta [US Consular Agency]	Mexico
Pusan [US Consulate]	Korea, South
P'yongyang	Korea, North
Quebec [US Consulate General]	Canada
Queen Charlotte Islands	Canada
Queen Elizabeth Islands	Canada
Queen Maud Land [claimed by Norway]	Antarctica
Quito [US Embassy]	Ecuador
Rabat [US Embassy]	Morocco
Ralik Chain	Marshall Islands
Rangoon [US Embassy]	Burma
Ratak Chain	Marshall Islands
Recife [US Consulate]	Brazil
Redonda	Antigua and Barbuda
Red Sea	Indian Ocean
Revillagigedo Island	United States
Revillagigedo Islands	Mexico
Reykjavik [US Embassy]	Iceland
Rhodes	Greece
Rhodesia	Zimbabwe
Rhodesia, Northern	Zambia
Rhodesia, Southern	Zimbabwe
Riga [US Embassy]	Latvia
Rio de Janeiro [US Consulate General]	Brazil
Rio de Oro	Western Sahara
Rio Muni	Equatorial Guinea
Riyadh [US Embassy]	Saudi Arabia
Road Town	British Virgin Islands
Robinson Crusoe Island (Mas a Tierra)	Chile

Name	Geographic Area
Rocas, Atol das	Brazil
Rockall [disputed]	United Kingdom
Rodrigues	Mauritius
Rome [US Embassy, US Mission to the UN Agencies for Food and Agriculture (FODAG)]	Italy
Roncador Cay	Colombia
Roosevelt Island	Antarctica
Roseau	Dominica
Ross Dependency [claimed by New Zealand]	Antarctica
Ross Island	Antarctica
Ross Sea	Antarctica
Rota	Northern Mariana Islands
Rotuma	Fiji
Ryukyu Islands	Japan
Saba	Netherlands Antilles
Sabah	Malaysia
Sable Island	Canada
Sahel	Burkina, Cape Verde, Chad Mali, Mauritania, Niger
Saigon (Ho Chi Minh City)	Vietnam
Saint Brandon	Mauritius
Saint Christopher and Nevis	Saint Kitts and Nevis
Saint-Denis	Reunion
Saint George's [US Embassy]	Grenada
Saint George's Channel	Atlantic Ocean
Saint Heliar	Jersey
Saint John's [US Embassy]	Antigua and Barbuda
Saint Lawrence, Gulf of	Atlantic Ocean
Saint Lawrence Island	United States
Saint Lawrence Seaway	Atlantic Ocean
Saint Martin	Guadeloupe
Saint Martin (Sint Maarten)	Netherlands Antilles
Saint Paul Island	Canada
Saint Paul Island	United States
Saint Paul Island (Ile Saint-Paul)	French Southern and Antarctic
Saint Peter and Saint Paul Rocks (Penedos de Sao Pedro e Sao Paulo)	Brazil
Saint Peter Port	Guernsey
Saint Petersburg [US Consulate]	Russia
Saint-Pierre	Saint Pierre and Miguelon
Saint Vincent Passage	Atlantic Ocean
Saipan	Northern Mariana Islands
Sakhalin Island (Ostrov Sakhalin)	Russia
Sala y Gomez, Isla	Chile

Name	Geographic Area
Salisbury (Harare)	Zimbabwe
Salvador de Bahia [US Consular Agency]	Brazil
Salzburg [US Consulate General]	Austria
Sanaa [US Embassy]	Yemen
San Ambrosio	Chile
San Andres y Providencia, Archipielago	Colombia
San Bernardino Strait	Pacific Ocean
San Felix, Isla	Chile
San Jose [US Embassy]	Costa Rica
San Juan	Puerto Rico
San Luis Potosi [US Consular Agency]	Mexico
San Marino	San Marino
San Miguel Allende [US Consular Agency]	Mexico
San Salvador [US Embassy]	El Salvador
Santa Cruz [US Consular Agency]	Bolivia
Santa Cruz Islands	Solomon Islands
Santiago [US Embassy]	Chile
Santo Domingo [US Embassy]	Dominican Republic
Sao Luis [US Consular Agency]	Brazil
Sao Paulo [US Consulate General]	Brazil
Sao Pedro e Sao Paulo, Penedos de	Brazil
Sao Tome	Sao Tome and Principe
Sapporo [US Consulate General]	Japan
Sapudi Strait	Indian Ocean
Sarajevo	Bosnia and Herzegovina
Sarawak	Malaysia
Sardinia	Italy
Sargasso Sea	Atlantic Ocean
Sark	Guernsey
Scotia Sea	Atlantic Ocean
Scotland	United Kingdom
Scott Island	Antarctica
Senyavin Islands	Micronesia, Federated States of
Seoul [US Embassy]	Korea, South
Serbia	Serbia and Montenegro
Serrana Bank	Colombia
Serranilla Bank	Colombia
Settlement, The	Christmas Island
Severnaya Zemlya (Northland)	Russia
Seville [US Consular Agency]	Spain
Shag Island	Heard Island and McDonald Islands
Shag Rocks	Falkland Islands (Islas Malvinas)
Shanghai [US Consulate General]	China
Shenyang [US Consulate General]	China

Name	Geographic Area
Shetland Islands	United Kingdom
Shikoku	Japan
Shikotan (Shikotan-to)	Japan
Siam	Thailand
Sibutu Passage	Pacific Ocean
Sicily	Italy
Sicily, Strait of	Atlantic Ocean
Sikkim	India
Sinai	Egypt
Singapore [US Embassy]	Singapore
Singapore Strait	Pacific Ocean
Sinkiang (Xinjiang)	China
Sint Eustatius	Netherlands Antilles
Sint Maarten (Saint Martin)	Netherlands Antilles
Skagerrak	Atlantic Ocean
Skopje	The Former Yugoslav Republic
Society Islands (Iles de la Societe)	French Polynesia
Socotra	Yemen
Sofia [US Embassy]	Bulgaria
Solomon Islands, northern	Papua New Guinea
Solomon Islands, southern	Solomon Islands
Soloman Sea	Pacific Ocean
Songkhla [US Consulate]	Thailand
Sound, The (Oresund)	Atlantic Ocean
South Atlantic Ocean	Atlantic Ocean
South China Sea	Pacific Ocean
Southern Grenadines	Grenada
Southern Rhodesia	Zimbabwe
South Georgia	South Georgia
South Island	New Zealand
South Korea	Korea, South
South Orkney Islands	Antarctica
South Pacific Ocean	Pacific Ocean
South Sandwich Islands	South Georgia
South Shetland Islands	Antarctica
South Tyrol	Italy
South Vietnam	Vietnam
South-West Africa	Namibia
South Yemen (People's Democratic Republic of Yemen)	Yemen
Spanish Guinea	Equatorial Guinea
Spanish Sahara	Western Sahara

Name	Geographic Area
Spitsbergen	
Stanley	Falkland Islands
Stockholm [US Embassy]	Sweden
Strasbourg [US Consulate General]	France
Stuttgart [US Consulate General]	Germany
Suez, Gulf of	Indian Ocean
Sulu Archipelago	Philippines
Sulu Sea	Pacific Ocean
Sumatra	Indonesia
Sumba	Indonesia
Sunda Islands (Soenda Isles)	Indonesia; Malaysia
Sunda Strait	Indian Ocean
Surabaya [US Consulate]	Indonesia
Surigao Strait	Pacific Ocean
Surinam	Suriname
Suva [US Embassy]	Fiji
Swains Island	American Samoa
Swan Islands	Honduras
Sydney [US Consulate General]	Australia
Tahiti	French Polynesia
Taipei	Taiwan
Taiwan Strait	Pacific Ocean
Tallin [US Embassy]	Estonia
Tampico [US Consular Agency]	Mexico
Tanganyika	Tanzania
Tangier	Morocco
Tarawa	Kiribati
Tartar Strait	Pacific Ocean
Tashkent [US Embassy]	Uzbekistan
Tasmania	Australia
Tasman Sea	Pacific Ocean
Taymyr Peninsula (Poluostrov Taymyra)	Russia
Tegucigalpa [US Embassy]	Honduras
Tehran [US post not maintained; representation by Swiss Embassy]	Iran
Tel Aviv [US Embassy]	Israel
Terre Adelie (Adelie Land) [claimed by France]	Antarctica
Thailand, Gulf of	Pacific Ocean
Thessaloniki [US Consulate General]	Greece
Thimphu	Bhutan
Thurston Island	Antarctica
Tibet (Xizang)	China
Tibilisi (Tbilisi) [US Embassy]	Georgia
Tierra del Fuego	Argentina; Chile

Name	Geographic Area
Tijuana [US Consulate General]	Mexico
Timor	Indonesia
Timor Sea	Indian Ocean
Tinian	Northern Mariana Islands
Tiran, Strait of	Indian Ocean
Tirane [US Embassy]	Albania
Tobago	Trinidad and Tobago
Tokyo [US Embassy]	Japan
Tonkin, Gulf of	Pacific Ocean
Toronto [US Consulate General]	Canada
Torres Strait	Pacific Ocean
Torshavn	Faroe Islands
Toshkent (Tashkent)	Uzbekistan
Transjordan	Jordan
Transkei	South Africa
Transylvania	Romania
Trieste [US Consular Agency]	Italy
Trindade, Ilha de	Brazil
Tripoli [US post not maintained; representation by Belgian Embassy]	Libya
Tristan da Cunha Group	Saint Helena
Trobriand Islands	Papua New Guinea
Trucial States	United Arab Emirates
Truk Islands	Micronesia
Tsugaru Strait	Pacific Ocean
Tuamotu Islands (Iles Tuamotu)	French Polynesia
Tubuai Islands (Iles Tubuai)	French Polynesia
Tunis [US Embassy]	Tunisia
Turin	Italy
Turkish Straits	Atlantic Ocean
Turkmeniya	Turkmenistan
Turks Island Passage	Atlantic Ocean
Tyrol, South	Italy
Tyrrhenian Sea	Atlantic Ocean
Udorn [US Consulate]	Thailand
Ulaanbaatar [US Embassy]	Mongolia
Ullung-do	Korea, South
Unimak Pass [strait]	Pacific Ocean
United Arab Republic	Egypt; Syria
Upper Volta	Burkina
Vaduz [US post not maintained; representation from Zurich, Switzerland]	Liechtenstein
Vakhan Corridor (Wakhan)	Afghanistan

Name	Geographic Area
Valencia [US Consular Agency]	Spain
Valletta [US Embassy]	Malta
Valley, The	Anguilla
Vancouver [US Consulate General]	Canada
Vancouver Island	Canada
Van Diemen Strait	Pacific Ocean
Vatican City [US Embassy]	Holy See
Velez de la Gomera, Penon de	Spain
Venda	South Africa
Veracruz [US Consular Agency]	Mexico
Verde Island Passage	Pacific Ocean
Victoria [US Embassy]	Seychelles
Vienna [US Embassy, US Mission to International Organizations in Vienna (UNVIE)]	Austria
Vientiane [US Embassy]	Laos
Vilnius [US Embassy]	Lithuania
Vladivostok [US Consulate]	Russia
Volcano Islands	Japan
Vostok Island	Kiribati
Vrangelya, Ostrov (Wrangel Island)	Russia
Wakhan Corridor (now Vakhan Corridor)	Afghanistan
Wales	United Kingdom
Walvis Bay	South Africa
Warsaw [US Embassy]	Poland
Washington, DC [The Permanent Mission of the USA to the Organization of American States (OAS)]	United States
Weddell Sea	Atlantic Ocean
Wellington [US Embassy]	New Zealand
Western Channel (West Korea Strait)	Pacific Ocean
West Germany (Federal Republic of Germany)	Germany
West Island	Cocos (Keeling) Islands
West Korea Strait (Western Channel)	Pacific Ocean
West Pakistan	Pakistan
Wetar Strait	Pacific Ocean
White Sea	Arctic Ocean
Willemstad	Netherlands Antilles
Windhoek [US Embassy]	Namibia
Windward Passage	Atlantic Ocean
Winnipeg [US Consular Agency]	Canada
Wrangel Island (Ostrov Vrangelya)	Russia [de facto]
Yamoussoukro	Cote d'Ivoire
Yaounde [US Embassy]	Cameroon
Yap Islands	Micronesia

Name	Geographic Area
Yellow Sea	Pacific Ocean
Yemen (Aden) [People's Democratic Republic of Yemen]	Yemen
Yemen Arab Republic	Yemen
Yemen, North [Yemen Arab Republic]	Yemen
Yemen (Sanaa) [Yemen Arab Republic]	Yemen
Yemen, People's Democratic Republic of	Yemen
Yemen, South [People's Democratic Republic of Yemen]	Yemen
Yerevan [US Embassy]	Armenia
Youth, Isle of (Isla de la Juventud)	Cuba
Yucatan Channel	Atlantic Ocean
Zagreb [US Embassy]	Croatia
Zanzibar	Tanzania
Zurich [US Consulate General]	Switzerland

Glossary of Trade Terms

Acceptance – This term has several related meanings: (1) A time draft (or bill of exchange) that the drawee has accepted and is unconditionally obligated to pay at maturity. The draft must be presented first for acceptance – the drawee becomes the "acceptor" – then for payment. The word "accepted" and the date and place of payment must be written on the face of the draft. (2) The drawee's act in receiving a draft and thus entering into the obligation to pay its value at maturity. (3) Broadly speaking, any agreement to purchase goods under specified terms. An agreement to purchase goods at a stated price and under stated terms.

Ad valorem – According to value. See **Duty.**

Advance against documents – A loan made on the security of the documents covering the shipment.

Advising bank – A bank, operating in the exporter's country, that handles letters of credit for a foreign bank by notifying the export firm that the credit has been opened in its favor. The advising bank fully informs the exporter of the conditions of the letter of credit without necessarily bearing responsibility for payment.

Advisory capacity – A term indicating that a shipper's agent or representative is not empowered to make definitive decisions or adjustments without approval of the group or individual represented. Compare **Without reserve.**

Agent – See **Foreign sales agent.**

Air waybill – A bill of lading that covers both domestic and international flights transporting goods to a specified destination. This is a nonnegotiable instrument of air transport that serves as a receipt for the shipper, indicating that the carrier has accepted the goods listed and obligates itself to carry the consignment to the airport of destination according to specified conditions. Compare **Inland bill of lading, Ocean bill of lading,** and **Through bill of lading.**

Alongside – The side of a ship. Goods to be delivered "alongside" are to be placed on the dock or barge within reach of the transport ship's tackle so that they can be loaded aboard the ship.

Antidiversion clause – See **Destination control statement.**

Arbitrage – The process of buying foreign exchange, stocks, bonds, and other commodities in one market and immediately selling them in another market at higher prices.

Asian dollars – U.S. dollars deposited in Asia and the Pacific Basin. Compare **Eurodollars.**

ATA Carnet – See **Carnet.**

Balance of trade – The difference between a country's total imports and exports. If exports exceed imports, a favorable balance of trade exists; if not, a trade deficit is said to exist.

Barter – Trade in which merchandise is exchanged directly for other merchandise without use of money. Barter is an important means of trade with countries using currency that is not readily convertible.

Beneficiary – The person in whose favor a letter of credit is issued or a draft is drawn.

Bill of exchange – See **Draft.**

Bill of lading – A document that establishes the terms of a contract between a shipper and a transportation company under which freight is to be moved between specified points for a specified charge. Usually prepared by the shipper on forms issued by the carrier, it serves as a document of title, a contract of carriage, and a receipt for goods. Also see **Air waybill, Inland bill of lading, Ocean bill of lading,** and **Through bill of lading.**

Bonded warehouse – A warehouse authorized by customs authorities for storage of goods on which payment of duties is deferred until the goods are removed.

Booking – An arrangement with a steamship company for the acceptance and carriage of freight.

Buying agent – See **Purchasing agent.**

Carnet – A customs document permitting the holder to carry or send merchandise temporarily into certain foreign countries (for display, demonstration, or similar purposes) without paying duties or posting bonds.

Cash against documents (CAD) – Payment for goods in whicn a commission house or other intermediary transfers title documents to the buyer upon payment in cash.

Cash in advance (CIA) – Payment for goods in which the price is paid in full before shipment is made. This method is usually used only for small purchases or when the goods are built to order.

Cash with order (CWO) – Payment for goods in which the buyer pays when ordering and in which the transaction is binding on both parties.

Certificate of inspection – A document certifying that merchandise (such as perishable goods) was in good condition immediately prior to its shipment (see chapter 12).

Certificate of manufacture – A statement (often notarized) in which a producer of goods certifies that manufacture has been completed and that the goods are now at the disposal of the buyer.

Certificate of origin – A document, required by certain foreign countries for tariff purposes, certifying the country of origin of specified goods (see chapter 12).

CFR – Cost and freight. A pricing term indicating that the cost of the goods and freight charges are included in the quoted price; the buyer arranges for and pays insurance (see chapter 10).

Charter party – A written contract, usually on a special form, between the owner of a vessel and a "charterer" who rents use of the vessel or a part of its freight space. The contract generally includes the freight rates and the ports involved in the transportation.

CIF – Cost, insurance, freight. A pricing term indicating that the cost of the goods, insurance, and freight are included in the quoted price (see chapter 10).

Clean bill of lading – A receipt for goods issued by a carrier that indicates that the goods were received in "apparent good order and condition," without damages or other irregularities. Compare **Foul bill of lading.**

Clean draft – A draft to which no documents have been attached.

Collection papers – All documents (commercial invoices, bills of lading, etc.) submitted to a buyer for the purpose of receiving payment for a shipment.

Commercial attache – The commerce expert on the diplomatic staff of his or her country's embassy or large consulate.

Commercial invoice – An itemized list of goods shipped, usually included among an exporter's collection papers (see chapter 12).

Commission agent – See **Purchasing agent.**

Common carrier – An individual, partnership, or corporation that transports persons or goods for compensation.

Confirmed letter of credit – A letter of credit, issued by a foreign bank, the validity of which has been confirmed by a U.S. bank. An exporter whose payment terms are a confirmed letter of credit is assured of payment by the U.S. bank even if the foreign buyer or the foreign bank defaults. See **Letter of credit.** (Also see chapter 13.)

Consignment – Delivery of merchandise from an exporter (the consignor) to an agent (the consignee) under agreement that the agent sell the merchandise for the account of the exporter. The consignor retains title to the goods until the consignee has sold them. The consignee sells the goods for commission and remits the net proceeds to the consignor.

Consular declaration – A formal statement, made to the consul of a foreign country, describing goods to be shipped.

Consular invoice – A document, required by some foreign countries, describing a shipment of goods and showing information such as the consignor, consignee, and value of the shipment. Certified by a consular official of the foreign country, it is used by the country's customs officials to verify the value, quantity, and nature of the shipment (see chapter 12).

Convertible currency – A currency that can be bought and sold for other currencies at will.

Correspondent bank – A bank that, in its own country, handles the business of a foreign bank.

Countertrade – The sale of goods or services that are paid for in whole or in part by the transfer of goods or services from a foreign country. (See **Barter.**)

Countervailing duty – A duty imposed to counter unfairly subsidized products.

CPT (carriage paid to) and **CIP (carriage and insurance paid to)** – Pricing terms indicating that carriage, or carriage and insurance, are paid to the named place of destination. They apply in place of **CFR** and **CIF,** respectively, for shipment by modes other than water.

Credit risk insurance – Insurance designed to cover risks of nonpayment for delivered goods. Compare **Marine insurance.**

Customhouse broker – An individual or firm licensed to enter and clear goods through customs.

Customs – The authorities designated to collect duties levied by a country on imports and exports. The term also applies to the procedures involved in such collection.

Date draft – A draft that matures in a specified number of days after the date it is issued, without regard to the date of acceptance. See **Draft, Sight draft,** and **Time draft.** (Also see chapter 13.)

Deferred payment credit – Type of letter of credit providing for payment some time after presentation of shipping documents by exporter.

Demand draft – See **Sight draft.**

Destination control statement – Any of various statements that the U.S. government requires to be displayed on export shipments and that specify the destinations for which export of the shipment has been authorized (see chapter 12).

Devaluation – The official lowering of the value of one country's currency in terms of one or more foreign currencies. For example, if the U.S. dollar is devalued in relation to the French franc, one dollar will "buy" fewer francs than before.

DISC – Domestic international sales corporation (see chapter 11).

Discrepancy – Letter of credit – When documents presented do not conform to the letter of credit it is referred to as a discrepancy.

Dispatch – An amount paid by a vessel's operator to a charterer if loading or unloading is completed in less time than stipulated in the charter party.

Distributor – A foreign agent who sells for a supplier directly and maintains an inventory of the supplier's products.

Dock receipt – A receipt issued by an ocean carrier to acknowledge receipt of a shipment at the carrier's dock or warehouse facilities. Also see **Warehouse receipt.**

Documentary draft – A draft to which documents are attached.

Documents against acceptance (D/A) – Instructions given by a shipper to a bank indicating that documents transferring title to goods should be delivered to the buyer (or drawee) only upon the buyer's acceptance of the attached draft.

Draft (or Bill of exchange) – An unconditional order in writing from one person (the drawer) to another (the drawee), directing the drawee to pay a specified amount to a named drawer at a fixed or determinable future date (see chapter 13). See **Date draft, Sight draft, Time draft.**

Drawback – Articles manufactured or produced in the United States with the use of imported components or raw materials and later exported are entitled to a refund of up to 99 percent of the duty charged on the imported components. The refund of duty is known as a drawback.

Drawee – The individual or firm on whom a draft is drawn and who owes the stated amount. Compare **Drawer.** Also see **Draft.**

Drawer – The individual or firm that issues or signs a draft and thus stands to receive payment of the stated amount from the drawee. Compare **Drawee.** Also see **Draft.**

Dumping – Selling merchandise in another country at a price below the price at which the same merchandise is sold in the home market or selling such merchandise below the costs incurred in production and shipment.

Duty – A tax imposed on imports by the customs authority of a country. Duties are generally based on the value of the goods (ad valorem duties), some other factor such as weight or quantity (specific duties), or a combination of value and other factors (compound duties).

EMC – See **Export management company.**

ETC – See **Export trading company.**

Eurodollars – U.S. dollars placed on deposit in banks outside the United States; usually refers to deposits in Europe.

Ex – **From.** When used in pricing terms such as "ex factory" or "ex dock," it signifies that the price quoted applies only at the point of origin (in the two examples, at the seller's factory or a dock at the import point). In practice, this kind of quotation indicates that the seller agrees to place the goods at the disposal of the buyer at the specified place within a fixed period of time.

Exchange permit – A government permit sometimes required by the importer's government to enable the import firm to convert its own country's currency into foreign currency with which to pay a seller in another country.

Exchange rate – The price of one currency in terms of another, that is, the number of units of one currency that may be exchanged for one unit of another currency.

Eximbank – Export-Import Bank of the United States.

Export broker – An individual or firm that brings together buyers and sellers for a fee but does not take part in actual sales transactions.

Export commission house – An organization which, for a commission, acts as a purchasing agent for a foreign buyer.

Export declaration – See **Shipper's export declaration.**

Export license – A government document that permits the licensee to export designated goods to certain destinations. See **General export license** and **Individually validated export license.** (Also see chapter 11.)

Export management company – A private firm that serves as the export department for several producers of goods or services, either by taking title or by soliciting and transacting export business on behalf of its clients in return for a commission, salary, or retainer plus commission (see chapter 4).

Export trading company – A firm similar or identical to an export management company. (See chapter 4.)

Factoring houses – See chapter 14.

FAS – **Free alongside ship.** A pricing term indicating that the quoted price includes the cost of delivering the goods alongside a designated vessel (see chapter 10).

FCA – **"Free carrier" to named place.** Replaces the former term "FOB named inland port" to designate the seller's responsibility for the cost of loading goods at the named shipping point. May be used for multimodal transport, container stations, and any mode of transport, including air.

FCIA – **Foreign Credit Insurance Association** (see chapter 14).

FI – **Free in.** A pricing term indicating that the charterer of a vessel is responsible for the cost of loading and unloading goods from the vessel.

Floating policy – See **Open policy.**

FO – **Free out.** A pricing term indicating that the charterer of a vessel is responsible for the cost of loading goods from the vessel.

FOB – **"Free on board" at named port of export.** A pricing term indicating that the quoted price covers all expenses up to and including delivery of goods upon an overseas vessel provided by or for the buyer.

Force majeure – The title of a standard clause in marine contracts exempting the parties for nonfulfillment of their obligations as a result of conditions beyond their control, such as earthquakes, floods, or war.

Foreign exchange – The currency or credit instruments of a foreign country. Also, transactions involving purchase or sale of currencies.

Foreign freight forwarder – See **Freight forwarder.**

Foreign sales agent – An individual or firm that serves as the foreign representative of a domestic supplier and seeks sales abroad for the supplier.

Foreign trade zone – See **Free-trade zone.**

Foul bill of lading – A receipt for goods issued by a carrier with an indication that the goods were damaged when received. Compare **Clean bill of lading.**

Free port – An area such as a port city into which merchandise may legally be moved without payment of duties.

Free-trade zone – A port designated by the government of a country for duty-free entry of any nonprohibited goods. Merchandise may be stored, displayed, used for manufacturing, etc., within the zone and reexported without duties being paid. Duties are imposed on the merchandise (or items manufactured from the merchandise) only when the goods pass from the zone into an area of the country subject to the customs authority.

Freight forwarder – An independent business that handles export shipments for compensation. (A freight forwarder is among the best sources of information and assistance on U.S. export regulations and documentation, shipping methods, and foreign import regulations.)

GATT – **General Agreement on Tariffs and Trade.** A multilateral treaty intended to help reduce trade barriers between signatory countries and to promote trade through tariff concessions.

General export license – Any of various export licenses covering export commodities for which **Individually validated export licenses** are not required. No formal application or written authorization is needed to ship exports under a general export license (see chapter 11).

Gross weight – The full weight of a shipment, including goods and packaging. Compare **Tare weight.**

Import license – A document required and issued by some national governments authorizing the importation of goods into their individual countries.

Individually validated export license – A required document issued by the U.S. Government authorizing the export of specific commodities. This license is for a specific transaction or time period in which the exporting is to take place. Compare **General export license.** (Also see chapter 11.)

Inland bill of lading – A bill of lading used in transporting goods overland to the exporter's international carrier. Although a through bill of lading can sometimes be used, it is usually necessary to prepare both an inland bill of lading and an ocean bill of lading for export shipments. Compare **Air waybill, Ocean bill of lading,** and **Through bill of lading.**

International freight forwarder – See **Freight forwarder.**

Irrevocable letter of credit – A letter of credit in which the specified payment is guaranteed by the bank if all terms and conditions are met by the drawee. Compare **Revocable letter of credit.** (Also see chapter 13.)

Letter of credit (L/C) – A document, issued by a bank per instructions by a buyer of goods, authorizing the seller to draw a specified sum of money under specified terms, usually the receipt by the bank of certain documents within a given time (see chapter 13).

Licensing – A business arrangement in which the manufacturer of a product (or a firm with proprietary rights over certain technology, trademarks, etc.) grants permission to some other group or individual to manufacture that product (or make use of that proprietary material) in return for specified royalties or other payment.

Manifest – See **Ship's manifest.**

Marine insurance – Insurance that compensates the owners of goods transported overseas in the event of loss that cannot be legally recovered from the carrier. Also covers air shipments. Compare **Credit risk insurance.**

Marking (or marks) – Letters, numbers, and other symbols placed on cargo packages to facilitate identification.

Ocean bill of lading – A bill of lading (B/L) indicating that the exporter consigns a shipment to an international carrier for transportation to a specified foreign market. Unlike an inland B/L, the ocean B/L also serves as a collection document. If it is a "straight" B/L, the foreign buyer can obtain the shipment from the carrier by simply showing proof of identity. If a "negotiable" B/L is used, the buyer must first pay for the goods, post a bond, or meet other conditions agreeable to the seller. Compare **Air waybill, Inland bill of lading,** and **Through bill of lading.**

On board bill of lading – A bill of lading in which a carrier certifies that goods have been placed on board a certain vessel.

Open account – A trade arrangement in which goods are shipped to a foreign buyer without guarantee of payment. The obvious risk this method poses to the supplier makes it essential that the buyer's integrity be unquestionable.

Open insurance policy – A marine insurance policy that applies to all shipments made by an exporter over a period of time rather than to one shipment only.

Order bill of lading – A negotiable bill of lading made out to the order of the shipper.

Packing list – A list showing the number and kinds of items being shipped, as well as other information needed for transportation purposes (see chapter 12).

Parcel post receipt – The postal authorities' signed acknowledgment of delivery to receiver of a shipment made by parcel post.

PEFCO – **Private Export Funding Corporation.** A corporation that lends to foreign buyers to finance exports from the United States (see chapter 14).

Perils of the sea – A marine insurance term used to designate heavy weather, stranding, lightning, collision, and sea water damage.

Phytosanitary inspection certificate – A certificate, issued by the U.S. Department of Agriculture to satisfy import regulations for foreign countries, indicating that a U.S. shipment has been inspected and is free from harmful pests and plant diseases.

Political risk – In export financing, the risk of loss due to such causes as currency inconvertibility, government action preventing entry of goods, expropriation or confiscation, and war.

Pro forma invoice – An invoice provided by a supplier prior to the shipment of merchandise, informing the buyer of the kinds and quantities of goods to be sent, their value, and important specifications (weight, size, etc.).

Purchasing agent – An agent who purchases goods in his or her own country on behalf of foreign importers such as government agencies and large private concerns.

Quota – The quantity of goods of a specific kind that a country permits to be imported without restriction or imposition of additional duties.

Quotation – An offer to sell goods at a stated price and under specified conditions.

Remitting bank – The bank that sends the draft to the overseas bank for collection.

Representative – See **Foreign sales agent.**

Revocable letter of credit – A letter of credit that can be canceled or altered by the drawee (buyer) after it has been issued by the drawee's bank. Compare **Irrevocable letter of credit.** (Also see chapter 13.)

Schedule B – Refers to Schedule B, Statistical Classification of Domestic and Foreign Commodities Exported from the United States. All commodities exported from the United States must be assigned a seven-digit Schedule B number.

Shipper's export declaration – A form required for all shipments by the U.S. Treasury Department and prepared by a shipper, indicating the value, weight, destination, and other basic information about an export shipment (see chapter 12).

Ship's manifest – An instrument in writing, signed by the captain of a ship, that lists the individual shipments constituting the ship's cargo.

Sight draft (S/D) – A draft that is payable upon presentation to the drawee. Compare **Date draft** and **Time draft** (see chapter 13).

Spot exchange – The purchase or sale of foreign exchange for immediate delivery.

Standard industrial classification (SIC) – A standard numerical code system used by the U.S. government to classify products and services.

Standard international trade classification (SITC) – A standard numerical code system developed by the United Nations to classify commodities used in international trade.

Steamship conference – A group of steamship operators that operate under mutually agreed-upon freight rates.

Straight bill of lading – A nonnegotiable bill of lading in which the goods are consigned directly to a named consignee.

Tare weight – The weight of a container and packing materials without the weight of the goods it contains. Compare **Gross weight.**

Tenor (of a draft) – Designation of a payment as being due at sight, a given number of days after sight, or a given number of days after date.

Through bill of lading – A single bill of lading converting both the domestic and international carriage of an export shipment. An air waybill, for instance, is essentially a through bill of lading used for air shipments. Ocean shipments, on the other hand, usually require two separate documents – an inland bill of lading for domestic carriage and an ocean bill of lading for international carriage. Through bills of lading are insufficient for ocean shipments. Compare **Air waybill, Inland bill of lading,** and **Ocean bill of lading.**

Time draft – A draft that matures either a certain number of days after acceptance or a certain number of days after the date of the draft. Compare **Date draft** and **Sight draft** (see chapter 13).

Tramp steamer – A ship not operating on regular routes or schedules.

Transaction statement – A document that delineates the terms and conditions agreed upon between the importer and exporter.

Trust receipt – Release of merchandise by a bank to a buyer in which the bank retains title to the merchandise. The buyer, who obtains the goods for manufacturing or sales purposes, is obligated to maintain the goods (or the proceeds from their sale) distinct from the remainder of his or her assets and to hold them ready for repossession by the bank.

Warehouse receipt – A receipt issued by a warehouse listing goods received for storage.

Wharfage – A charge assessed by a pier or dock owner for handling incoming or outgoing cargo.

Without reserve – A term indicating that a shipper's agent or representative is empowered to make definitive decisions and adjustments abroad without approval of the group or individual represented. Compare **Advisory capacity.**